LINGUISTICS AND READING

Charles C. Fries

LINGUISTICS
AND
READING

IRVINGTON PUBLISHERS, INC.
551 FIFTH AVENUE NEW YORK, N.Y. 10017

First Irvington Edition 1983

Copyright© 1963 by Charles Carpenter Fries

Library of Congress Cataloging in Publication Data

Fries, Charles Carpenter, 1887-
    Linguistics and reading.

    Reprint. Originally published: New York: Holt, Rinehart, and Winston, 1963.
    Bibliography: p.
    Includes index.
    1. Reading. 2. Linguistics. I. Title.
LB1050.F7   1982   428.4   82-7746
ISBN 0-8290-0980-9

Printed in the United States of America

To
Eve and Sue and Peter
and especially to
Carol
who taught them

Introduction

This book attempts to bring to the study of the problems of learning to read and of the teaching of reading a body of knowledge not hitherto fully explored for help in this fundamental part of our education.

For many years I have held the view that, in order to achieve basically sound solutions to educational problems, we must, in some way, learn how to bring to bear upon the pressing problems of education all the knowledge that has been won, and all the new knowledge that is continually being won, in every one of the "subject-matter" disciplines. I have firmly believed also that, in order to accomplish that end, some of us who have worked primarily in academic disciplines must struggle to understand sympathetically the work, the methods, and the language of those devoted to the professional study of education. We must achieve such an understanding as to make complete communication and thorough cooperation possible. The bridging of the gap between the academic scholar-teacher and the education specialist demands that kind of communication and that kind of cooperation.

Throughout most of my career I have tried to develop this kind of understanding in my special field — the historical and descriptive study of the English language. In spite of some widely circulated statements to the contrary, I have never been a "Professor of Education." I have, however, throughout my years as Professor of English in the Department of English of the University of Michigan, been welcomed as a member of the staff of the School of Education, have attended their faculty meetings, and through seminars and as chairman of doctoral committees have contributed to the advanced study of the problems of teaching English. In the field of English linguistics I have tried, not only to understand and to contribute to the developing knowledge of the nature and functioning of human language, but also to explore the applications of that knowledge to the problems of teaching. Some examples of the results of this work appear in my *The Teaching of the English Language* (1927), reprinted with the title *The Teaching of English* (1949); *Teaching and Learning English as a Foreign Language* (1945); and *Foundations for English Teaching* (1961).

This book, *Linguistics and Reading,* continues my striving to explore the applications of linguistic knowledge. It presents a non-technical survey of the knowledge concerning the nature and functioning of language that has been built up by the scientific study of language during the last 140 years, and an analysis of the reading process in the light of that knowledge. This book does *not deal with linguistics as content material that should be taught to children in the elementary schools.* As a matter of fact, the book does not deal with the *teaching of linguistics* to any level of student. It is true that teachers, or lay readers, or even linguistic students, who desire a brief account of the changing linguistic attitudes from 1825 to 1960, will find Chapter Two a useful unit apart from the rest of the book. But this book does not seek to provide for the teaching of linguistics as such. It is concerned with the *teaching of reading* and it seeks to analyze and restate a number of the fundamental questions about reading *not in the terms of the procedures of linguistic science* but against *the background of the knowledge concerning human language* which linguistic science has achieved.

The general analysis of the reading process in terms of language meanings and language signals is set forth in Chapter Four, "The Nature of the Reading Process." But Chapter Four rests upon an understanding of the developing views of the nature and functioning of human language that are surveyed in Chapter Two, "Linguistics: The Study of Language," and in Chapter Three, "Language Meanings and Language Signals." The reader will find Chapter Four, "The Nature of the Reading Process," much easier to grasp in its full significance if he comes to it fresh from the summaries of Chapter Two and the materials treated in Chapter Three. This general analysis of the reading process forms the theoretical basis upon which to build a detailed linguistic examination of the kinds of materials to which a reader must develop high-speed recognition responses. (See Chapter Six, "English Spelling: Background and Present Patterns," and Chapter Seven, "Materials and Methods: The Essentials of a Linguistically Sound Approach.") These five chapters constitute the chief burden of the book.

Chapter Two, the descriptive survey of linguistics, does *not* center attention upon the techniques and procedures of linguistic analysis — the problems that linguistic scholars faced, and the tools and increasingly rigorous methods they developed to solve those problems. If the purpose of Chapter Two had been a full history of the scientific study of language these matters of problems and procedures would have bulked much larger than they do. For the purpose of this book the descriptive survey of Chapter Two was limited primarily to a statement of the new views of the nature and functioning of human language that gradually emerged as unexpected results of the use of the new techniques and procedures. In the text of this survey chapter, brief summaries are given at the end of each of the three sections covering the three time periods: 1820 to 1875, 1875 to 1925, and 1925 to 1950. At the end of the third section, all three summaries are brought together.

This survey of the knowledge and understanding developed over a period of 140 years should help to dispel the image of the "linguist" as one who devotes himself primarily to the destruction of all the qualities that make for precise and full expression — an irresponsible speaker of the language for whom "anything goes."

The reader of this book should *not* attempt to read Chapters Six and Seven before he has read at least the summaries of Chapter Two and the whole of Chapters Three and Four. Throughout the discussions of the teaching of reading the arguments concerning the use of *phonics* bulk large. For many teachers the word *phonics* seems to stand for almost any procedure that seeks to make connections between the pronunciation of a word and its spelling. Particularly confusing and distressing to a linguist who tries to read these discussions is the lack of discrimination in the uses of the words *phonic* and *phonetic,* and *phonics* and *phonetics.* Chapter Five of this book tries to provide the basis for a mutual understanding in the uses of these terms and to relate to them the somewhat newer terms *phonemic* and *phonemics.* Only from such a basis of understanding can one proceed to a satisfactory treatment of the structural significance of the alphabet that English uses in its spelling patterns. Chapter Five, therefore, must also be read before Chapters Six and Seven. It can be read first or immediately after Chapter One.

Chapter One, "Past Practice and Theory in the Teaching of Reading," rests upon a first-hand study of two sets of materials. The first set of materials examined consisted of the professional studies of reading problems — studies published from 1910 to 1960, the period of what has been called "the scientific study of education." (For a brief summary of the bibliographical resources covering the tremendous number of these professional publications see Note 1 of Chapter One.)

The second set of materials studied consisted of the actual textbooks from which reading was taught in the home and in the school as well as the books and journal articles discussing the teaching of reading, and the sections of other books dealing with orthography and pronunciation — all of these published during the years from 1551 to 1900. I had already done a first-hand historical study of the grammars and the dictionaries in the light of the developing attitudes toward the English language from the fifteenth century to 1925.

The chapter itself, although it touches briefly the earlier reading materials, emphasizes the practice and the theory developed during the years from 1800 to 1900. It seeks primarily to bring into focus the contributions of the nineteenth century to the practices of today.

My special interest in the problems of reading was aroused by conversations with Leonard Bloomfield nearly thirty years ago when we were both members of a small committee of the Linguistic Society of America appointed to consider some of the problems of the practical applications of linguistic knowledge. Bloomfield himself developed a set of materials through which he taught his boy to read and Agnes Fries and I, starting with the writing of a little book for a three-year-old boy in 1940, have, since that time, whenever an opportunity could be found from the press of other duties, continued our efforts to build up a satisfactory and linguistically sound approach to the teaching of reading. This present book on *Linguistics and Reading,* which attempts to set forth the fundamental principles of our thinking, has been taking shape slowly over a considerable period. In the meantime we have found a number of opportunities to experiment in a variety of situations with our new materials for teaching beginning reading. We have taught not only the normal five and six year olds but also children of three and four, as well as "retarded" children of eleven and twelve of very low intelligence quotients.

In this book, therefore, the approach to the problems of reading assumes the primacy of language and talk. This view of the fundamental relation of language to reading will appear throughout all the discussion, as it attempts to analyze (a) the nature of the reading process, (b) the sets of habits which must be acquired in order to read satisfactorily, (c) the essential features of materials adjusted to various stages of reading competence, and (d) the principles of procedure and teaching method that grow out of this approach.

If such a book is to be really useful, there must be considerable cooperation on the part of both author and reader. As author I have tried to realize something of the difficulties that readers have in grasping the significance of a new and different approach to problems they have studied for a long time with a different set of assumptions. The mere elimination of technical terms will not provide the answer. It will help, but the difficulties lie deeper. The new statements of the problems, the consideration of matters not hitherto thought to be related to reading processes, the new views of language must in some way be attached to the experience of the readers. There is no easy road to this end. I believe, however, that the workers investigating reading problems, those who devise reading programs, those who train the teachers of reading, and the parents who are concerned with the educational development of their children cannot afford to neglect exploring fully the contribution which present-day linguistic knowledge could make to the developing of a more effective teaching of reading at all levels.

SUMMARY OF CONTENTS

This book presents the first attempt to bring together a non-technical descriptive survey of modern linguistic knowledge, an analysis of the nature of the reading process in the light of that knowledge, and a somewhat detailed linguistic examination of the kinds of materials to which the reader must develop high-speed recognition responses. It lays the foundation for an integrated program that will not only provide materials for the beginner and his progress through the first stage of reading achievement, but also a brief map of the course for his continued development through the stage of "productive reading" to the mature reading of literature.

The book begins with a survey of past practice and theory in the teaching of reading (Chapter One) in order to give some perspective to the discussion of the new materials to follow. Because the early discussions of the methods and materials for the teaching of reading English seem to have been neglected (or misunderstood) the survey began with John Hart's book of 1570 entitled

A Methode or comfortable beginning for all unlearned, whereby they may bee taught to read English, in a very short time with pleasure.

On the whole, however, it gives major attention to the developments in the teaching of reading before 1900. It brings together the materials to demonstrate that the important changes in approach that characterize the history of the teaching of reading in the schools have grown out of the earnest struggle of the teachers and administrators themselves to find better ways — ways to achieve specific types of skills that the approach then in use neglected, ways to make their teaching measure up to their ideals of all that must be accomplished. The mere chronology of some of the major emphases in the teaching of reading as shown in the "directions for the teachers" and "explanations of method" that appear in the prefaces and introductions of widely distributed textbooks, in the manuals used for teacher training in the annual teachers institutes, and in the journals for teachers, sheds considerable light upon this struggle. This chronology also demonstrates that the chief methods and combinations of methods now discussed so vigorously were actually in use long before the time of modern educational research. As early as 1842 the Word-Method was vigorously discussed, and fully worked out in widely used books published in 1850, 1856, 1874, 1883. As a general practice these books also provided for the teaching of new words by using the methods of "word analysis by sound," usually preceded by a period of "preparation" activity to put the pupils "on their own" in approaching new words in their reading.

The Sentence-Method received considerable discussion and practice from 1870 on. Farnham's book, first published in 1881 with later editions of 1886 and 1895, was widely used in teacher training institutes in the East, especially in New York State, and in the Middle West, chiefly in Iowa and Nebraska. As explained and practiced by Farnham and his followers this approach through the "whole sentence" was well conceived and thoroughly worked out in a teachable program. It stressed the need for preparation exercises to make the pupils "ready" for reading, constantly insisted upon the getting of meaning and thought as the basic objective, made use of supplementary reading material and selection on the basis of pupil interest, and, asserting that "true education is a growth," based the teaching of reading upon the experience of the pupils. The leading teachers and administrators before 1890 did not conceive the task of teaching reading in any narrow fashion, and their practical classroom experimentation led to a continuing development in theory and in method. These achievements all antedate the rise of "modern educational research" by at least a generation.

Among the great mass of studies devoted to the problems of teaching reading during the first half of the twentieth century one can find but one or two that have given any consideration to the new knowledge concerning the nature and functioning of language achieved by the labors of a host of linguistic scholars over more than a century.

Chapter Two, entitled "Linguistics: The Study of Language" attempts to explain to the educated lay reader the succession of problems to which the "scientific study of language" has devoted itself during the last 140 years, and the results of that work. Linguists themselves, of course, usually center attention upon the progress in the development of increasingly satisfactory techniques and procedures of linguistic analysis and description. But for those not professional linguists — teachers and educated laymen — of vastly greater importance is the new knowledge concerning the nature and functioning of human language that has come as the unexpected result of this century and a half of scientific linguistic work. It is this new understanding of the language that has shed new light upon the nature of the reading process and the problems of learning to read — the problems of beginning reading as well as those of mature reading.

Chapter Three carries further the descriptive explanation of each language as an arbitrary code of signals. We assume for our purpose here that our particular language provides the tool by which English speaking communities grasp and share meanings. These meanings constitute the storehouse of all the knowledge of our society. Our language is not the meanings themselves but rather the system of arbitrary patterns by means of which the meanings are signalled or communicated. Learning to use a language means learning (a) to recognize the significant patterns of the functioning units that identify the lexical items or "words," and those that identify the grammatical structures, and (b) to recall instantly the meanings that attach to these patterns, and (c) to produce these significant patterns for the recognition of other members of the community. In other words, a child has learned to "talk" his native language when he can make the regular responses to these language signals as produced by others and also can produce these same language signals to elicit the regular responses in others of his linguistic community. Learning thus to "talk" (learning to produce and to receive the oral signals of his language) constitutes the basis upon which a child must build to learn to read.

Learning to read (as set forth in Chapter Four) is *not* a process of learning new or other language signals than those the child has already learned. The language signals are all the same. The difference lies in the medium through which the physical stimuli make contact with his nervous system. In "talk," the physical stimuli of the language signals make their contact by means of sound waves received by the ear. In reading, the physical stimuli of the same language signals consist of graphic shapes that make their contact with his nervous system through light waves received by the eye. The process of learning to read is the process of transfer from the auditory signs for language signals which the child has already learned, to the new visual signs for the same signals.

Learning to read, therefore, means developing a considerable range of high-speed recognition responses to specific sets of patterns of graphic shapes. In the transfer from a succession of sound patterns in a time dimension to a succession of graphic patterns in a space direction there are many (often little understood) arbitrary features that must be specifically and thoroughly learned by much practice. Insufficient practice of these seemingly insignificant details of contrastive shape and direction often lies back of the need for "remedial" teaching later.

Perhaps the most important weaknesses of the present approaches to the teaching of reading arise out of a misunderstanding or an ignoring of the structural significance of alphabetic writing, and the nature of the spelling patterns of present-day English. To help remove these misunderstandings Chapter Five seeks to clarify the uses of the words *phonics, phonetics,* and *phonemics,* and to show something of the place of our alphabet in the history of writing. Chapter Six furnishes a brief history of English spelling in order to show that although the alphabet as used for English is phonemically based, it is not a "phonemic alphabet," in the sense that there is a single letter for each phoneme and a single phoneme for each letter. Throughout the history of

English spelling the letters of the alphabet have never had a one for one correspondence with English phonemes. The phonemes, especially the vowel phonemes, have always been graphically represented by *spelling patterns*. English spelling today cannot be satisfactorily dealt with by trying to match individual letters with individual sounds. To say this, however, does not deny the basic relation that does exist between sounds and spellings. To grasp that relation, the beginning reader must learn to respond to the significant features of the major patterns of spelling rather than try to learn the many various sounds that each letter can be said to represent. From this point of view, all but a very small number of the spellings of English words fit into one of the spelling patterns. The comparatively few that do not fit, the "orphans," are primarily problems for the writer, who must produce in his writing the proper spellings for all of these "irregulars." The reader, as a reader, however, must learn to identify the words *as spelled for him by the author* of the text he is reading; for reading, it is not necessary for him to spell them himself. The major spelling patterns of present-day English are fortunately few in number, but for these the reader must develop, through long practice, high-speed recognition responses. These responses must become so habitual that practically all the clues that stimulate them eventually sink below the threshold of attention leaving only the cumulative comprehension of the meaning.

But, for the efficient development of these habits of automatic recognition on the part of the pupil, the materials for his practice cannot ignore these clues. They must be selected and organized in such a sequence as to lead him through all of the major and some of the minor spelling-patterns. The progression of the material must be so programmed that each new item of whatever length is tied by a simple contrast to an item formerly practiced. The simple contrasts used should always be of items within a whole pattern, never of items less than a word. The basic principle of the learning and the teaching should always be contrast within a frame.

The spelling-pattern approach differs fundamentally from the phonics approach. Underlying the phonics approach is the assumption that much of learning to read is learning to match words as written, letter by letter, with words as pronounced, sound by sound,

It is perfectly true that for a certain range of spelling-patterns, notably the first major set of spelling-patterns described in Chapter Six, the phonics approach has been helpful and this fact accounts for the persistence of phonics in the schools. But the "phonics way" does not lay the basis for the kinds of responses to spelling-patterns that can be used for all the materials. One can learn such words as MAN, MAT, MEN, MET, the phonics way, and project similar letter-sound correspondences through a substantial number of words. But even for the three letter words like MAN it is not the single letter A that indicates the vowel sound [æ]. It is the spelling-pattern MAN in contrast with the spelling-patterns MANE and MEAN that signals the different vowel phonemes that identify these three different word-patterns /mæn/ /men/ /min/; or MAT /mæt/ — MATE /met/ — MEAT /mit/.

Although the spelling-pattern approach always gives attention to whole words rather than to individual isolated letters it differs fundamentally from any of the common "word-method" approaches in that there is no uncertainty in the identifying characteristics that mark off one written word from another. These are the identifying characteristics of the language itself as incorporated in the patterns of our alphabetic spelling.

The handling of these beginning materials need not be mechanical, but they must be subjected to rigorous criteria of selection and programmed into a progression of small, coherent, contrastive steps. Even from the beginning there must be complete meaning responses not only to words but to complete utterances and, as soon as possible, to sequences of utterances. The *cumulative* comprehension of the meanings must become so complete that the pupil reader can as he goes along supply those portions of the language signals which the bundles of spelling-patterns alone do not represent. The case for the use of a considerable amount of properly directed oral reading rests primarily on the need to develop this kind of *productive* reading.

During the long period through which active observation, systematic reading, and concentrated investigation continued to build the understanding upon which the thinking of this book rests I have gained much stimulation and many very helpful insights from talks with colleagues, students, teachers in the schools, and especially with children. I cannot list here even those who contributed most but I want them to know that I am grateful. The book would not have given attention to a considerable variety of what now seem especially important details had not the realization of their significance been stimulated by the revealing comments of these informal "consultants." Throughout the years devoted to work upon the materials of this book various members of my family have given their very active cooperation. The manuscript had the benefit of keen critical comments by my son, Peter H. Fries, at several stages in its development. But the book would not have been written without the very patient, self-sacrificing participation in every phase of the work by my wife, Agnes C. Fries. She has borne the chief responsibility in providing materials for our experimental teaching of beginners.

Charles C. Fries

Ann Arbor, Michigan
February 1963

Contents

CHAPTER ONE

Past Practice and Theory in the Teaching of Reading

The discussions in English concerning the methods and materials for the teaching of reading began at least four hundred years ago. And John Hart's book of 1570, entitled *A Methode or comfortable beginning for all vnlearned, whereby they may bee taught to read English, in a very short time, with pleasure,* reaches back to the first century of the Christian era, for in the Preface he insists that "This maner of teaching is after the councell of the excellent Latine rhetorician Quintilian, who died aboue .xv.C. yeres past."

The four hundred years since John Hart's work have produced a tremendous amount of material bearing upon the problems of reading.[1] If "Johnny can't read," it is not because his teachers, or the principal of his school, or the superintendent of his school system, or the professors of education, or the psychologists, or the directors of reading clinics, have ignored or neglected the problems created by the innumerable and diverse Johnnies and Janes that must, for modern living, have an increasingly high

1

standard of literacy. Whatever the causes of the "failure of modern education," no one can insist that they have arisen out of willful neglect of the problems or an unwillingness to labor hard in their study.

One must remember that people have been learning to read and have taught others to read from the time of the first graphic symbols that deserve the name of "writing." One must remember too that most of the early teaching of the reading process (in distinction from the teaching of oral public reading) occurred in the home rather than in school. Even today some of the best-known private schools of England—schools which receive pupils of five years of age—will not accept those of this age who cannot already read. For many years only a portion of the population sent their children to the free public elementary schools, and the practices and standards of those schools do not give us a complete picture for those years. To grasp the practices of teaching reading before the beginning of the nineteenth century and for a considerable time thereafter, one must know something of the materials and methods used in the home. Many books made special appeals to parents for home use.

The teaching of reading became a public problem with the development of democratic forms of government and the growth of schools to educate the children of all the people. Compulsory school attendance for all children from six to fourteen and then to sixteen increased the problems and stressed the obligation to teach reading with maximum efficiency. One response to the increasing pressures of the problems of public elementary schools has been the movement for the "scientific study of education"—a type of investigation depending in large part upon statistical procedures applied to data gathered through the use of various types of objective tests and measurements. In this trend toward the measurement-statistical approach to educational problems, which got under way during the first two decades of the twentieth century, the number of studies directed to matters connected with the teaching of reading far exceeds that given to any other single subject of the school curriculum.

Through the patient work of such men as William S. Gray, Arthur Traxler, and Emmett A. Betts, in listing, classifying, and summarizing these studies, the bibliographical resources in the field of reading deserve the gratitude of everyone who attempts to grasp coherently just what this kind of research has contributed to an understanding of the nature of the reading process and of the materials and procedures for teaching. Even with the aid of Gray's yearly *Summaries,* however, which reach back to the very beginnings of this type of educational study, and Traxler's four volumes covering the productions from 1930 to 1958, together with the digests of research on specific problems, the very mass of the materials creates great difficulty. But the difficulties do not arise out of the volume of the materials alone. One comes away from a concentrated study of hundreds out of the thousands of these investigations much distressed. He seeks in vain for the cumulative continuity that has characterized all recognized sound scientific research. He struggles hard, without success, to find the strands of fundamental assumptions and accepted criteria of sound procedure running through a series of studies attacking any of the major problems of the teaching of reading.

The few quotations given here from men like Gray and Traxler, who have carried the main burden of recording and summarizing the published research on reading during the last thirty-five years and who have sought diligently and sympathetically for the studies that make sound contributions, give something of the reasons for the feeling of frustration with which one comes from an intensive study of these research materials.

Unfortunately, much of the scientific work relating to reading has been fragmentary in character. As pointed out by various writers the investigator frequently attacks an isolated problem, completes his study of it, and suggests that he will continue his research at some later time but often fails to do so. In the second place, there is far too little coordination of effort among research workers in the field of reading. . . . In the third place, many of the studies reported have been conducted without adequate controls.[2] (W. S. Gray)

Phonics—The sum total of the available research on phonics continues to be inconclusive so far as evidence on the value of phonetic training is concerned. (A. E. Traxler)

Dominance—The results of available research in this controversial area continue to be conflicting. (Traxler)

Vocabulary—Studies of elementary school primers and readers indicate that the tendency toward a smaller and more nearly uniform reading vocabulary is even more pronounced than it was during the periods reviewed in the preceding bulletins. [For 1930–1940 and for 1940–1945] Nevertheless, the vocabulary of modern readers seems not greatly different from that of the time-honored McGuffey series with the grade placement one step lower in the McGuffey books than in modern ones.[3] (Traxler)

Of the various weaknesses of reading research, these three seem most important. Inadequate controls, poor control groups, and weak criteria of success. . . .
The most tantalizing and stimulating characteristic of reading research findings is their inconclusiveness. In reviewing a recent summary of studies on mixed eye-hand dominance Gray concluded, "Obviously final conclusions relating to this problem cannot be stated at present." This statement could be written large after every area of reading research. The situation is desirable in a number of respects, but to the extent that it arises from faulty or uncoordinated research it is inexcusable.[4] (See Winfield Scott)

The research studies themselves certainly do not justify the vigorous assertions frequently appearing concerning the "scientific" basis of so-called "modern procedures" of teaching reading. In fact, the discussions of methods and the published opinions of reading "experts" seem often to ignore the limitations given in the research studies themselves, and, in the spirit of "science fiction," project the claims to knowledge far beyond anything that the studies are prepared to deliver. In these discussions also, in order to sharpen the contrasts, all the period before the appearance of the "scientific study of education" (approximately 1920) is usually pictured as a time in which only absurdly mechanical and ineffective methods of reading instruction were employed. The following quotations come from a published "summary of a presentation" entitled *Why Do the Schools Teach Reading as They Do?*[5]

Methods of the Past.
For hundreds of years reading was taught by having children spell words and sound letters. For many weary weeks after pupils had entered first grade their reading instruction consisted of dull drill on the alphabet and the sounds of the letters. Nothing was considered of any importance except to teach the child these word elements as a means of enabling him to pronounce reading symbols. The child, himself, felt no particular need for memorizing these elements; they had no meaning for him, and such work must have been extremely uninteresting and boring to him. . . . [p. 2]

READING FOR MEANING
What Did Schools of the Past Do About Teaching Meanings?
For centuries absolutely no attention was given to teaching children how to get the thought from what they read. If they had learned to "pronounce the words" their reading achievement was supposed to have been completed. The reading recitation throughout the elementary grades was given over to oral reading in which pupils took turns in calling words aloud to see whether or not they "could pronounce them." No attempt was made to teach pupils to read for meanings nor to check their reading after it was done to find out how much of the content they had absorbed. . . . [p. 5]

THE GREAT CHANGE
What Happened to Bring About This Change in Regard to Reading?
Why do the schools go to all of this trouble in teaching children to get meanings from reading when nothing was done in regard to this phase of reading instruction in the past?

One part of the answer to this question is found in a growing philosophy that was developing for a couple of centuries in regard to making all phases of education more meaningful. This was a cumulative philosophy which was talked about by leaders in education for many years before anyone did anything about it. Such historical figures in education as Rousseau, Pestalozzi, Herbart, Froebel and Parker successively wrote and talked about making instruction in all subjects more meaningful. The application of their advice, however, didn't take hold in reading instruction until as recently as the first quarter of our present century. . . . [p. 7]

There was even a more potent reason than this, however, for adding instruction in meanings to the reading program. This reason is revealed in the findings of investigators. . . . [p. 8]

The kind of reading instruction which the schools are now putting into practice is deeply and firmly embedded in a triad of hundreds of scientific investigations, great accumulations of knowledge in regard to child development, and a keen sensitiveness to the demands of a changing civilization. [p. 15]

As a matter of fact, however, the educational research of the last forty years seems to have had comparatively little effect in originating new approaches to the teaching of reading. That research studies from 1916 to 1960 (or what some people believed these research studies had "proved") may have, from time to time, supported particular practices of certain teachers, or may have contributed to practical decisions concerning materials and methods

can not be denied; but the important changes in approach that characterize the history of the teaching of reading in the schools have
grown out of the earnest struggle of the teachers and the administrators themselves to find better ways—ways to achieve specific types
of ability that the approach then in use neglected, ways to make their
teaching measure up to their ideals of all that must be accomplished.
The mere chronology of some of the major emphases in the teaching of reading as shown in the "directions for teachers" and "explanations of method" that appear in the prefaces and introductions
of widely distributed textbooks, in the manuals used for teacher
training in the annual teachers institutes, and in the journals for
teachers, sheds considerable light upon this struggle. This chronology also demonstrates that the chief methods and combinations of
methods now discussed so vigorously were actually in use long
before the time of modern educational research.

To build up an understanding of the methods and materials
used to teach "reading" in English during the three centuries before
1900 and to arrive at an evaluation of these practices in terms of
the "reading" experience of the last fifty years is exceedingly difficult. The very word "reader" as applied to a schoolbook in 1831
meant something quite different then from what this same word
"reader" meant in 1931. The "readers" in 1831 and for a considerable span of time thereafter had, for the most part, the objective
of public oral rendering of stories, essays, and poems for the sake
of communication. Distinctness, pleasing voice tone, standing position, the method of holding the book were all matters of importance.
Pupils usually came to the "readers" after progress in the process
of reading through exercises in the "spellers." Lyman Cobb, in the
Preface to his *Juvenile Reader No. 1,* has this note "To Teachers":

> The practice of teaching a child to read before he is familiar
> with the orthography and pronunciation of words, is productive of
> great injury, and tends to retard rather than facilitate correct reading.
> No person should attempt to read until he is able to call or pronounce
> at sight the words most commonly met with in composition; and, this
> can be more easily acquired by reading words in a judicious and ana-
> logical classification in a Spelling Book, than in detached reading
> lessons. The Author . . . would respectfully suggest the propriety of
> accustoming the child to pronounce the words in the spelling lessons,
> without naming the letters, until he shall be quite familiar with them,
> a practice which will tend greatly to facilitate his reading by enabling

him to associate the pronunciation of words with the characters which compose them, to render his enunciation clear and distinct, and free him from the embarrassments which too frequently terminate in a confirmed habit of stammering. This practice the Author pursued for years while engaged in the business of teaching with results entirely satisfactory.[6]

There is, however, no sharp break in the use of the word "reader" and some of the problems of understanding the evidence for the history of reading instruction arise out of ambiguities attached to this word during the long period of its use. One obtains a very false impression of the practices of teaching reading in the past if he superficially compares the school "readers" of the preceding century with the "readers" of the last forty years.

Nor can we today easily understand the social-cultural meaning of the content of the older "readers" and "spellers." Our own social-cultural reactions to the religious and moral lessons and the sometimes very formal style will differ completely from those of the people who lived in the eighteenth and nineteenth centuries. Only by bringing into attention some of the social practices of those days can one begin to realize how differently they responded. For example, when Benjamin Franklin learned that his sister Jane was about to be married he sent her the following letter.[7] He himself was only twenty-one at the time and she was fifteen.

Philadelphia, January 6, 1726–7

Dear Sister,

I am highly pleased with the account Captain Freeman gives me of you. I always judged by your behaviour when a child, that you would make a good, agreeable woman, and you know you were ever my peculiar favorite. I have been thinking what would be a suitable present for me to make, and for you to receive, as I hear you are grown a celebrated beauty. I had almost determined on a tea-table; but when I considered, that the character of a good housewife was far preferable to that of being only a pretty gentlewoman, I concluded to send you a *spinning-wheel*, which I hope you will accept as a small token of my sincere love and affection.

Sister, farewell, and remember that modesty, as it makes the most homely virgin amiable and charming, so the want of it infallibly renders the most perfect beauty disagreeable and odious. But, when that

brightest of female virtues shines among other perfections of body and
mind in the same person, it makes the woman more lovely than an
angel. Excuse this freedom, and use the same with me. I am, dear
Jenny, your loving brother,

B. Franklin.

It is extremely hard for us even to understand intellectually
the eighteenth-century social-cultural meanings of a letter like this
and practically impossible for us to respond to it emotionally as
people then would. We have the same difficulty with much of the
content of the early materials for "reading" instruction. In the
effort here to establish some realization of the struggle of conscientious and able teachers of the past to improve the teaching of
reading, I shall ignore all those matters (such as the religious and
moral content of the readers) that are peripheral and extraneous
to the immediate problems of teaching the *process of reading*. I
shall try to center attention upon a few key materials, quoting at
considerable length in order to let the authors speak for themselves
in showing something of their actual practice in applying the
new views as they develop, and in combining them with the
successful features of older procedures.

THE ALPHABET AND PHONICS

The difficulties of English spelling, "the vices and faultes of
our writing: which cause it to be tedious, and long in learnyng: and
learned hard, and evill to read," first drew the fire of John Hart
in his *The Opening of the Unreasonable Writing of Our English
Toung* (1551).[8] This was followed in 1569 by his important *An
Orthographie, conteyning the due order and reason, howe to write
or paint thimmage of mannes voice, most like to the life or nature.*
Here Hart specifically deplores the difficulties of learning to read
a spelling in which the same letter stands for entirely different
sounds and same-sounding words have different writings. Here,
too, he first points out the difficulties arising from the "misnaming
of the letters."

In 1570 he applied the materials of his earlier writing to the
teaching of reading in a little book entitled *A Methode or comfortable beginning for all vnlearned, whereby they may bee taught
to read English, in a very short time, with pleasure.* In this book

he carried farther his comments concerning the difference between the names of the letters and the "powers" of the letters, insisting that "they [the letters] are misnamed much from their offices and natures, whereby the desirous are much the more hindered from learning to reade, though they were neuer so willing."[9] Hart thus is perhaps the first to have published a strong objection to the so-called "alphabetic" method of teaching reading—that is, to spell a word by naming the letters and then to pronounce the word.[10] He proposes instead a type of "phonic" approach in which the sound of the word is produced through a combining of the sounds indicated by the "offices" of the letters.[11]

Hart's method also takes account of the diversity of sounds attaching to some of the letters and provides certain special symbols so that his spelling follows the rule of each symbol having only one sound and the same sound having only one symbol. His method is, therefore, a "phonic" approach using a rather consistent "phonetic" alphabet.

Hart was followed by others who during the end of the sixteenth and through the seventeenth and early eighteenth centuries dealt with English sounds and the alphabetic representations of these sounds. Some, like Charls Butler (1634), also used a rather consistent phonetic alphabet. Butler thus seeks to overcome the "inconveniences" in the usual spelling—"Uncertain writing, and Difficulti of learning," which is "as trubblesom to the novice Reader, as to the Writer." Through this approach will, Butler insists, "the learners attein unto a more perfect and reddy reading in one yeer, than otherwise they have doon in three."[12]

Through the years of the seventeenth and eighteenth centuries the books which lay back of the "spellers" were the English Grammars and the works of the Orthoepists.[13] In practically all of the grammars of this period, the first large division of each book was devoted to Orthography—the letters of the alphabet, their kinds and uses, the formation of syllables, and the spelling of words. The "spellers," making practical use of these materials, were the books out of which the early steps in reading were taught.

Meaning

In these materials there is no ignoring of the meaning of the material read. Concern for the understanding of what is read appears repeatedly from the very beginning. Quotations are abundant from 1570 to 1900.

. . . the effect of writing consisteth not in the letter, but to shew what is ment by the letter [Hart, *Methode,* 1570].[14]

A leading object of this work is to enable the scholar, while learning to *read,* to *understand,* at the same time, the *meaning* of the words he is reading. . . . if, for example, when the pupil is taught to read, he is enabled, at the same time, to discover the *meaning* of the words he repeats, he will readily make use of the proper inflections, and place the emphasis where the sense demands it. The monotonous sing-song mode of reading, which is common in schools and which is often retained in after life, is acquired from the exercise of reading what is not understood. . . .

The bad effects resulting from this practice have led teachers to adopt one of the only two modes, which have as yet been invented for avoiding them. They either place in the hands of their pupils books reduced to the level of their capacities; or, if the compositions are more elevated, direct them to seek definitions from the pages of a common dictionary. . . .

The common mode of teaching the definitions of words is also very objectionable; the pupil is obliged to commit to memory the definitions of a certain number of isolated and unconnected words, in a dictionary. . . .

The plan of the present work relieves the scholar from this difficulty. It presents the word to be defined in connexion with others, and supplies a train of ideas, with which the word itself may be associated [Putnam, *The Analytical Reader,* 1836].[15]

It is recommended that the pupil be required to master everything as he goes along. . . . The Definition ought to be made out by the exercise of the pupil's own judgment (aided by the instructor) from the sense which the connection requires; for, to seek out and memorize definitions from a dictionary, or defining vocabulary, is injurious rather than beneficial [McGuffey, *The Eclectic Third Reader,* 1838].[16]

First and chiefest, in reading, let the lesson be understood; its words, its phrases, its connections; its object, if it have any object; if not, it is not proper for a reading lesson. Every word and sentence to which no meaning is attached is an enemy, lying in ambush [*The Common School Journal,* 1842].[17]

Reading consists: first, in gaining the thoughts of an author from written or printed language:—second, in giving oral expression to these thoughts in the language of the author, so that the same thoughts are conveyed to the hearer.

It is important that this two-fold function of reading should be fully recognized. The first, or silent reading, is the fundamental process. . . . The second, oral reading, or "reading aloud," is entirely subordinate to silent reading. While oral expression is subject to laws of its own, its excellence depends upon the success of the reader in comprehending the thought of the author [Farnham, *The Sentence Method*, 1881].[18]

. . . we would guard instructors against teaching words without first developing the ideas they represent.

To aid the teacher in this work, most of the lessons of this book are illustrated.

Begin the lesson by showing the children the picture. Let them tell all they see in it. Have a familiar talk about it. Call upon one to name an object in the picture. Show them on the board the word by which the object is known [E. H. Butler, *The First Reader*, 1883].[19]

THE "WORD" METHOD

The "word" method approach to reading appeared early in the nineteenth century. Two quite different practices were included in what was called "word" method. The first was the revolt against using for practice, at the beginning, sequences of two or three letters which represented syllables but did not make "words"—"those cadaverous particles, *ba, be, bi, bo, bu,* etc.," "the stiff perpendicular row of characters, lank, stark, immovable, without form or comliness, and as to signification, wholly void."[20] It was insisted that the learning to recognize and to pronounce letters in combination must be built up through practice upon units that have meaning for the child, real words. Even the *New-England Primer* reduced the number of two-letter syllables, that did not make words, to the simple tables of the five vowel letters before each of the consonant letters except *q, w, y,* and *h,* and after each of the consonant letters except *q* and *x.* The rest of the tables before the consecutive reading contained full words, grouped in small lists of one, two, three, four, five, and six syllables. There were only three small pages even of these lists.

In the discussions of the teaching of reading published in the early nineteenth century, it is not always easy to separate this insistence upon the use of whole words rather than nonsense syllables from the second and later use of the term *word method.* In this later use of the term *word method,* the words as wholes were first presented as unanalyzed units to be connected with meanings just as pictures of dogs, cats, and horses represent these animals. In fact some of the nineteenth-century books in this method used "object exercises" in which small pictures were inserted for key words.

OBJECT EXERCISE

See the   and the

The   ran at the

The   ran at the

Can the   get the

The   is in the

The   is in the

SOURCE: Barnes, *New National First Reader,* New York, Chicago: A. S. Barnes & Company, 1883, p. 13.

The methods and procedures of the "word" method were discussed at length throughout the nineteenth century. Many such discussions appear in the early volumes of *The Common School Journal* which began in 1839. The following quotations come from a letter to the editor, signed simply "M," which appeared in the Journal of 1842. The heading of the letter, entitled "How to Teach Reading and the Alphabet," is preceded by the note in brackets which follows.

live live live live live

Can a   live

with a   ?

Can an   live

with a   ?

SOURCE: Pollard, *Synthetic First Reader*, 1889, p. 23.

[Let all teachers of young children read the following article attentively—Ed.] My theory is, that words can be more easily remembered than letters, for two reasons. In the first place they are not such minute objects, and the faculty by which the forms are distinguished can therefore more readily perceive them; in the second place, every word that a child learns, will (if judiciously selected), convey a distinct image of a thing, or an act, to his mind, and can be more easily remembered than the name of a letter with which he can have no natural associations.

What is invaluable in this method is, that children are always happy to learn thus . . . it is altogether an unnatural one [effort] to learn writing signs to which nothing already known can be attached. Until I was convinced that this was the best method, I always found myself instinctively helping innocent children along, through their first steps, by means which, at the time, I half thought were tricks and pernicious indulgences. I feared I was depriving them of some wholesome and desirable discipline. . . . But I will never again force helpless children of three or four years, to learn the alphabet and the *abs*, until reading is so charming to them that every letter is interesting from its position and its association with the word it helps to form. When letters are learned in the ordinary manner, they are often associated artificially with some image as *a* stands for *apple, b* for *boy* etc; and these associations are so many hindrances to the next step in the process, because they must all be unlearned before the letters can be applied to other words. . . . I frequently tell little children who know the alphabet to look at the word, rather than to spell it over with the lips, and then tell me, without the book, what the letters are, assisting them sometimes by saying, "Observe what two letters are in the middle, or what two are at the end, or in the beginning." . . .

I therefore say to those who make the objection, that this mode of teaching to read leaves spelling out of the question, that it only defers spelling a little, and that the first words spelled should be those which are already perfectly familiar to the eye. . . .

It is desirable that in the first book there should be many repetitions of the same words, and experience has convinced me that nothing can be learned easily or remembered well that is not so arranged as to have some natural sequence. For this reason I would arrange the first words in natural groups. (In a story of a bird, for instance, after some of the principal names of things, such as *bird, tree, wings, feathers, bill*, etc. have been mentioned, several actions may be introduced. These are the things birds do;—*build, fly, sing,* etc. Then the names of colors are easily associated, and even the words *the, which,* and *and*.) . . .

After learning a few groups of words often repeated on a page, let these be combined in short sentences. These sentences children will learn with great ease, and they will remember the particles that necessarily connect the names of things and actions. They will, of their own accord, turn back to the pages where they first became familiar with the words; and when this process of comparison has gone on a little while, if no pain is associated with it, the improvement will be rapid. . . .

Children of six, who begin to read thus by learning words instead of letters, will be able in three months to read simple stories very easily. . . . One or two instances have quite astonished me, however. . . . My present class of that age are beginning to emerge from all their puzzles, and their desires to read are perfectly insatiable. One boy of seven, who has been much neglected is still in the Slough of Despond, and cannot yet read better than little L., who began three or four months ago. His knowledge of letters does not help him forward; but light is dawning upon him since he has been made to spell only the words he knows. . . .

I would also have the stories in the first book attractive to the imagination, that they may be frequently recurred to with pleasure,—and the first words well impressed before the vocabulary is much enlarged. Repetition is a great secret of real progress. . . .

After the process of spelling has become familiar, classes of words of similar pronunciation and appearance should be given; as, *boy, toy, joy.* It is also an admirable exercise to let children spell over their reading lesson from the book after reading, pronouncing each word distinctly before they read the letters. The good effect of this mode of drilling will soon be perceived both in oral spelling and writing.

Let me impress it upon all teachers, if I have not already made it sufficiently clear, that spelling is only to be deferred a little while, till it can be begun with advantage; and then there cannot be too much of it. A quick ear for music will assist some children, a good organ of form will aid others, and frequent repetition of the sight and sound of letters, in their various combinations, will help all. Above all, let the whole process be made agreeable, and there is no fear of want of co-operation on the part of the little people.[21]

Here in 1842 is the word-method not only practiced but grasped clearly in theory—the beginning with whole words as meaning units, learned without analysis until "the child is ready for it," usually after thoroughly learning approximately "fifty words," and these words then supported by attention to the letters related to sounds and to their names.[22]

As often happens, textbook writers adopted various types of the word-method—some with little or no selection of the words with regard to similar shapes and others with considerable attention to this feature. There was much difference of opinion among the nineteenth-century advocates of the word-method concerning when and how to teach "sounds" and spelling. Usually the textbooks appeared with no acknowledgment of the sources of their views. Before these textbooks, exceedingly valuable discussions of the methods and materials of teaching reading appeared in the early annual reports of Horace Mann as Secretary of the Board of Education for the state of Massachusetts and in his articles on "The Best Mode of Preparing and Using Spelling-Books." These and other articles published in *The Common School Journal,* of which Horace Mann was editor, show not only the devotion with which those responsible for the schools of Massachusetts struggled with the problems of reading but also the probable source of many of the developing practices in the schools in the second half of the nineteenth century.

WIDELY USED WORD-METHOD TEXTBOOKS OF THE NINETEENTH CENTURY

Webb's Series

In 1850, with revised and enlarged editions in 1856 and 1874, J. Russell Webb[23] published what he called "A New Method of Teaching Children to Read: Founded on Nature and Reason." It was the word-method, "proved and commended by many practical teachers." The following quotations come from the Preface and from the "Directions for Teaching" for Book I of the series.

It is a lamentable fact, and one which the community is beginning to understand, that children have been wrongly taught their first lessons in reading. . . .

It may be asked by some, why we have commenced with words instead of letters. We answer, a word can as easily be learned as a letter; and, in addition, a word has some meaning—a letter none. A word conveys to the mind an idea, the mind acts to receive it; the letter has no such effect. The former necessarily teaches a child to think; the latter teaches—nothing.

The child, in this part, is not to be taught a *letter*, or to *spell* a *word*, but is simply to learn the words by their *forms*, the same as he learns the names of animals, by looking at them as a *whole* as an *animal*—associating the *name* with its *form*. The child thus reads naturally, by sight, the same as all persons read, and understanding the meaning of every word, of course, reads with ease and pleasure.[24]

The following quotation shows the content and the method of the first step in Webb's approach. There is no neglect of the meaning of what is read.

The first word which the child is to be taught is the word *BOY*. When this is learned so as to be readily known, questions, similar to those at the close of the lesson, should be used, thus giving the child to understand that the word MEANS something. The next word is *GOOD*. This, when learned, can be combined with the word *boy*, making the first phrase, "good boy," in the reading lesson. The meaning of the phrase "good boy" should be talked about, till the child understands it. Two words are now learned, each of which has a meaning which the child understands. The two words have conveyed to the mind two ideas—the mind has acted to receive them—the child has begun to think—the mind has begun to expand, thus accomplishing the principal objects designed by reading: viz.; the expanding and disciplining of the mind. The word "girl" should next be learned, and various questions relative to the being, "girl," should be asked. This word combined with the word "good," forms the second phrase in the reading lesson. These phrases should be read as soon as the words forming them are learned.[25]

Throughout the second half of the nineteenth century the word method of introducing pupils to the process of reading spread widely, as indicated by the number of different textbooks using this approach and their various editions and distribution. The specific practices of applying the method varied, but in practically all it was assumed that the word method would be combined with one or more of the other methods then in use.

Note A.—Some Teachers prefer teaching spelling, and the letters, at the same time they teach the words. These Teachers first teach the word by its form, then teach the child to spell it, after which they teach the forms of the letters, or, in other words, the letters.
To this method we will not object, though we decidedly prefer that marked out in "Directions for Teaching." . . .
The difference in the two methods is, we teach nothing but words and reading at first, leaving the letters and spelling till the 6th lesson, when it is believed the child will understand the object and nature of reading, and be prepared to commence the Alphabet understandingly.[26]

Webb himself, for example, gives the title "Word Method" only to Part I of his book *No. 1*. Part II is entitled "Teaching New Words, Reading, Spelling, the Alphabet, and the Sounds of the Letters."

Note.—The teacher may now pursue *either* of the following ways, or any combination of them, as may be thought best; though *we* give a *decided preference to the fourth:* Spelling by Sound.
1. The Word Method, heretofore used, may be continued—the words being taught from Column 3d.
2. The words may be taught from Column 3d—Spelled by sound, from Columns 1st and 2d, and the names of the letters learned from the Alphabet on the margin.

3. The letters may be taught first from Col. 1st—put together or spelled, as in Col. 2d, and pronounced as in Col. 3d.

The spelling may be done in two ways:

1st. In the ordinary way calling each letter by name; or,

2d. By uniting the *last two* letters; as *a-n,* making *an;* then using this combination as one character, with the letters preceding it; thus *m-an, man.* Of course, these words, as soon as learned, will be read in connection with other words, as in the reading lesson following.

4. Spelling by Sound.

The words may be taught by the *sounds* of their letters. First teach the sound of *a,* then *n,* being careful to teach only those sounds of the letters which they represent in the word *an.* Require the pupil to utter these sounds in quick succession, as represented in Col. 2d, [following] till the combination in Col. 3rd is distinctly given.

Next, the sound of *m* should be taught, and given in connection with the combination in the 3d Column, as represented in Col. 2d, till the perfect word in Col. 3d is heard.

This word should now be read in the reading lesson below.

When the next word, *fan,* is wanted, it can be had by simply teaching the letter *f.* As fast as new words are wanted they should be taught, and *no faster.*

A similar course should be continued through Part II., when the Alphabet (except q and z) is learned, *its use,* and the use of words. If the teacher prefers, the *names* of the letters can be taught in connection with their sounds.

LESSON 1.

Column 1st.	Column 2d.	Column 3d.
ā n	ā-n	ān
m	m-ān	mān
f	f-ān	fān
r	r-ān	rān
p	p-ān	pān[27]

Webb's teaching of new words followed the methods of "word analysis" by sound and was preceded by a period of "preparation" or "readiness" activity designed to put the pupils "on their own" in approaching new words in their reading. The suggestions to the teacher concerning methods for this "readiness" work begin on page 18 about halfway through Part I. In that place, taking up nearly half the page, appears the box on page 19 with a note.

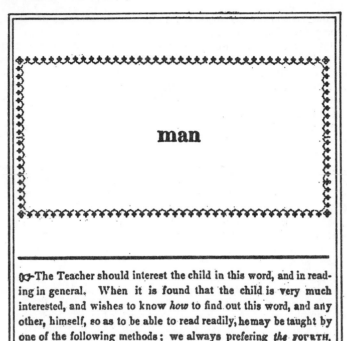

man

☞The Teacher should interest the child in this word, and in reading in general. When it is found that the child is very much interested, and wishes to know *how* to find out this word, and any other, himself, so as to be able to read readily, he may be taught by one of the following methods; we always prefering *the* ᴘᴏᴜᴛʜ, as referred to on pages 37 and 38.

Part III has the title "Union Method": "In this method we unite those given in Part I and II, and also bring in such words as come under the head of no method, except the Method of 'Application', which include all words not spelled as pronounced."[28]

In order to stress the need for comprehension and understanding on the part of the child Webb provides a series of suggested questions at the end of each reading lesson.

Questions.—What is this story about? Where did the quail set? Where was the boy? Was he a lazy boy? What girl is mentioned in the story? Did the quail have a mate? Where was its mate?

Butler's Series

"Butler's Series," published in 1883, uses a somewhat different procedure, as outlined in the "Suggestions To Teachers."

The first step in any work is the most important. Of no subject is this more true than of reading.

It is recommended that teachers using this book should employ the Word Method in connection with the Phonic Method. We are satisfied that the Alphabetic Method is a hindrance rather than a help. A child can more readily learn twenty-six words than twenty-six letters. Words have interest to a child because they mean something. Letters are merely arbitrary signs.

After a child names the letters of a word he pauses until he is told what the word is. Why not tell him the word at once?

Spelling should not be taught until a child can read fairly. A child is unconsciously learning to spell while he reads. He should be taught to write the words. In writing them he is really learning something about spelling them. Spelling may be learned to a limited extent, from reading; but reading never can be learned from spelling.

While advocating the Word Method, we would guard instructors against teaching words without first developing the ideas they represent.

To aid the teacher in this work, most of the lessons of this book are illustrated.

Begin the lesson by showing the children the picture. Let them tell all they see in it. Have a familiar talk about it. Call upon one to name an object in the picture. Show them on the board the word by which the object is known. Be careful to print the word as nearly like the one in the book as possible. Let the children find the word upon the page wherever it occurs, and pronounce it.

Teach *a* and *the* in connection with the word following each. . . .

After the lesson has been mastered by the Word Method, let the child pronounce the word to be analyzed just as it was pronounced in the lesson. The teacher should then pronounce the elements of the word slowly, and ask the child or the class to say what word they form.[29]

The words at the end of each reading lesson are designed for a phonic review, and not for a spelling lesson.

The first lessons in the book are not confined to very short words, for the reason that a child can as readily recognize a word of five or six letters as he can a shorter one.[30]

The McGuffey Readers

The famous *Eclectic Series,* the readers originally produced by William H. McGuffey, President of Cincinnati College, Ohio, first appeared during the 1830s.

In preparing the first two books, President McGuffey has taken a class of young pupils into his own house, and has taught them Spelling and Reading for the express purpose of being able to judge with the greatest accuracy of the best method of preparing the "Readers."

The lessons and stories which he has adopted in the First and Second Books, are probably the most simple and yet most instructive, amusing and beautiful for the young mind that can be found in our language.[31]

Later revisions, of course, changed much of this content. In that of 1879 appears the following note: "The credit for this revision is almost wholly due to the many friends of *McGuffey's Readers,*— eminent teachers and scholars, who have contributed suggestions and criticisms gained from their daily work in the school room."[32]

These books were "especially adapted to the Phonic Method, the Word Method, or a combination of the two."

III. Word Method.—Teach the pupil to identify at sight the words placed at the head of the reading exercises, and to read these exercises without hesitation. Having read a few lessons, begin to teach the names of the letters and the spelling of words.

IV. Word Method and Phonic Method Combined.—Teach the pupil to identify words and read sentences, as above. Having read a few lessons in this manner, begin to use the Phonic Method, combining it with the Word Method, by first teaching the words in each lesson *as words;* then, the elementary sounds, the names of the letters, and spelling.[33]

From the very beginning, as for example in the "Suggestions To Teachers" of the edition of 1838, the McGuffey readers emphasized the getting of *meaning* and especially the guiding of the pupils in the use of the context for that meaning.

It is recommended that the pupil be required to *master* every thing as he goes along. . . . The Definitions ought to be made out by the exercise of the pupil's own judgment (aided by the instructor) from the sense which the *connection requires:* for, to seek out and memorize definitions from a dictionary, or defining vocabulary, is injurious rather than beneficial. It is mere exercise of memory, and nothing else. . . . The plan of teaching the pupil to *spell,* in conjunction with the exercises in reading, will, it is believed, be found eminently beneficial in fixing in the memory the *orthographical form of words,* not only as they appear in the columns of a spelling-book or dictionary, but in all the variety of their different numbers, oblique cases, degrees of comparison, moods, tenses, etc.—while the exercise of *defining* produces a similar effect in regard to the *meaning* of the terms employed; since the learner is required to find out the meaning of each term defined, from the *connection,* without having recourse to the expositor. It is the *connection alone,* that can convey to the mind the true meaning of words.[34]

THE SENTENCE METHOD

The "Sentence" Method, as such, received considerable discussion and practice from 1870 on. It is best set forth in a small book first appearing in 1881,[35] followed by editions of 1886 and 1895. This book was widely used in teacher training institutes in the East, especially in New York State, and in the Middle West, chiefly in Iowa and Nebraska.

The Preface contains an account of the circumstances giving rise to the practices described in the book.

In his experience as teacher and superintendent of schools, it became evident to the author, many years ago, that there was something fundamentally wrong in the ordinary methods of teaching reading, writing and spelling. Viewed from the standpoint of economy, the result bore no just ratio to the time and effort devoted to these branches; and viewed from the standpoint of education, the first years of instruction seemed imperfect and unsatisfactory. This conviction, which he shared with many teachers throughout the country, led to examination and experiment.

In 1858, the phonetic system was introduced into the schools of Syracuse, N.Y., and for a time it was thought that the true method of teaching children to read had been discovered. After a trial of five years, however, it was seen that while pupils learned to read by this method in much less time than usual, and attained a high state of excellence in articulation, their reading was nearly as mechanical as before, and few of them became good spellers. The two systems of analysis, phonic and graphic, had so little in common that permanent confusion was produced in the mind.

The word method, next tried, was much more productive of good results than any that had preceded it; yet by this method words were treated as units, independent of sentences, and reading [oral] almost of necessity became a series of independent pronunciations, perpetuating the mechanical results of the old methods.

These experiments and their results led to further investigation, especially in the line of psychology. From a close observation of the action of the mind, and of the relations of language to thought, it was seen that the unit of thinking is a thought, and therefore that the sentence ought to be made the basis of reading exercises.

In 1870 a series of experiments was instituted in the schools of Binghamton, N.Y., to subject this theory to a practical test. The results far exceeded expectation in the direct teaching of reading, spelling and writing, and led to other results in awakening the mind and in influencing conduct which were unexpected and gratifying. It is safe to assume that the problem, how to teach these branches successfully, has been solved.

The methods here presented are not merely theoretical. They were elaborated after careful study, and then subjected to experiment and correction, and as here given they are such as have survived the ordeal and have borne abundant fruit.

It is believed that parents will find here a simple process of teaching reading, writing and composition to their children which will cause little interruption of their daily duties. Indeed the well regulated home is without doubt the very best primary school.[36]

Farnham's little book, widely used as a manual for teachers, puts into precise and effective expression much that one hears offered as good doctrine in educational circles today—the emphasis on "growth," the need for preparation exercises to make the pupils ready for reading, the constant insistence upon meaning and thought as the basic objectives for which anything that interferes (phonics, for example) must be abandoned, the use of much supplementary reading material, and selection on the basis of "interest." Farnham's own words in quotations will demonstrate his views, but separate brief excerpts would not really represent the helpful clarity achieved by the greater surface of his complete discussion in the book. The following quotations come from the 1881 edition. Chapter I, entitled "First Principles," sets forth the views underlying his "Sentence Method."

Reading consists: first, in gaining the thoughts of an author from written or printed language:—second, in giving oral expression to these thoughts in the language of the author, so that the same thoughts are conveyed to the hearer.

It is important that this two-fold function of reading should be fully recognized. The first, or silent reading, is the fundamental process. It is often called "Reading to one's self," a phrase significant as indicating a wrong conception of the true end to be accomplished. The second, oral reading, or "reading aloud," is entirely subordinate to silent reading. While oral expression is subject to laws of its own, its excellence depends upon the success of the reader in comprehending the thought of the author. The importance of these distinctions is so great that I will consider them in detail.

SILENT, OR EYE READING

It is scarcely possible to exaggerate the importance of correct "eye reading;"—of the ability to look over the written or printed page, and, with the least possible consciousness of the words used, to fully comprehend the thoughts expressed.

A common process is indicated by the expression, "reading to one's self." This means the translation of written into oral language.

The reader either pronounces each word so that he can actually hear it, or he thinks of the pronunciation. In either case the thought is not formed in his mind directly through the written language, but indirectly after the written words have changed into oral expression. This process is slow and laborious, it becomes painful when long continued; and its practice will account for the antipathy which so many persons have to reading books and articles of considerable length.

The object in teaching should be to make every pupil an eye reader,—to give him the ability to look directly through the written expression to the meaning, or to at once detect the unknown elements that prevent the accomplishment of this object.

A New Use of the Eye.

The ordinary function of the eye is to take in the visible characteristics of objects. This is the use to which all children have become accustomed, and they form judgments in accordance with perfect confidence. No child doubts his ability to distinguish his friends, his toys, or any object to which he may direct his attention. Through this sense, aided by touch, he comes into possession of most of his knowledge of the external world. The knowledge so obtained is direct and tangible.

With hearing it is different. While the ear recognizes sound, it has been accustomed from the earliest period to recognize thought through the sound of oral language, until the thought becomes primary in one's consciousness, and his sound of the language secondary. Indeed, language becomes so purely representative of thought, that, as sound, it scarcely appeals to consciousness. The child associates speech with thought divined from his experience, and never regards it as having a separate existence. The words he hears quicken thought into conscious activity, and he in turn is impelled to express his thought by the use of words.

The child has come into possession of his powers, both of thought and of expression, by a gradual and unconscious process. He has simply been shaped by his surroundings. By association with those who talk, he has acquired the power of understanding speech and of speaking. The kind of speech, whether perfect or imperfect, which he hears he reproduces.

This fact should be distinctly understood and realized. The powers of speech and of understanding what is said, both come to the child by a process so simple and natural that he is conscious of no effort to acquire them. Speech, objectively considered, is only a combination of sounds uttered in quick succession, having not the slightest resemblance to the thoughts represented; but by the child it is understood with exactness and uttered with precision. The whole complicated process is matured without effort, and without the intervention of teachers.

To make the eye perform the office of the ear, and the hand that of the organs of voice, is the problem that presents itself in attempting to teach a child to read and write. The vital point is to so change the function of the eye that it will look upon written or printed characters, not as objects to be recognized for their own sake, but as directly calling into conscious being past experiences, and so becoming representative of thought. All the efforts of the teacher should be directed to this end.

At this point our education has often failed. The process of translating the written language into speech is so slow and difficult that a large share of the pupils in our schools are condemned to comparative ignorance. The words as they appear have no meaning to them. One who acquired the power of directly receiving thought from the printed page, is endowed with a new intellectual faculty. His eye flashes along the pages of a book, and he comprehends whole sentences at a glance. It would not do to say that these rapid readers do not understand what they read. The fact is they understand much better than the slow reader. The mental power, being relieved from the necessity of translating, concentrates itself upon the thought, and the thought is understood and remembered. Our endeavor should be to give pupils this power of eye reading from the first so that they may continually profit by it, and have no evil habits to overcome.

Oral Reading.

When the habit of sight-reading is acquired, oral reading will need but little attention. The oral expression is subordinate to correct eye-reading, and its acquisition is largely incidental. When the pupil has power to take in the thought from the printed page directly, he will have but little difficulty in giving it proper oral expression in the language of the author. The pupil, being under the control of the thought obtained, must read the thought as naturally as he speaks.

In oral reading there are always two parties, the readers and the hearers. It is as important that pupils should be taught to obtain thoughts by listening as by reading; and to this end the other members of the class should close their books while one is reading, the test of the value of the exercise being their ability to reproduce the thoughts which they have heard.

FIRST PRINCIPLE

The first principle to be observed in teaching written language, is, "that things are cognized as wholes." Language follows this law. Although it is to be taught by an indirect process, still, in its external characteristics, it follows the laws of other objects.

The question arises, what is the whole? or what is the unit of expression? It is now quite generally conceded that we have no ideas not logically associated with others. In other words, *thoughts,* complete in their relations, are the materials in the mind out of which complex relations are constructed.

It being admitted that the thought is the unit of thinking, it necessarily follows that *the sentence is the unit of expression.* One may assure himself of the correctness of this view by watching the operations of a little child, even before it is able to talk. You give such a child any direction which you expect will control its action, and leave out any part of the sentence that is essential to its completeness, and the child will not be influenced by it. It is true that elliptical expressions are sometimes used, but the missing portions are supplied in the mind, before action is produced. Let anyone attempt to remember a series of words so arranged as to express no complete thought, and he will see how absolutely we are dependent upon the logical arrangement of language. A speaker will have no difficulty in making himself understood in any part of a large room, if he addresses the audience in connected and logical discourse. No one listening will be conscious of losing a single word of what is said. But let the same speaker attempt to read the names of a dozen persons, or give a list of disconnected words, and he will hardly be able to pronounce them with sufficient distinctness to be understood, without repetition.

SECOND PRINCIPLE

A second principle is, we acquire a knowledge of the *parts* of an object by first considering it as a whole. Repeated recognitions reveal the characteristics of the whole, so as to separate it from other things. We descend from the contemplation of the whole to the parts that compose the whole. Otherwise the parts would be more distinctly remembered than the whole. But this is contrary to experience. We have no difficulty in distinguishing one person from another, but if called upon to state exactly in what this difference consists, we shall be at a loss for a satisfactory reply, unless we have made the matter an object of special attention.

That words are no exception to this rule is obvious from the almost universal practice of writing out the word and looking at it as a *whole* to determine whether it is properly spelled. We have more confidence in our judgment of the appearance of a word as a whole, than upon our ability to reproduce it in detail, notwithstanding this latter method is the one in which we have been drilled.

The sentence, when properly taught, will, in like manner, be understood as a whole, better than if presented in detail. The order indicated is, first the sentence, then the words, and then the letters. The sentence being first presented as a whole, the words are discovered, and after that the letters composing the words.

THIRD PRINCIPLE

The third principle, is that while language, oral and written, follows the laws of other objects so far as its material characteristics are concerned, it differs from other objects studied for their own sake, by being only representative in its character. While it is to be recognized, it must be so recognized as to make the thought expressed by it the conscious object of attention.[37]

In Chapter II Farnham gives in detail a step-by-step procedure for making the pupil ready to read, under the heading "Exercises Before Books are Used." Three steps are discussed in detail.

(a) ". . . to awaken thought in the mind of the child by means of objects, and to give the thought complete oral expression."

(b) ". . . to awaken in the mind of the child the exact thought contained in oral expression, and to lead him to make the appropriate concrete representation. . . .

"In observation we pass from the thought to the expression; in reading, from the expression to the thought. This step is to make clear that thought may be obtained from oral expression, as preparatory to the final step of obtaining thoughts from written expression."

(c) ". . . to awaken in the mind of the child the exact thought contained in written expression, and to enable him to express the thought in the language used."[38]

Chapter III deals with the process of "reading from books." The preparatory steps before books are introduced will take on the average approximately three months but, as he says, "the time necessary for each step cannot be precisely given, as it must vary with the capacity of the pupil, the tact of the teacher, and various conditions of the school."

Farnham would cast out "phonics" and its uses—or rather "phonic analysis"—as he understands it. His vigorous condemnation follows.

The phonic analysis of words should have no place in the primary schools. Until the habits of thought reading and correct spelling are well established, such analysis is a positive evil. It makes the child conscious of the oral element of words, and as these do not correspond with the written elements, a double evil ensues: the mind has become directly conscious of language which it should use unconsciously or nearly so; and it introduces a new set of elements antagonistic to the ones used in the graphic expression. The habitual action of the muscles coming from one stimulus, upon which good spelling depends, is directly interfered with by another stimulus which urges to different results. The antagonism is radical and irreconcilable, and bad spelling must result. The reason for the early introduction of the phonic element:—the securing of correct pronunciation, may be accomplished in another way. The pupils should be required to pronounce their words slowly, so as to give to each sound its proper force, and here imitation of the words as spoken by others is the only way to secure correct results.

The letter, word, or phonic method will each day accomplish certain specific results, which can be weighed and measured. Teachers, parents, and friends see this, and are satisfied. But the results leave little impress of true mental growth. Naming letters and words, no matter in what order, and remembering them, is not necessarily reading. The thought must be reached, and everything else must be subordinated to this end.[39]

Farnham thus makes the getting of the "thought" the first aim of reading and demands that every technique and method used in teaching reading must contribute to the pupils' growth in habits of "thought" reading.

Farnham also stresses the need to supplement the reading material of any single book.

A great difficulty is experienced in obtaining a sufficient supply of appropriate reading matter. The book given to any class should be within their comprehension and it should be read through, or such parts of it as are found interesting. An ordinary first or second reader will last but a few weeks, and hence there should be in every school several such readers, or some equivalent reading matter. . . .

In general, children should be induced to read what they desire to know, and what is worth knowing, and for the purpose of knowing. Hence, all through the course, silent reading, followed by reproduction,[40] should receive special attention. . . .

The children may bring their own little books and each one may read a story, which the others will reproduce. In these exercises another important educational interest is served;—the pupils are taught to listen to what is said, and to repeat accurately what they heard.[41]

Toward the end of his little book, Farnham again insists upon the goal of real comprehension and understanding, which can only be achieved by starting from the growing experience of the child himself.

A very common mistake should be carefully avoided, and that is the endeavor to fill the mind with the matured and condensed results of scientific investigation. *True education is a growth.* The knowledge upon which the mind feeds[42] must be assimilated. This knowledge must be administered in such proportions and under such conditions as will best promote assimilation. The effort to cram ideas is as fatal as that of cramming words.[43] [The italics are mine.]

Whatever our opinion concerning the validity of the "sentence" method of teaching reading, we must agree that, as explained and practiced by Farnham and his followers, this approach through the "whole sentence" was well conceived and thoroughly worked out in a teachable program. As early as 1881, the schools in the systems of which Farnham was superintendent stressed the need for preparation exercises to make the pupils "ready" for reading, constantly insisted upon the getting of meaning and thought as the basic objective, made use of supplementary reading material and selections on the basis of pupil interest, and, asserting that "True education is a growth," based their teaching of reading upon the experience of the pupils.

The inclusion here of rather long quotations from the "Directions to Teachers" in the prefaces of textbooks, from the journals containing the discussions of teachers' practices, and from the "method books" widely used in the very common short-term annual "institutes for teachers" seemed necessary in order to demonstrate in some detail what the struggles of teachers and superintendents of city schools had achieved before 1890. The leading teachers and administrators of those days did not conceive the task of teaching reading in any narrow fashion and their practical classroom experimentation led to a continuing development in theory and in method. These achievements all antedate the rise of "modern" educational research by at least a generation.

Without doubt there was much poor teaching of reading in the schools of the nineteenth century and many very poor teachers. The condemnations of many of the then current practices of such teachers appeared abundantly in the letters and journals from 1828 to 1900. Such condemnations, however, have appeared both before and after the nineteenth century, and with considerable justification. On the other hand, there have been in our schools many excellent teachers thoroughly devoted to the task of improving the education provided for our children. And such teachers developed most of the methods and combinations of methods of teaching reading that are vigorously discussed today.

I have not been able to find the evidence to justify the assertion that the published findings of recent educational research [since 1916] have provided the basis of most of the modern reforms in reading instruction.[44]

EYE MOVEMENTS

Those somewhat familiar with the steady stream of educational research devoted to the teaching of reading during the last forty years will raise the question of the contribution made through the research done on eye movements. The study of eye movements began in Europe with the work of Professor Émile Javal of the University of Paris, published in 1878–1879.[45] Building upon this early work, continuing studies in France and in Germany, and, after 1900, in the United States, produced not only much more accurate and satisfactory techniques of observation but also a large body of knowledge that constitutes one large sector of what is usually studied as the "psychology of reading."[46]

From the many studies that since 1900 have concentrated upon "the eye movements in reading," much has been learned concerning the eye movements of good readers and the eye movements of poor readers, the eye movements of college professors and of elementary-school pupils, of graduate students reading the materials of their special field of concentration and those of subject-matter outside their special experience. Many, too, have tried to take this knowledge about the eye movements in reading and find ways by which to use it in practical exercises that would result in improved reading performance of readers. Most of the efforts in the practical application of knowledge concerning the characteristics of "eye movements in reading" have centered upon those who have failed to learn to read during the school years usually devoted to acquiring literacy. It has been used in the attempts to cure bad habits set up in some way during the first years of the teaching of reading. It is in the greatly increased remedial work that eye movements have been given their chief consideration and exercises with various types of mechanical apparatus have been developed in the struggle to apply the rather considerable body of knowledge concerning eye movements.[47] But on the whole, practically nothing has appeared that has utilized the knowledge gained from the study of eye movements in order to improve the reading efficiency of normal children in the first stages of learning to read. In spite of the great number of studies dealing with eye movements (or better, "eye pauses"), very little of a positive nature has been contributed from these studies to our understanding of reading ability and to our knowledge of how to develop it in either children or adults. The research studies have, it is true, shown some correlations between rhythmic movements with few fixations and superior reading ability. But nonrhythmic eye movements with an increased number of fixations and some reversals do not always mark poor reading ability. They often appear in the records of those of superior reading ability and mark the reader's struggle with points of meaning. *In other words, the rhythmic or nonrhythmic eye movements, the few or many fixations, the reversals, are all symptoms of a successful or unsuccessful performance of reading at a particular time.* Unfortunately many have regarded the nonrhythmic eye movements and frequent eye pauses as *causes* of poor reading and have sought to change the eye-movement habits of children, even by the use of mechanical devices. I can find no evidence in the research studies that nonrhythmic eye pauses cause poor reading. The reported correlations in the studies of the past thirty years do not furnish any ground for doing anything concerning the eye-movement patterns of children.[48] In fact the authors of a number of research studies on various aspects of eye movements include in their conclusions very definite statements to the contrary.

Since there is tremendous variation in eye-movement pattern from child to child, and, since eye-movement patterns tend to remain stable for a given child in various reading situations, a question arises regarding the advisability of eye-movement training. Eye-movement patterns seem to express the child's individuality and any exterior mechanical attempt to regulate or change these patterns would seem to be contraindicated.[49]

. . . recent research, like earlier research, failed to provide convincing support for the value of training of eye movements through mechanical procedures.[50]

In the early enthusiasm for the new "scientific" study of educational problems, it was perhaps inevitable that conclusions reported at second-hand in summaries of research should appear without the guarded qualifications of the original articles. It was also perhaps inevitable that considerable pressure should develop to apply at once in practical teaching what it was believed research had "proved." In the commendable effort to use for the improvement of teaching in the schools the knowledge made available by research, three things have happened.

(a) Conclusions that have been barely suggested as possibilities or opinions by the authors of research studies have been made absolute in the practical materials for teachers.

Regular rhythmical movements of the eye are prerequisite to rapid silent reading.

Rapid readers read with more comprehension than slow readers.

This habit [lip movement] is an outgrowth of the exclusive use of oral reading which characterized the practice of most American schools until the year 1915 and which is still common in many elementary schools.

(b) Symptoms have been regarded as causes. Some correlations have shown a connection between poor reading and irregular nonrhythmical eye movements, but the attacks of teachers upon the eye movements themselves have assumed that the irregular eye movements were the *cause* of poor reading. Some correlations have seemed to indicate that the rapid readers examined in certain studies read with more comprehension than did the slow readers,[51] and the teachers have tried to improve comprehension by increasing the speed of reading, assuming that the slow rate was the cause of the lower comprehension.

(c) Many conscientious teachers have come to believe not only that the major principles of the reading program of the school system in which they teach (as they understand these principles) are supported by widely accepted research evidence, but also, by inference, *that whole sets of former practices must now be considered wrong.* This negative point of view of many teachers, combined with their fear of being censured, seems to me to be one of the most disturbing elements in the present situation.

Among the professional articles and books dealing specifically with the problems of reading appear the works not only of teachers, school administrators, and professors of education, but also those of psychologists, ophthalmologists, neurologists, and librarians— practically nothing by linguists.[52] Kenneth L. Pike's *Phonemics: A Technique for Reducing Language to Writing* (University of Michigan Press, 1947) seems to be known only to linguists and has not been listed in the bibliographies of the materials concerning reading. Leonard Bloomfield's article "Linguistics and Reading"[53] is listed in the bibliographies but the few comments that have been made upon it demonstrate that it has not been understood. Rudolf Flesch in *Why Johnny Can't Read* used it to support his "back to phonics" plea in spite of the fact that Bloomfield in his article (p. 129) specifically points out the "serious faults" of the "so-called 'phonic' methods of teaching children to read." Irving H. Anderson and Walter F. Dearborn, in *The Psychology of Teaching Reading* (pp. 209, 210), seem to use it to support the word method, in spite of Bloomfield's criticisms of that method and the following direct statement: "The most serious drawback of all the English instruction known to me, regardless of the special method that is in each case advocated, is the drawback of the word-method." William S. Gray, in *On Their Own in Reading* (pp. 29–32) ignores the fact that Bloomfield's approach always uses "whole words," never separate or isolated sounds of letters, and says of it, "One recent proposal for a mechanical approach roundly denounces any learning of words as wholes in the early stages—and proposes, instead, use of the alphabetical principle."

Throughout all these publications on the teaching of reading there seems to be no awareness whatever of any aspect of the "scientific study of language"—not even of the rich resources made available by the great *Oxford English Dictionary*. Those dealing professionally with educational problems quite naturally think that the linguist's field of central activity is very remote from that of those who deal with the process of reading. They forget that the final deciphering of many types of ancient writing was achieved by linguists, that the historical study of language has rested upon and must rest primarily upon written evidence, and that the historical linguist has had to determine the precise relations between the graphic signs and the language itself. The linguist, especially the historical linguist, has also had to learn to read more varieties of "writing" than perhaps any other type of scholar. Unfortunately his experience and knowledge have not been part of that brought to bear upon the problems of teaching and learning reading. As a result, the studies devoted to reading problems have given no consideration to the new knowledge concerning the nature and functioning of language achieved by the labors of a host of linguistic scholars over more than a century. It is perhaps not overstating the situation to say that the most important deficiency of the studies devoted to reading problems arises out of misunderstanding or ignoring

(a) the nature of the various types of signals which constitute language in general and the English language in particular, and

(b) the actual structural significance of the alphabet in comparison with the other writing systems.

What then is a "linguist," and what is the "linguistics" to be explored here for possible help in defining more sharply the problems of teaching reading?

CHAPTER TWO

Linguistics: The Study of Language

For many of those who deal with the practical problems of the schools and for the general public the word *linguistics* has the ring of something quite new. It seems to stand for something that has grown up very recently—something radical. On the other hand, there are those who understand *linguistics* as simply a new label for the familiar struggle to learn foreign languages. To them a *linguist* is one who can speak several languages. To be a "good linguist" for a large part of even the well-educated public means to speak foreign languages fluently.

Linguistics, however, in the special sense of that word as used in the title of this book and of this chapter, does not concern itself primarily with the practical study of languages. Linguists do study languages. Good linguists find it necessary to study a great variety of languages—especially languages that differ fundamentally in structure from their own native language. But this study of languages by "linguists" does not have as its primary aim and purpose the building up of the habits of use required to speak them fluently or even well enough to communicate through reading or writing. Most "linguists" study languages in order to know and to understand their structures—the particular ways in which these languages use their linguistic units to achieve their communicative function. They seek primarily, knowledge *about* the units and the working processes of each language, rather than the ability to speak them. Of course, some linguists, like Bloomfield and the workers of the Summer Institute of Linguistics, do strive to learn to speak the languages they set out to describe scientifically. The linguist, as linguist, however, studies a wide variety of languages because he seeks primarily to understand *the processes of human language*. He is somewhat like the zoologist, who studies animal life in a wide variety of forms—from protozoa to vertebrates. He is perhaps more like the anthropologist, who studies the life of humans in a great variety of the groups of mankind. In other words, a linguist is a "scientist" whose field of research and knowledge is human language, not the practical mastery of languages. Languages constitute the specific material upon which he works, but through the concrete evidence of the workings of each of these languages the linguistic scientist tries to understand the nature of human language and the processes of its functioning. The fruit of his work constitutes "linguistic science."

The special way in which the linguistic scientist studies languages to achieve his purpose we shall call here the "scientific study of language" or *linguistics,* and use the phrase "the practical study of languages" whenever we wish to designate that language study which seeks to master one or more languages for practical use.

This "scientific study of language" is not very new. It seems new to many people because only comparatively recently have vigorous popular discussions used the particular terms "linguist," "linguistics," and the "scientific study of language." In most of these recent popular discussions, the more than a century-long history of this type of study is not only never mentioned but the views attributed to linguists are often attacked as the private theories of a small group of radicals devoted to a program of undermining the defenses of "accurate and elegant expression."[1] But modern linguistics, as the scientific study of language through the work of a great host of linguistic scholars, has, since the first quarter of the nineteenth century, built up a tremendous body of new knowledge concerning the nature and functioning of human language which has not yet been assimilated by or even known to the general public.

It is true that the knowledge so gained has made it necessary for linguists to abandon many of the traditional views of language vigorously set forth in the seventeenth and eighteenth centuries, especially those dominating the grammars and dictionaries of the second half of the eighteenth century—the English grammars of Archbishop Lowth, of William Ward, of Charles Coote, and of Lindley Murray, and the dictionaries of Samuel Johnson, and of Thomas Sheridan. But linguists have abandoned these conventional views not because of any deliberate purpose on their part to oppose the conventional views but because their use of the newer methods of language study forced them to conclusions that made the traditional views of language untenable.

LINGUISTIC SCIENCE FROM 1820 TO 1875

It is, of course, quite arbitrary to fix a precise date for the "beginning" of any significant intellectual advance. The best we can do is to place in time some specific evidence of a breakthrough into the new ways of working and the new understandings upon which later scholars have built. In linguistics such a breakthrough into a new way of studying the problems of language diversity and relationship occurred with the publication in 1818 of Erasmus Rask's *Investigation on the Origin of the Old Norse or Icelandic Language*[2] and the publication of the second edition of the first volume of Jakob Grimm's *Deutsche Grammatik* in 1822. These two publications started a succession of workers upon a long series of studies that had the two fundamental characteristics of a science—that it be *cumulative* and *impersonal*. It must be *cumulative* in the sense that all contributions must build upon, or take cognizance of, all that has preceded; and *impersonal* in the sense that the techniques used must lead to generalizations that are verifiable by all competent persons.[3] To be "science" the results obtained cannot remain private theories perpetuated by authority.

The scientific study of language has had since 1825 a host of devoted workers building upon, refining, and extending the techniques that proved most productive of verifiable conclusions. From time to time linguistic scholars have tried to summarize for the general public the results of this scientific study of language.

During the month of March 1863, Professor William Dwight Whitney of Yale University delivered six lectures "On the Principles of Linguistic Science" at the Smithsonian Institution in Washington, D.C. A brief abstract of these lectures was printed in the Institution's Annual Report.[4] These lectures were expanded to twelve and delivered before the Lowell Institute in Boston in December 1864 and January 1865. Rewritten and expanded again, they were published in 1867 in a book of 505 pages under the title *Language and the Study of Language: Twelve Lectures on the Principles of Linguistic Science*. Their substance constituted the basis of his "instruction in the science of language" in Yale University. Professor Whitney believed

. . . that at least so much knowledge of the nature, history, and classifications of language as is here presented ought to be included in every scheme of higher education, even for those who do not intend to become special students in comparative philology. Much more necessary, of course, is it to those who cherish such intention. It is, I am convinced, a mistake to commence at once upon a course of detailed comparative philology with pupils who have only enjoyed the training in the classical or the modern languages or in both. They are liable either to fail of apprehending the value and interest of the infinity of particulars into which they are plunged, or else to become wholly absorbed in them, losing sight of the grand truths and principles which underlie and give significance to their work, and the recognition of which ought to govern its course throughout.[5]

Invited to contribute a volume on language to *The International Scientific Series,* begun in London in 1873, Whitney produced his *Life and Growth of Language: An Outline of Linguistic Science,* a book of 327 pages, in 1875. Several of the comments from his introductory chapter should be added to the statements quoted from his earlier book.

Yet the body of truth [concerning the general problems of language] has been so small, that the science of language is to be regarded as a modern one, as much so as geology and chemistry; it belongs like them to the nineteenth century. . . . Although of so recent growth, the science of language is already one of the leading branches of modern inquiry. It is not less comprehensive in its material, definite in its aims, strict in its methods, and rich and fruitful in its results, than its sister sciences. Its foundations have been laid deep and strong in the thorough analysis of many of the most important human tongues, and the careful examination and classification of nearly all the rest. It has yielded to the history of mankind as a whole, and to that of the different races of men, definite truths and far-reaching glimpses of truth which could be won in no other way. It is bringing about a recast of the old methods of teaching even familiar and long-studied languages, like the Latin and Greek; it is drawing forward to conspicuous notice others of which, only a few years ago, hardly the names were known. It has, in short, leavened all the connected branches of knowledge and worked itself into the very structure of modern thought, so that no one who hears or reads can help taking some cognizance of it. No educated person can afford to lack a clear conception of at least a brief connected outline of a science possessing such claims to attention. The design of this volume, accordingly, is to draw out and illustrate the principles of linguistic science, and to set forth its results, with as much fullness as the limited space at command shall allow.[6]

Especially significant was Whitney's clear-sighted grasp of the distinction to be made between the building up of an extensive body of exact information concerning a wide range of different languages and the conclusions relating to the nature and functioning of language to be derived from this information—the conclusions which constitute the heart and substance of linguistic science.

Comparative philology and linguistic science, we may say, are two sides of the same study: the former deals primarily with the individual facts of a certain body of languages, classifying them, tracing out their relations, and arriving at the conclusions they suggest; the latter makes the laws and general principles of speech its main subject, and uses particular facts rather as illustrations. The one is the working phase, the other the regulative and critical and teaching phase of the science. The one is more important as a part of special training, the other as an element of general culture—if, indeed, it be proper to raise any question as to their relative importance, even to the special student of language; for the lack of either will equally unfit him for doing the soundest and best service. . . .

Yet the two are certainly different enough to make it possible that a scholar should excel in the one and not in the other. The science of language runs out, on its comparative side, into an infinity of details, like chemistry or zoölogy; and one may be extremely well versed in the manipulation of its special processes while wholly wrong as regards its grander generalizations: just as one may be a skillful analyst while knowing little or nothing of the philosophy of chemistry, or eminent in the comparative anatomy of animals with no sound knowledge or judgment as to the principles of biology. To illustrate this, it would be easy to cite remarkable examples of men of the present generation, enjoying high distinction as comparative philologists, who, as soon as they attempt to reason on the wider truths of linguistic science, fall into incongruities and absurdities; or, in matters of minor importance, they show in manifold ways the lack of a sound and defensible basis of general theoretical views. Comparative work of the broadest scope and greatest value has long been done and is still doing; but the science of language is only in the most recent period taking shape; and its principles are still subjects of great diversity of opinion and of lively controversy. It is high time that this state of things, tolerable only in the growing and shaping period of study, should come to an end, and that, as in other sciences of observation and deduction—for example, in chemistry, zoölogy, geology—there should be acknowledged to exist a body, not of facts only, but of truths, so well established that he who rejects them shall have no claim to be considered a man of science.[7]

These two books by Whitney on the principles and results of "linguistic science" appeared in 1867 and in 1875, nearly a century ago, but almost fifty years after the first breakthrough in the struggle to find sound techniques by which to explore and establish the relationships of diverse languages. Before 1818, questions concerning language—of origin, of diversity, of relationship, of structure, of meaning—were approached primarily through speculation and appeals to authority.[8] The fifty years from the linguistic ground-breaking of Rask and Grimm to the publication of Whitney's books saw the development of a considerable body of verifiable knowledge concerning language, built up through the use of techniques accessible to all who would become proficient workers in linguistics. The special technique from which the first steps in modern linguistic science started was based upon correspondences of sounds.

Rask and Grimm, by means of the law of Lautverschiebung [sound change, or the Law of Permutation of Consonants] established the fact that the changes of sounds, or as it was then expressed, of *letters,* into one another take place in accordance with laws, and above all, that a fixed historical relation can be observed between the sounds of the German on the one side and of the classical languages on the other. . . .

[This law] . . . goes by Grimm's name, although already pro-claimed by Rask in its main features.[9]

With Rask, this phonological technique was generalized as the means of exploring and proving a genetic relationship between any languages, and it became the firm basis for establishing language "families." Rask's statement, in translation, follows.

A language, however mixed it may be, belongs to the same branch of languages as another when it has the most essential, concrete, indispensable words, the foundation of the language, in common with it. . . . When agreement is found in such words . . . , and so frequently that rules may be drawn up for the shift in letters from one to the other, then there is a fundamental relationship between the two languages. . . .[10]

This principle of rules for the "correspondences in the shift of sounds" or "laws of sound change" provided the beginnings of a new and scientific approach to etymology and the ground upon which to repudiate conclusions based on chance likenesses. It furnished a criterion from which to evaluate both the evidence and the conclusions concerning linguistic relationships. Linguistics thus began to achieve the status of a "science" with the developing of the techniques and procedures for identifying and analyzing the linguistic evidence significant for determining the genetic relationship (or non-relationship) of diverse languages. The developing of these techniques and procedures throughout the fifty years from 1820 to 1875 was the cumulative contribution of an increasing body of workers. As Whitney expressed it in 1867,

A host of worthy rivals and followers of the men whose names we have noted [Rask, Bopp, Grimm, Pott, Burnouf] have arisen in all parts of Europe and even in America, to continue the work which those had begun; and by their aid the science has already attained a degree of advancement that is truly astonishing considering its recent origin.[11]

Whitney also indicated something of the breadth of the field of linguistics:

The material and subject of linguistic science is language, in its entirety; all the accessible forms of human speech, in their infinite variety, whether still living in the minds and mouths of men, or preserved only in written documents, or carved on the scantier but more

imperishable records of brass and stone. It has a field and scope limited
to no age, and to no portion of mankind. The dialects of the obscurest
and most humbly endowed races are its care, as well as those of leaders
in the world's history. Whenever and wherever a sound has dropped
from the lips of a human being, to signalize to others the movement of
his spirit, this science would fain take it up and study it, as having a
character and office worthy of attentive examination. Every fact of
every language, in the view of the linguistic student, calls for his investigation, since only in the light of all can any be completely understood. To assemble, arrange, and explain the whole body of linguistic
phenomena, so as thoroughly to comprehend them, in each separate
part and under all aspects, is his endeavor.[12]

Thus even during the first fifty years the scientific study of
language was not narrowly conceived. The heart and substance of
the linguistic science of even this first period of its development
was not simply in its new tools of operation but rather in the
growing understanding of the nature of language itself. This growing understanding of certain basic characteristics of language did
not, in most instances, come as the conclusions of conscious inquiry into these characteristics, but rather as the *unexpected results*
of the use of the new linguistic techniques and procedures as
applied to the study of a great variety of languages. Some of the
basic characteristics of language that have thus formed part of the
knowledge that constituted the linguistic science of this period are
the following:

(1) All living language is in a condition of constant growth and
change. It matters not to what part of the world we may go: if we find
for any existing speech a record of its predecessor at some time distant
from it in the past, we shall perceive that the two are different—and
more or less different, mainly in proportion to the distance in time that
separates them. . . . An English speaker even of only a century ago
would find not a little in our every-day speech which he would understand with difficulty, or not at all; if we were to hear Shakespeare read
aloud a scene from one of his own works, it would be in no small part
unintelligible. . . . Chaucer's English (500 years ago) we master by dint
of good solid application, and with considerable help from a glossary;
and King Alfred's English (1000 years ago), which we call Anglo-
Saxon, is not easier to us than German. All this, in spite of the fact that
no one has gone about of set purpose to alter English speech, in any
generation among the thirty or forty that have lived between us and
Alfred, any more than in our own. Here, then, is another side of the
life of language for us to deal with, and to explain, if we can.[13]

(2) Language and dialect . . . are only two names for the same thing, as looked at from different points of view. Any body of expressions used by a community, however limited and humble, for the purposes of communication and as the instrument of thought, is a language; no one would think of crediting its speakers with the gift of dialect but not of language. On the other hand, there is no tongue in the world to which we should not with perfect freedom and perfect propriety apply the name of dialect, when considering it as one of a body of related forms of speech. The science of language has democratized our views on such points as these; it has taught us that one man's speech is just as much a language as another man's; that even the most cultivated tongue that exists is only the dialect of a certain class in a certain locality—both class and locality limited, though the limits may be wide ones. The written English is one of the forms of English, used by the educated class for certain purposes, having dialectic characters by which it is distinguished from the colloquial speech of the same class, and yet more from the speech of other classes or sections of the English-speaking community—and each one of these is as valuable to the comparative student of language as their alleged superior. But English and Dutch and German and Swedish, and so on, are the dialects of Germanic speech; and the same, along with French and Irish and Bohemian, and the rest, are dialects of the wider family whose limits we have drawn above. This is the scientific use of the terms. . . .[14]

(3) The constant changes in language are not corruptions that can or should be eliminated or prevented. The actual changing usage of people constitutes the basis of all the "correctness" there can be in language, and the facts upon which to state the history of a language. There can be no other approach upon which to build a scientific history of a language. It was in this first period of the development of linguistic science that the two great historical dictionaries were begun. The collecting of the evidence for the *Deutsches Wörterbuch* began in 1837 and that for the *Oxford English Dictionary* (earlier called *A New English Dictionary on Historical Principles*) was undertaken in 1858. For the *Oxford English Dictionary* the editing, under the direction of Sir James Murray, started in 1878, twenty years after the collecting began. The first part was published in 1884 and the first volume in 1888. The final part came from the press in 1928, seventy years after the collecting started. This dictionary set out to do, and actually accomplished, the most complete survey of usage ever attempted in any language. Altogether the editors of the *Oxford English Dictionary* had in hand, as the basis for their conclusions, more than

six million dated quotations with exact references to their place of occurrence so that they could each be verified. The following two excerpts from the Preface to the first edition of Volume I of that dictionary give the first editor's own statement of their aim and approach.

It was proposed that materials should be collected for a Dictionary which, by the completeness of its vocabulary, and by the application of the historical method to the life and use of words, might be worthy of the English language and of English scholarship. With this view, it was resolved to begin at the beginning, and extract anew typical quotations for the use of words, from all the great English writers of all ages, and from all writers on special subjects whose works might illustrate the history of words employed in special senses, from all writers whatever before the 16th century, and from as many as possible of the more important writers of later times.

The aim of this Dictionary is to furnish an adequate account of the meaning, origin, and history of English words now in general use, or known to have been in use at any time during the last seven hundred years. It endeavours (1) to show, with regard to each individual word, when, how, in what shape, and with what signification, it became English; what development of form and meaning it has since received; which of its uses have, in the course of time, become obsolete, and which still survive; what new uses have since arisen, by what processes, and when; (2) to illustrate these facts by a series of quotations ranging from the first known occurrence of the word to the latest, or down to the present day; the word being thus made to exhibit its own history and meaning; and (3) to treat the etymology of each word strictly on the basis of historical fact, and in accordance with the methods and results of modern philological [linguistic] science.[15]

Although the editing of the *Oxford English Dictionary* lasted through the whole of the second period of the development of linguistic science, it can, in respect to its principles and design, still be regarded as one of the products of the linguistic achievements of the years from 1820 to 1875. The producing of such a dictionary was discussed during the years before 1858, when the collection of materials was formally undertaken by The Philological Society.[16] The basic design of the use of these materials and the statement of the aims of the *Oxford Dictionary* stemmed directly from the new linguistic approach here discussed. It thus differed fundamentally from that of Dr. Samuel Johnson (1755) which had become the model for all succeeding commercial dictionaries, even those of recent times. Johnson's *Dictionary* very clearly rested upon and in itself supported the views of the nature and functioning of language that dominated the second half of the eighteenth century. The *Oxford English Dictionary,* which was planned and undertaken a century later, rested upon and became an important tool in the application of the startlingly new views of the nature and functioning of language that began to arise out of the very different techniques and procedures of the linguistic work from 1820 to 1875.

Johnson's *Dictionary* depended on and attached to the lexicographical work of Nathaniel Bailey (especially the second edition of Bailey's *Dictionary* of 1730). Bailey, for example, was the first of the completely English dictionaries (that is, English dictionaries for English people as distinct from two-language dictionaries) to try to include the whole English vocabulary. The preceding English dictionaries had confined themselves to the "hard" words, especially those borrowed from Latin and Greek. Bailey first included words like *cat, dog,* and *horse.* Johnson followed Bailey in this feature as have the "unabridged" dictionaries following him. The *Oxford English Dictionary,* however, from its much more thorough survey of usage, records six times as many vocabulary entries as does Johnson.

In a feature that differed from Bailey, Johnson first consistently gave quotations from English literature to illustrate the meanings which he described in the definitions. These quotations, however, served merely as illustrations and were not designed to furnish the evidence for his explanations and comments as shown by the fact that in many instances the comments contradict the evidence furnished by the quotations.

The third special feature of Johnson's *Dictionary* is of particular concern for our discussion here. In this dictionary, as editor, Johnson gave judgments concerning the status of the forms, the meanings, and the uses of many of the vocabulary items he included.[17] In a considerable number of instances Johnson condemns words and expressions for which he gives quotations showing their use in English literature by generally approved authors. It is in this feature especially that Johnson became the "father" of most of the later commercial dictionaries. Four examples of such judgments follow.

For the word *budge,* he gives as definition "To stir, to move off the place," and then, in spite of two quotations from Shakspere and one from Samuel Butler's *Hudibras,* he calls it "a low word."

For *fun,* he quotes from Moore and defines it as "Sport; high merriment; frolicsome delight," but calls it "a low cant word."

For *clever* he gives three separate definitions,—(1) "dextrous; skilful," (2) "just; fit; proper; commodious," (3) "well shaped; handsome"—with quotations from L'Estrange, Addison, Pope, and Arbuthnot. Then his judgment follows: "This is a low word, scarcely ever used but in burlesque or conversation; and applied to anything a man likes, without settled meaning."

For *excepting,* in spite of quotations from Dryden and Collier, he calls it "an improper word."

In contrast with this typical eighteenth-century authoritarian attitude toward language, the *Oxford English Dictionary* as a matter of principle gives no such status judgments. It presents a selection of the significant evidence, from the dated quotations collected, as the ground for the conclusions concerning the history of each word and of its various meanings in English. The "definitions" simply state the conclusions that can be drawn from the evidence in hand. In Johnson's *Dictionary* and in others the definitions and comments of the editors are the important matter; they often go beyond or even contradict the illustrative quotations. The *Oxford Dictionary* treatment of the word *nice* represents the new view of language. There is no condemnation of any of the ways in which the word *nice* has been used since its first introduction into the English language in the latter part of the thirteenth century. The editors give the quotations that show that it came into English from Old French, with the meaning of foolish, stupid, senseless (Latin *nescius,* ignorant). It passed through several developments of meaning: "wanton, loose-mannered"; "slothful, lazy, indolent"; "coy, shy, reserved"; "fastidious, dainty, hard to please"; "strict, careful"; "requiring or involving great precision"; "minutely or carefully accurate"; and then our modern common use, "agreeable, that one derives pleasure or satisfaction from, delightful"; "a general epithet of approval." The *Oxford Dictionary* shows that this meaning of *general approval* has been attached to the word *nice,* and has appeared in our literature with that meaning, ever since the middle of the eighteenth century.

By 1875, the end of the first fifty years of this "modern scientific study" of language, the following views of language became for linguists the ground upon which they based their procedures.

(1) Constant change is to be expected in all languages at every period of their history. It was these changes that formed the object of study.

(2) These changes are not a succession of unrelated events in which anything can happen at random. These changes, in spite of what seemed to be many exceptions, showed a surprising regularity. They showed so much regularity, in fact, that it was possible to grasp this regularity in generalizations upon which to determine language relationships, and to establish "families" of languages. This assumption of basic regularity of change made possible scientific linguistic investigation.

(3) These changes of language could not have been the result of corruptions arising out of the mistakes of the ignorant or the careless. Only by assuming that the usage of the speakers and writers of a language is the only basis of "correctness" could such a dictionary as the *Oxford English Dictionary* have been produced. The editorial work upon this dictionary was preceded (beginning in 1858) by a tremendous labor of collecting the evidence for the facts of usage.

LINGUISTIC SCIENCE FROM 1875 TO 1925

But the achievements in linguistic science, the new views of the nature and functioning of language arising unexpectedly out of the broadening use of the new techniques for the study of language, as discussed in Whitney's two books, constitute only the first steps in the development of linguistics. A second breakthrough into new understanding concerning our knowledge of language occurred in the 1870s with the publishing of a series of brilliant articles solv-

ing the problems arising out of the large number of seeming irregularities or "exceptions" to the sound-laws postulated for the
Indo-European family of languages.

"Phonetic Laws Without Exceptions"

We would mark the beginning of the second period of linguistic science, again a span of about fifty years, with the publishing of
Karl Verner's paper[18] establishing what has been called "Verner's
Law of Accent." It was one of a number of papers dealing with the
apparent exceptions to the "sound-laws" (the generalizations concerning correspondences of forms) that had been established for
the Indo-European family of languages. Verner's article disposed
of the greatest body of "exceptions" to the Germanic sound-
shift.

. . . the effect of Verner's article . . . was immeasurable. Now there were
no more exceptions to the Germanic sound-shift, and this absence of
exceptions necessarily had quite as strong an effect upon the whole
conception of linguistics as the chief laws applying to the sound-shifts
had exerted in their time. Then, scholars were beginning to understand
that there were laws of phonology; now, they were awaking to the
fact that such laws operate regularly [or without exception].[19]

As Verner expressed it in 1875, "There must be a rule for
irregularity; the problem is to find it." Or as he had earlier phrased
the general principle, in 1872, "No exception without a rule."[20]

But Karl Verner, a Dane, was not alone in building the evidence that now induced linguists "to postulate complete adherence
to laws in the development of sounds," and to seek a scientifically
verifiable explanation for every deviation. Others made notable
contributions, including Graziadio Ascoli, an Italian; August Les-
kien and Karl Brugmann, both Germans; and the French Swiss
Ferdinand de Saussure.

It became clear, however, that, although in the mass of
changes to be observed in languages through a period of time,
phonological changes were fundamental for a scientific approach,
yet there were other changes that lay outside the area of sound-
changes. The more rigorously linguistic scholars sought the supplementary sound laws that would explain the residues of exceptions to the generalizations tentatively set up, the more precisely

they could identify and isolate the portions of these residues for which other types of explanation were necessary. Two kinds of changes other than sound-changes were now recognized:

(a) those that came about through *analogical creation,* and
(b) those that arose through *borrowings* from other languages and dialects.

Analogical Creation

Through *analogical creation,* or *levelling,* new forms were brought into line with some pattern that for some reason had become especially strong. For example, of the nouns in Old English, only masculine *"-a* stems" like *stān* (Modern English *stōne*) had an *"s"*-form plural, *stānas.* This pattern of an *"s"* form for the plural gradually supplanted other forms for the plural, until now in Modern English, less than five percent of the nouns, even in running discourse, have plural forms other than *"s"*[21]: *boy - boys; bed - beds; rock - rocks; bush - bushes; church - churches; judge - judges.* This so-called *s*-form plural became such a strong pattern that nearly all foreign words, even those borrowed from Greek and Latin, have now regular *"s"* plurals; as, for example, *ideas, families, sciences, operas, formulas.*

These changes have come about through the process of *analogy,* not through the processes of a sound-change that can be grasped by the kind of generalization that constitutes a *phonetic law.* The recognition of the principle of analogy, together with the effort to treat analogy rigorously, helped to remove one large body of the "exceptional" forms that made up the residues not explained by the accepted sound-laws.

Borrowings

The recognition of the fact that sound-laws operated within a certain period of time and within a particular language or dialect also made it possible to remove "borrowed" words from the body of what seemed to be exceptions. For example, although our word *kitchen* (Old English *cycena*) appears even in Old English texts, it is not a native English word, cognate with Latin *coquina.* If it were it would be an exception to Grimm's Law of Consonant Shift. It was borrowed from Latin long after the period of the operation of the Germanic sound-change (Grimm's Law) and therefore has the same initial consonant it had in Latin. But the borrowing must have occurred before the operation of the prehistoric English sound-change called "i-umlaut," for only in this way can one account for the particular change of vowel from the Latin [o] to English [ɪ] in the first syllable. Thus borrowed words, through the evidence of their sound features reveal not only the fact that they are borrowed and not native, but also something of the time at which they were borrowed.

The assumptions concerning the nature of human language that grew out of the more rigorous treatment of sound-change, supplemented with new insights into the processes of analogical creation and borrowing, marked the special growth of linguistic science in the latter part of the nineteenth century. The acceptance of the strict "regularity" of sound-change became general in linguistic science—acceptance not as a dogma of belief, but as a basic assumption that has proved most productive in practice. The principle of "regularity" in language change—so regular that from adequately stated generalizations linguistic predictions have been possible—also provided the ground upon which to evaluate both the evidence and the conclusions of linguistic studies.

Linguistics may be said to have begun its scientific career with the comparative study and reconstruction of the Indo-European languages. In the course of their detailed researches Indo-European linguists have gradually developed a technique which is probably more nearly perfect than that of any other science dealing with man's institutions. Many of the formulations of comparative Indo-European linguistics have a neatness and a regularity which recall the formulae, or the so-called laws, of natural science. . . .

The methods developed by the Indo-Europeanists have been applied with marked success to other groups of languages. It is abundantly clear that they apply as rigorously to the unwritten primitive languages of Africa and America as to the better known forms of speech of the more sophisticated peoples. . . . The more we devote ourselves to the comparative study of the languages of a primitive linguistic stock, the more clearly we realize that phonetic law and analogical leveling are the only satisfactory key to the unravelling of the development of dialects and languages from a common base. Professor Leonard Bloomfield's experience with Central Algonkian and my own with Athabaskan leave nothing to be desired in this respect and are a complete answer to those who find it difficult to accept the large scale regularity of the operation of all those unconscious linguistic forces which in their totality give us regular phonetic change and morphological readjustment on the basis of such a change. It is not merely theoretically possible to predict the correctness of specific forms among unlettered peoples on the basis of such phonetic laws as have been worked out for them—such predictions are already on record in considerable number.[22]

The following statement attempts to summarize briefly the chief features of what is meant by the heading of this section— "Phonetic Laws Without Exceptions."

From evidence such as the following,

(a) correspondences in the representations of certain words in several languages,
(b) certain changes in the representations of the same word in the records of the same language separated by a period of time,

we infer that there was a change in the native speaker's manner of pronouncing a particular "sound," and that this change

(1) affected every occurrence of that "sound" in essentially the same phonetic surroundings,

(2) operated within a particular span of time and within a particular dialect or group of dialects,

(3) was not interfered with by any nonphonetic factors such as meaning, homonymy, etc.

Statements of such changes have often been called "phonetic laws." They are rather descriptive generalizations of the observed correspondences of forms, the result of historical change. They do not set forth the processes of these changes nor indicate their causes. By assumption, these descriptive generalizations, if they are accurately and completely stated, must apply "without exception" to the whole body of the "native" words of a language, or a dialect or a group of dialects. Whatever residues there may be must be strictly accounted for by the processes of analogy or borrowing.

In addition to this major linguistic contribution leading to a practical understanding of the assumption of "Phonetic Laws Without Exceptions," two other linguistic developments of the period from 1875 to 1925 need brief comment before concluding this section. They are linguistic geography and phonetics.

Linguistic Geography

The increasing number of studies in the history of a variety of languages brought to light more and more evidence that the "standard" language, or the prestige form of a language, had, because of particular historical circumstances, arisen out of the dialects, rather than that the dialects had diverged from the "standard" language. "Standard" English, for example, arose out of the old dialect of London, as that speech gained more and more prestige when London, in the fourteenth century, became increasingly the center of affairs for a more unified England. The divergent linguistic forms of the speech of other dialects were not, as was earlier believed, corrupted forms derived through ignorance or carelessness from those of standard or literary English. In many instances these divergent forms proved to be older. The efforts to understand the relationships of dialect to standard language and dialect to dialect led again to the gathering and recording of these facts of usage in dialect dictionaries, dialect grammars, and the assortment of maps that constitute a dialect atlas. As Whitney had insisted in 1867

> The material and subject of linguistic science is language, in its entirety. . . . The dialects of the obscurest and most humbly endowed races are its care, as well as those of leaders in the world's history. . . . Every fact of every language, in the view of the linguistic student, calls for his investigation, *since only in the light of all can any be completely understood.* [The italics are mine.][23]

The period from 1875 to 1925 saw an increasing variety of language and dialect surveys with constant improvements in the techniques of making the surveys and interpreting the data. Of these, the following are the best-known examples:

Georg Wenker in 1876 began the work which led to the *Sprachatlas des deutschen Reichs.*

Jules Gilliéron planned and edited the *Atlas linguistique de la France* (1902–1908) based on the survey material gathered by Edmond Edmont.

K. Jaberg and J. Jud began the publication of the *Sprach- und Sachatlas Italiens und Südschweiz* in 1928, just when the formal collecting of material began for the *Linguistic Atlas of the United States and Canada.*[24]

Linguistic geography thus supplemented language history in leading to a much clearer understanding of the significance of dialect differences in a language, of the centers of language dispersion, and of the basis for the special prestige through which one regional dialect out of many becomes a "standard" language.

Phonetics

It is not surprising that "phonetics" should have had an especially vigorous development during the years from 1875 to 1925. The generalizations upon which the "new" linguistic science was founded were generalizations concerning the sounds of the languages. It was the sound-changes of language that were especially stable, and sound-changes rather than grammatical changes that showed amazing regularity. To understand all that could be learned concerning the nature of speech sounds, therefore, became quite naturally one of the flourishing major interests. Phonetics as the science of speech sounds[25] began to develop new techniques for the analysis and description of the sounds of all languages. *Articulatory phonetics* had growing success in attempting to analyze and describe the physical movements by which speech sounds are differentiated. *Instrumental phonetics,* beginning with the simple laryngoscope, the x-ray, and the false palate, to increase the range of direct observation, advanced to more complex devices like the kymograph and the oscillograph to study the physical or acoustic properties of sounds and to "photograph" them. Out of this increasing study of speech sounds came the realization that there are a great many more differences of sound used, even in our own native language, than we had thought possible.

The feeling that the average speaker has of his language is that it is built up, acoustically speaking, of a comparatively small number of distinct sounds, each of which is rather accurately provided for in the current alphabet by one letter or, in a few cases, by two or more alternative letters. As for the languages of foreigners, he generally feels that, aside from a few striking differences that cannot escape even the uncritical ear, the sounds they use are the same as those he is familiar with but that there is a mysterious "accent" to these foreign languages, a certain unanalyzed phonetic character, apart from the sounds as such, that gives them their air of strangeness. This naïve feeling is largely illusory on both scores.[26]

G. B. Shaw's well-known *Pygmalion* (1900)[26a] makes dramatic use of some of the enormous number of phonetic differences in the various kinds of pronunciation of English. Higgins, the phonetician in the play, says,

You can spot an Irishman or a Yorkshireman by his brogue. *I* can place any man within six miles. I can place him within two miles in London. Sometimes within two streets.

Of the Flower Girl, Higgins says,

You see this creature with her kerbstone English: the English that will keep her in the gutter to the end of her days. Well, sir, in three months I could pass that girl off as a duchess at an ambassador's garden party. I could even get her a place as lady's maid or shop assistant, which requires better English.

Later he asks Pickering (a phonetician of ability but of somewhat less skill):

HIGGINS: Tired of listening to sounds?
PICKERING: Yes. It's a fearful strain. I rather fancied myself because
    I can pronounce twenty-four distinct vowel sounds; but your
    hundred and thirty beat me. I can't hear a bit of difference between
    most of them.
HIGGINS: Oh, that comes with practice. You hear no difference at
    first; but you keep on listening, and presently you find they're all
    as different as A and B.

Not only did the analyses of the phoneticians bring to light and describe the tremendous number of differences of vocal sounds that appear in a language like English—differences of sound of which the native speakers are not aware, except as broad differences of "accent"—but they required a greatly increased set of graphic symbols in order to pin them down and discuss them.

HIGGINS. . . . I'll show you how I make records. We'll set her [the
    Flower Girl] talking; and I'll take it down first in Bell's Visible
    Speech; then in broad Romic; then we'll get her on the phonograph
    so that you can turn her on as often as you like with the written
    transcript before you.

In the quotation from *Pygmalion* just given Higgins suggests that he will "write down" the Flower Girl's pronunciation exactly, so that the "written transcript" can be compared with the actual sounds recorded on the phonograph. The conversation just preceding had already indicated that Pickering could distinguish 24 different vowel sounds and that Higgins could identify 130. The writing proposed must therefore have available sufficient distinctly different letters (or symbols) to record these differences. At the opening of the play the Note Taker (Higgins) had already demonstrated that he could make such a record and from it repeat accurately the precise sounds of the Flower Girl's utterances. Obviously he must have used some type of writing that had more than the five vowel letters of the Roman alphabet. He was using a *phonetic alphabet* and making a *phonetic transcription.*[27]

Because of the insufficient number of letters (especially the lack of letters to represent more than five vowel sounds) scholars who have tried to write about pronunciation matters and to identify the many differences that occur in the speech sounds people use have devised phonetic alphabets. In English the invention and use of special phonetic alphabets goes back at least as far as the work of John Hart, who in 1570 published and used such an alphabet in the teaching of reading. He had already used the "newe maner of writing" in his *Orthographie* of 1569 and discussed it in his manuscript *The Opening of the Unreasonable Writing of Our English Toung* in 1551.

> For even so I have opened the vices and faultes of our writing: which cause it to be tedious, and long in learnyng: and learned hard, and evill to read. . . . And then have I sought the meanes (herin writen) by the which we may use a certaine, good and easi writing, onli folowing our pronunciation; and keping the letters in their auncient, Simple, and Singular powers. . . .[28]

Others, like Sir Thomas Smith, William Bullokar, and Edmund Coote in the sixteenth century, Alexander Gill, Charls Butler, and John Wilkins in the seventeenth century, and Benjamin Franklin in the eighteenth century advocated and used phonetic alphabets for English. A. J. Ellis and Isaac Pitman struggled with their Phonotype through the middle of the nineteenth century. But it was the International Phonetic Association (founded in 1886), that

56 Linguistics and Reading

took up Otto Jespersen's suggestion and established in 1888 an alphabet designed to be really international and applicable to all languages.[29] In general it was derived from Henry Sweet's Broad and Narrow Romic rather than from Alexander Melville Bell's Visible Speech or Otto Jespersen's Analphabetic System.

The International Phonetic Alphabet (IPA) with additions and improvements has been used ever since 1888 in the *Maître Phonétique*, the official publication of the International Phonetic Association. The chart shows this alphabet as published in 1912. At that time it had symbols for twenty-six different vowel sounds and fifty-two different consonant sounds.

THE INTERNATIONAL PHONETIC ALPHABET

		Lips	Lip-teeth	Point and Blade	Front	Back	Uvula	Throat
CONSONANTS	Plosive	p b		t d	c ɟ	k g	q ɢ	ʔ
	Nasal	m		n	ɲ	ŋ	ɴ	
	Lateral			l ɫ	ʎ	(ɫ)		
	Rolled			r ř			R	
	Fricative	ʍ w ɥ / ɸ β	f v	θ ð s z / σ ρ ʃ ʒ ɹ	ç j (ɥ)	(ʍ w) x ɣ	ʁ ʀ	h ɦ

		Lips		Front	Mixed	Back	
VOWELS	Close	(u ü y) (ʊ ʏ)		i y / ɪ ʏ	ɪ ʉ	ɯ u / ʊ	
	Half-close	(o ö ø)		e ø	ɘ ö / ə	v o	
	Half-open	(ɔ ɔ œ)		ɛ œ / æ ɐ	ɜ ɞ	ʌ ɔ	
	Open			a		ɑ	

(Sounds appearing twice on the chart have a double articulation, the secondary articulation being shown by the symbol in brackets.)
From the Supplement to the Maître Phonétique Sept.-Oct. 1912, entitled, The Principles of the International Phonetic Association. Page 10.

SOURCE: Supplement to the *Maître Phonétique*, September-October 1912, entitled *The Principles of the International Phonetic Association*, p. 10.

But *phonetic transcription*, the use of a phonetic alphabet, is but one of the tools of phonetics, the science of speech sounds. Frequently, however, among those who are actively using phonetic transcriptions in their study of a foreign language, the term *phonetics* has become the equivalent of phonetic transcription. Among those who discuss the problems of teaching reading, *phonetics* and *phonics* have become equivalent terms. Among linguists, *phonetics* is a science devoted to the study of speech sounds. Phonetics in this sense made great progress during the years 1875–1925, especially in the acoustic analysis of speed sounds.

Just as the "sounds" of languages in their relationships formed the basic materials of the first break-through of modern linguistic science, and constituted the special features of the investigations that led to the second break-through of the 1870s, so it was a new view of the "sounds" as units in a structural system that will appear to lead the way into the linguistic developments from 1925 to 1950.

By 1925, the end of the second fifty years of the modern scientific study of language, the following views of language, of special significance for us, had become for linguists common ground upon which to base their study.[30]

(1) The sound-features of a language (the pronunciation) even of unwritten languages or of the language of the illiterate and uneducated are its most stable characteristic. Sound-changes operate as massive, uniform, and gradual alterations within a particular language or dialect, and within a particular period of time. Sound-changes are neither hindered nor helped by features of meaning, nor by the conscious choices of individuals. The regularity of these sound-changes has made it possible to predict the precise forms of words in a dialect, before actual instances of them have been found.

(2) It became clear, from the fifty years of editorial work upon the *Oxford English Dictionary* and the other collections of usage, that multiple meanings for words is normal, not "queer." We must everywhere in language expect to find that the frequently used words have a variety of meanings—not just one so-called literal meaning and a few figurative or transferred meanings. The number of different meanings for each of the commonly used words of English as recorded and illustrated in the *Oxford English Dictionary* will not be believed without a thorough study of the evidence. For example, for the 500 most used words in English (as listed by the Thorndike word-count) the *Oxford Dictionary* records 14,070 separate and different meanings—an average of 28 different meanings for each word.

(3) The development of the work in phonetics provided the techniques for the successful analysis and description of speech sounds. Now we know that all the "mysterious" qualities of the sounds and "accents" in human languages are matters that can be

analyzed and described in terms of the physical movements by which they are produced, and also in terms of the specific kinds of vibrations that make up their acoustic characteristics. The increasing accuracy and completeness of the recording, reproduction, and transmission of vocal sounds grew out of the work of the phonetics laboratories.

(4) The continued work on the historical dictionaries, and the new work on the surveys of dialect areas which constituted the development of linguistic geography, produced greater understanding not only of the necessity of gathering the facts of usage upon as broad a base as possible but also of the need for more and more rigorous techniques both for collecting these facts and for studying them in order to have them yield sound and significant results.

Usage materials which are mere chance observations, or even usage materials more consistently collected but without the necessary information of all the historical, geographical, and class circumstances in which they occurred, or usage materials without collections of the alternate forms with which they must be compared, or usage materials that provide no basis for quantitative evaluation—such usage materials cannot provide the basis for scientific linguistic study. And even usage materials that provide all the necessary kinds of information in an adequate sampling must be handled rigorously with the accepted appropriate techniques of linguistic analysis.

Just as in 1867 and 1875 William Dwight Whitney's two books attempted to summarize and interpret the new linguistic understanding achieved during the first fifty years of the "new linguistic science," so the second fifty years of that science had its contemporary authors who, in spite of the immensely more complex achievements of the years from 1875 to 1925, tried to bring the summary and interpretation of the new linguistic knowledge up to date:

(1) Hermann Paul, *Prinzipien der Sprachgeschichte,* first edition 1880, fifth edition 1920. The second edition (1886) was translated in 1889 into English by H. A. Strong, entitled *Principles of the History of Language.* An adaptation for English readers was produced by H. A. Strong, W. S. Longman, and B. L. Wheeler, entitled *Introduction to the Study of the History of Languages.*

(2) Leonard Bloomfield, *An Introduction to the Study of Language*, 1914.
(3) Otto Jespersen, *Language, Its Nature, Development, and Origin*, 1921.
(4) Holger Pedersen, *Linguistic Science in the Nineteenth Century*, 1924, translated by John Webster Spargo, 1931.
(5) Edward Sapir, *Language*, 1921.
(6) Leonard Bloomfield, "On Recent Work in General Linguistics," in *Modern Philology* XXV (1927), 211–230.

The last two items of this list not only help to sum up the achievements to 1925 but also lead the way into the new materials of the next thirty-five years.

LINGUISTIC SCIENCE FROM 1925 TO 1950

In general the scientific study of language as practiced in the United States throughout the nineteenth century and during the first quarter of the twentieth century was based upon and did not depart greatly from that of the long line of European scholars working in historical-comparative linguistics, in phonetics, and in linguistic geography. With the breaking of contacts during the two world wars and the difficulty of intimate communication and the interruption of the flow of journals and books during at least ten of the years between the two wars, linguistics or the scientific study of language in the United States has had a somewhat independent but more or less parallel development with that of Europe. Here we shall center attention upon the American developments without special comment upon points of similarity or difference in the European approach.[31]

In America the development of "descriptive" linguistics (*synchronic* rather than *diachronic* description) grew out of the efforts to record and analyze the enormous number of individual languages that were members of the more than fifty separate families of American Indian languages on the North American continent.[32] In Europe, in a quite different way, Ferdinand de Saussure contributed greatly to the broadening of the field of scientific linguistics to include "descriptive" study. De Saussure's contribution did not come from any large amount of detailed descriptive analyses of living languages. It was rather a discussion and demonstration of fundamental linguistic principles. Bloomfield, in reviewing the second edition (1922) of de Saussure's book (composed primarily from notes taken by his students) praised it in enthusiastic terms, "The essential point . . . is this, that de Saussure has here first mapped out the world in which historical Indo-European grammar (the great achievement of the past century) is merely a single province; he has given us the theoretic basis for a science of human speech."[33]

Edward Sapir contributed tremendously to the newer trend which made "descriptive" language study acceptably scientific. The influence of his *Language,* 1921, is still strong. Leonard Bloomfield, in his review of that book in 1922, welcomed it as part of the changing emphasis in linguistics: "We are coming to believe that restriction to historical work is unreasonable and, in the long run methodically impossible. One is glad to see, that Dr. Sapir deals with synchronic matters (to use de Saussure's terminology) before he deals with diachronic, and gives to the former as much space as to the latter."[34]

The Break-through of American "Structural Linguistics"

For American "structural linguistics" that has given special vigor to the linguistic work in this country since 1925, Edward Sapir furnished the basic point of view and Leonard Bloomfield provided the detailed statement of principles of analysis. To mark the beginning then of the third, the present period of linguistic science in the United States, we would point to the publishing of Edward Sapir's "Sound Patterns in Language" in the first volume of the official journal of the Linguistic Society of America, *Language* (1925). This article represents, I believe, the break-through into the new approach which has developed into our "structural linguistics." Indeed, the present period of the scientific study of language has become the period of "structural linguistics."[35] But Sapir's paper of 1925 was not his first statement of the new point of view. In his book *Language* (1921), in the latter part of Chapter III, "The Sounds of Language," he had already expressed the beginnings from which his "structuralism" grew. Back of it lay his experience with his informant when he was trying to record, analyze, and describe some of the languages of the Athabaskan family of American Indian languages.

I found that it was difficult or impossible to teach an Indian to make phonetic distinctions that did not correspond to "points in the pattern of his language," however these differences might strike our objective ear, but that subtle, barely audible phonetic differences, if only they hit the "points in the pattern," were easily and voluntarily expressed in writing. . . .

Two historically related languages or dialects may not have a sound in common, but their ideal sound-systems may be identical patterns.[36]

Sapir's article of 1925 is a fully developed demonstration with the evidence of both the negative and the positive aspects of his general statement.

It is very necessary to understand that it is not because the objective difference is too slight to be readily perceptible that such variations as the quantitative alternations in *bad* and *bat, bead* and *beat, fade* and *fate* stand outside of the proper phonetic pattern of the language (e.g., are not psychologically parallel to such qualitative-quantitative alternations as *bid* and *bead, fed* and *fade*, or to such quantitative alternations as German *Schlaf* and *schlaff*, Latin *āra* and *ārā*), but that the objective difference is felt to be slight precisely because it corresponds to nothing significant in the inner structure of the phonetic pattern. In matters of this kind, objective estimates of similarity or difference, based either on specific linguistic habits or on a generalized phonetic system, are utterly fallacious. As a matter of fact, the mechanical English vocalic relation *bad : bat* would in many languages be quite marked enough to indicate a relation of distinct points of the pattern, while the English pattern relation -t : -d, which seems so self-evidently real to us, has in not a few other languages either no reality at all or only a mechanical, conditional one.

After what we have said, it almost goes without saying that two languages, A and B, may have identical sounds but utterly distinct phonetic patterns; or they may have mutually incompatible phonetic systems, from the articulatory and acoustic standpoint, but identical or similar patterns.

Phonetic patterning helps also to explain why people find it difficult to pronounce certain foreign sounds which they possess in their own language. Thus, a Nootka Indian in pronouncing English words with ŋ or *l* invariably substitutes *n* for each of these sounds. Yet he is able to pronounce both ŋ and *l*. He does not use these sounds in prose discourse, but ŋ is very common in the chants and *l* is often substituted for *n* in songs. His feeling for the stylistic character of ŋ and for the *n-l* equivalence prevents him from "hearing" English ŋ and *l* correctly. Here again we see that a speech sound is not merely an articulation or an acoustic image, but material for symbolic expression in an appropriate linguistic context.[37]

Two facts, especially important for us here, came out of Sapir's experience.

(a) The same phonetic difference may have (and probably will have) entirely different structural values from language to language.

(b) There is power or force in the structural system itself. The habits that constitute the control of one's native language are not habits concerning items as items, but habits concerning contrastive items as functioning units of an *ordered system of structural patterns*.

In 1926 Leonard Bloomfield published his "Postulates for the Study of Language."[38] In 1927 appeared his article "On Recent Work in General Linguistics."[39] But the most important single publication concerning the scientific study of language during the last thirty-five years was Bloomfield's book, *Language* (1933). Professor Bernard Bloch, of Yale, writing the following sentences in 1949, does not overstate the situation.

It is not too much to say that every significant refinement of analytic method produced in this country since 1930 has come as a direct result of the impetus given to linguistic research by Bloomfield's book. If today our methods are in some ways better than his, if we see more clearly than he did himself certain aspects of structure that he first revealed to us, it is because we stand upon his shoulders.[40]

Bloomfield considered his book of 1933 a revision of his *Introduction to the Study of Language* of 1914, of which he said:

Its purpose is the same . . . as that of Whitney's *Language and the Study of Language* and *The Life and Growth of Language,* books which fifty years ago represented the attainments of linguistic science, and, owing to their author's clearness of view and conscious discrimination between ascertained fact and mere surmise, contain little to which we cannot today subscribe.[41]

Bloomfield's *Language,* 1933, therefore, was an effort again to bring to the educated public the new knowledge and understanding of human language that had been achieved up to the time of writing. It is especially noteworthy that this book that presents a large part of the substance of the linguistic achievement of the period beginning in 1925 was published in 1933 when the new work had hardly got under way. In contrast, Whitney's books of 1867 and 1875 came at the end of a period of fifty years, as did those that gathered the new knowledge for the second fifty years. Bloomfield's book led the way into the achievements of present-day American "structural linguistics."

The present wide use of the term *structural linguistics* does not mean that all practicing linguists today agree upon what constitutes the special identifying features of this structuralism. The evidence for this great diversity of view shows itself in the articles listed by Kenneth and Eunice Pike in their bibliography covering the *Live Issues in Descriptive Linguistics* (1960) and in the references with critical comments that appear in the three parts of Kenneth Pike's *Language in Relation to a Unified Theory of the Structure of Human Behavior* (1954, 1955, 1960).

Rather than attempt to show the strands of this variety I shall here try simply to give a brief statement of some of the views of language and the principles of practice of a structural approach that stems primarily from the writings of Edward Sapir and Leonard Bloomfield.[42]

Structural Units and Word-Patterns

Our "structural" approach requires a basic shift in the usual thinking about language. For most people, that thinking is *word-centered.* As a child develops during his first and second years, we try to count the "words that he knows" as the measure of his progress in learning to talk. In the schools, the practical considerations of language problems have almost completely dealt with the words. Books are examined and rated on the basis of the kind and number of the words used. Readability scales and measures of grade placement for reading materials give primary attention to vocabulary items. Many of the discussions of the teaching of reading center upon the problems of word recognition and the learning of "new" words. Foreign language study usually features the number and range of the words mastered. Everywhere there is the pressure for increasing the size of one's vocabulary. Words and their meanings have held the central place in our thinking about language for so long a time that it has become extremely difficult for many people to realize even the existence of the kind of *structural base that constitutes the essential feature of every part of language*. It will probably be a long time before all who teach the language arts appreciate fully the significance of Sapir's comment of more than forty years ago: "The linguistic student should never make the mistake of identifying a language with its dictionary."[43]

This structuralism not only requires us to abandon our word-centered thinking about language; it demands that in every aspect of language we must shift from an *item-centered* view to one that is *structure-centered*. Language learning, in the thinking of both laymen and teachers, most frequently has meant the mastering of *items*—the items of sound that must be pronounced, the individual words that must be identified with meanings, the parts of sentences that must be classified.

From our structural point of view, items such as these have no linguistic significance by themselves. Only as such items contrast with other items in the patterns of an arbitrary system do they have linguistic significance. In other words, all the significant matters of language are linguistic features in contrast. Of course any difference between two items can be said to establish a basis upon which to assert that the two items are in contrast. But for the purposes of language—that is, language as a code of signals to transmit meanings[44]—not every possible physical contrast that makes two items different is used by every language or any particular language. We are concerned here with the special linguistic contrasts that English uses as the functioning units to identify and distinguish the patterns that constitute its structure.

For example, in English, as in other languages, of the many differences between vocal sounds that occur, only a very limited number are used as the units that function to identify lexical items or "words." English uses the difference between sounds made by the stopping of the breath in the mouth by the tip of the tongue against the alveolar ridge (the gums) and the sound made by stopping it by the base of the tongue against the palate (the roof of the mouth). This is the contrastive difference of sound between /tɪn/ *tin* and

/kɪn/ *kin*, /tæn/ *tan* and /kæn/ *can*, /ton/ *tone* and /kon/ *cone*, /pɪt/ *pit* and /pɪk/ *pick*, /pæt/ *pat* and /pæk/ *pack*, /nat/ *knot* and /nak/ *knock*.[45] This contrastive difference between /t/ and /k/ as used in English to identify and distinguish a large number of word patterns makes /t/ and /k/ two of the functioning units of the structure of our sound system—of our pronunciation.

But the particular sounds represented by *p* in *pin, pan, pun* differ phonetically from those represented by *p* in *spin, span, spun*. The initial consonant of *pin, pan, pun* is followed by a strong puff of breath, an aspiration, which does not occur after the same consonant in *spin, span, spun*. This difference between the aspirated consonant sound and the unaspirated consonant sound, however, is never used in English to distinguish word patterns. Therefore the aspirated consonant sound [pʰ] is not a separate functioning unit of our pronunciation structure.

In similar fashion, the initial /k/ in each of the following words /kɪl/ *kill*, /kol/ *coal*, /kɔl/ *call* differs phonetically from the other two. The initial consonant sound in *kill* is made by the base of the tongue touching the roof of the mouth farther forward than it does in making the initial consonant sound in *coal*, and much farther forward than in making the initial consonant sound in *call*. But these phonetic differences do not make these three different sounds separate functioning units of our pronunciation structure. These three instances of /k/ (the /k/ in *kill*, the /k/ in *coal*, the /k/ in *call*), differ phonetically, but English does not use these particular phonetic differences to identify and distinguish word patterns. They constitute a single functioning or signaling unit of our word patterns—a *phoneme*.

"Structural" linguistics has attempted to discover and to describe the contrastive sound units (the bundles of contrastive sound features) that function in each language to identify and separate the various lexical units (morphemes or "words"). To this end it has developed sets of special techniques. For example, to determine for English the number and kind of vowel sounds that are structurally significant (the vowel structural units of English) one can seek quite simply the words differentiated solely by different vowels. He will not find, as functioning units in the sound patterns that identify words, the 130 different vowel sounds that Higgins could hear, nor even the 24 that Pickering could distinguish. In each cf

the following sets of words the sounds of the consonant frames in
which the vowel appears are the same: /p—l/ and /h—t/. The
vowel sounds alone (we must ignore the conventional spellings)
make the difference.

peal, /pil/;	*pell*, /pɛl/	(as in pell-mell);	*pool*, /pul/;
pill, /pɪl/;	*pal*, /pæl/;		*pull*, /pʊl/;
pale, /pel/;	*poll*, /pal/	(as in poll parrot);	*pole*, /pol/;
			Paul, /pɔl/.

But we do not have in English a word of this consonant frame
/p—l/ with the vowel unit /ə/, as in the words *hut, but, cut.* In
the series with the consonant pattern /h—t/, however, this vowel
/ə/ appears as a distinguishing feature, as in *hut* /hət/. The /h—t/
series uses the following contrastive vowels in addition to the /ə/
in *hut:*

heat, /hit/;	*hat*, /hæt/;
hit, /hɪt/;	*hot*, /hat/;
hate, /het/;	*hoot*, /hut/.
het, /hɛt/ (in "nonstandard" English)	

There is no /hʊt/ to rhyme with *foot*, and no /hot/ to rhyme with
boat.

Of vowel clusters or diphthongs there are in English *file*,
/faɪl/ (/a + ɪ/), *fowl*, /faʊl/ (/a + ʊ/), and *foil* /fɔɪl/ (/ɔ + ɪ/).

From this structural point of view, English uses, as contrastive
units to identify and distinguish words, eleven single vowels and
three vowel clusters. There are in English speech a tremendous
number of different vowel sounds that can be heard, isolated, and
described, but I can find in my speech only these eleven vowel units
or bundles of phonetic features that contrast with each other to
form the functioning units of the sound patterns that identify words.
Structural linguistics thus seeks to identify the contrastive units that
function in some particular language like English to distinguish or
separate the various word patterns.

Structural linguistics also seeks to discover the particular sequences in which these units occur within the word-patterns, for, in
the languages that have been described, it appears that the permitted
sequences differ for each language and are strictly limited. In Eng-

lish, for example, the last consonant of the word *king* /kɪŋ/ - /ŋ/ - never occurs initially in a word. It always comes after a vowel. In English, there are at least 100 different consonant clusters that occur at the ends of words, as /nd/ in *sand, bend, wind;* /lt/ in *wilt, built, bolt;* /gd/ in *tagged, wagged, sagged;* /lθ/ in *health, wealth, stealth;* /kt/ in *walked, talked, looked;* /lz/ in *calls, holes, peals.* And there are at least 40 other consonant clusters that occur at the beginnings of words, as /gl/ in *glad, glisten, gloom;* /br/ in *bread, broom, brick;* /sn/ in *sneeze, snare, snow;* /tw/ in *twist, twine, tweezers.* But of all these clusters, *only three—*/st/, /sp/, /sk/*—occur both at the beginnings and at the ends of words* *—stain, rust; spell, lisp; skin, mask.* Many possible clusters of consonants do not occur at all either initially or finally in English, /dm/ (except internally with syllable division as in *Skidmore* College); /mk/ (except internally with syllable division as in the compound *tram-car*), /šn/ (except by those who show signs of intoxication).

With these developments in structural analysis it has become clear that practical pronunciation problems are for the most part not matters of the phonetic character of the sound segments *per se,* but rather, matters of the units and the *patterns of the structure* of the pronunciation system. The habits of pronunciation that the child develops in learning his native language are not habits of producing and hearing the separate sounds as isolatable items in individual words but rather habits of patterns of functioning contrasts in the unique structured system of a particular language.

The child learns to hear and to pronounce with speed and precision the contrastive features of the units in the sequences used to identify and separate the word patterns. But his speed and precision are achieved also, in part, by learning to *ignore* the phonetic features that are not structurally significant for his particular language. Thus the automatic habits through which we manipulate our native language signals have also developed blind spots for contrastive language features outside the structural system of our own particular language. We would now measure the child's first progress in learning to talk, not by counting the number of "words" he is said to "know," but by the degree to which he has achieved the production of, and responses to, the functioning contrasts by which *words* (and the other types of language signals) are identified.

To "know" a word means, in the first place, the instant recognition, in the stream of speech, of the particular pattern of functioning contrasts that identifies that word. To "know" a word means also, in the second place, a similarly instant recognition of some bundle of experience with which the word pattern is associated. The bundle of experience thus brought into attention with a word pattern in an utterance constitutes its "meaning." A child "learns" the physical word patterns /faðər/ *father* and /məðər/ *mother* only once; but as he matures he keeps constantly changing and enlarging the content of the bundle of experience which he correlates with these word patterns, until it comprehends an adult understanding of male and female parenthood. In respect to words, then, a child's competence at any particular age consists of the physical word patterns he recognizes *and* the bundles of experience with which the word patterns correlate for him. Practice in the use of the language makes the recognition and the correlation extremely rapid, until the signaling physical pattern itself sinks completely below the threshold of attention, leaving only the bundles of experience or the meaning of the utterance as a whole.

Structural Units and Grammar

Our structural linguistics does not confine itself to the bundles of contrastive sound features that in special sequences identify the word patterns of our language. The identification of the word patterns constitutes only the beginnings of the efforts of the structuralist to discover the chief features of the nature of language and the processes by which it accomplishes its communicative purposes. "Knowing" at least some of the thousands of words that a language uses constitutes only one of the essentials of communication.

As indicated above, words have held the central place in the layman's thinking about language. Examples of this word-centered thinking are abundant. During the past six years I have found views practically identical with those expressed in the following quotation vigorously put forward and argued by language teachers in countries as far apart as Germany and Japan.

In English, words are formed into sentences by the operation of an invisible power, which is like magnetism. Each one is charged with a meaning which gives it a tendency toward some of those in the sentence, and particularly to one, and which repels it from others; and he who subtly divines and dexterously uses this attraction, filling his words with a living but latent light and heat, which makes them leap to each other and cling together while they transmit his freely-flowing thought, is a master of the English language, although he may be ignorant and uninstructed in its use.[46]

Present-day examples of the continuation of word-centered thinking concerning sentences are abundant. In the UNESCO monograph on *The Teaching of Reading and Writing* (1956), Professor W. S. Gray, of the University of Chicago, writes of what he calls "fusing the meanings of words into ideas." He gives the following sentence and then attempts to account for the meaning it conveys.

The water in our village well is good to drink.

As one reads the first two words in this sentence various associations are aroused. This grasp of meanings is restricted and made more definite as the third, fourth, fifth and sixth words are recognized. The thoughts then retained are held in mind, as the reader continues to the end of the sentence. When he recognizes the words, "good to drink," the meaning already acquired is greatly expanded and clarified. The final idea is the result of the fusion of the meanings of the separate words into a coherent whole.[47]

As it stands, this sentence, "The water in our village well is good to drink," is a report or statement of the fact that the water is drinkable. But the simple shifting of the word *is* to the beginning, as in "Is the water in our village well good to drink," makes the "final idea" from these same words a question rather than the report or statement of a fact. To use these identical words in other positions would give us entirely different "final ideas."

To drink the well water in our village is good.

To water well the drink in our village is good.

Even the very different meanings to be attached to the same word-pattern, *well*, are indicated by the contrasting structural sets in which the word appears—*the well water, to water well*.

From the structural point of view adopted here, the "final idea" of this sentence as a whole—"The water in our village well

is good to drink"—does *not* result from "the fusion of the meanings
of the separate words into a meaningful whole." The full linguistic
meaning of this sentence cannot be derived from a fusion of any or
all of the meanings of these ten separate words—even with the
amazing number of different meanings recorded for each of them
in the *Oxford Dictionary*. There is a layer of meanings apart from
those of the words as separate lexical items. These meanings can be
called *grammatical meanings*.

Grammatical meanings are not merely vague inferences from
the context—whether of the words used or of the features of the
practical situation in which an utterance occurs. They are definite
and sharp, essential features of every utterance; and, like the
bundles of experience arbitrarily attached to physical word-patterns,
also arbitrarily attached to specific patterns of contrastive features
of arrangement and form. Since the connections of these "meanings" with the patterns of contrastive arrangement and form are
arbitrary they must be definitely learned. As in the case of the
physical word-patterns and their meanings, also with long practice
and use, the recognition responses to the specific patterns of contrastive arrangement and form sink below the threshold of attention
and leave only the grammatical meanings that are signaled.

In the matter of word-patterns and their meanings, the learning continues throughout life and we remember many of the instances of vocabulary learning. For grammatical meanings and the
patterns of arrangement and form with which they are tied, the
learning for each of us in our native language took place so early
that we do not remember any of that learning, nor even that there
is anything on this level that had to be learned.

The traditional grammar that has been taught in our schools
for more than 150 years has simply assumed that the meanings
here called grammatical meanings are intuitive and has never raised
the question as to the means by which they are identified. For
example, given the sentence,

Employers usually pay their workers good wages.

the traditional grammar calls attention to some of the meanings it
communicates, and assigns names to those meanings.

(a) This sentence makes a *statement* or a *report* of a fact. It
does not ask a question nor does it make a request or give a com-

mand. This sentence is therefore assigned the technical name *declarative sentence*. A question sentence would be assigned the technical name *interrogative sentence,* and a request or command sentence given the technical name *imperative sentence.*

(b) The given sentence identifies the *performers of the action* as *employers.* This word *employers* is therefore assigned the technical name *subject.* The *action performed* is identified as that of *paying.* Therefore the word *pays* is assigned the technical name *predicate (verb).* The *thing paid* is identified as *wages;* therefore the word *wages* is assigned the technical name *direct object.* And so on through the whole sentence.

In other words the traditional grammar starts from the meanings, which are assumed to be intuitive responses to the whole string of words as lexical items, and requires that the particular words and the groups of words to which these meanings are applied be assigned certain technical names. The whole process seems to be one of an analysis of the meanings for the sake of assigning certain technical names to particular words and word groups.

Our structural approach to grammar differs fundamentally in purpose and assumptions from that of the traditional school grammar. It recognizes all the grammatical *meanings* of the traditional grammar but does not accept either of the assumptions—(a) that the recognition of these meanings are intuitive responses, or (b) that they arise out of the fusion of the meanings of the separate words. This structural approach assumes that whatever "grammatical meanings" there are, are definitely conveyed by signals; that these signals consist of structures, identified by contrastive patterns of functioning structural "units"; and that these patterns can be described in terms of the contrastive arrangements and forms of these functioning "units."

Classification as such does not constitute any part of the goal of the structural linguistics here presented. Our structural approach seeks to identify and describe the *contrastive patterns of form and arrangement* which *regularly elicit predictable responses in a particular linguistic community.*[48] As in the case of the patterns of sound that identify the lexical items or "words," the structural approach to grammar differentiates sharply between those items that are functioning contrasts in the identifying of grammatical signals and those features of form and arrangement which do not so function. In grammar, too, the number of units that, in any particular language, function in regularly eliciting predictable responses is only a strictly limited part of those that exist.

For example, in all languages, the "words" of the utterances must occur in some order—in some sequence in a time dimension. But in only a limited number of languages does a contrast of position in the utterance sequences signal any grammatical meanings. In Old English the meaning of "performer of the action" in *"þone beran slōh sē mann"* is signalled by a structure identified solely by the contrastive forms of the article, *sē,* the nominative form, as attached to *mann* in contrast with *þone,* the accusative form, as attached to *beran.* The actual position of these words in the time sequence, *þone beran* as preceding *slōh* (the verb) in contrast with *sē mann* as following *slōh,* has no grammatical signalling value in distinguishing the "performer" of the action of "killing" from the "undergoer." These words *þone beran* and *sē mann* could occur in any position of the sequence (*sē mann þone beran slōh,* or *þone beran sē mann slōh,* or *sē mann slōh þone beran*) and we could predict that the regular response of any native speaker of Old English would be a recognition of the fact that the man (*sē mann*) performed the act of killing and that it was the bear (*þone beran*) that did not survive. In Modern English, however, with no contrasting forms of the article, the sentence "The man killed the bear" is just as definite and precise in eliciting the recognition response that *the man* performed the action and *the bear* did not survive. In Modern English it is the contrastive position of *the man* and *the bear* in the sequence that constitutes the structure that signals the meaning identifying the "performer" and the "undergoer." A shift in the position in the sequence to "The bear killed the man" would elicit a very different response—the recognition now of *the bear* as "the performer" and *the man* as "undergoer." The sequence "The man the bear killed" would elicit no predictable response as to which was the performer and which the undergoer.

The structuralist assumes that the habits that constitute the control of one's own native language are not habits concerning items of language as separate items—that is, of separate segments of sound as represented by the separate letters of an alphabet, or of individual grammatical forms. He assumes rather that practical language habits are always habits concerning contrastive forms and arrangements of linguistic items, in patterns of structure functioning as signals in a system. He attempts to discover and to describe

(a) the basic contrastive bundles of sound features that constitute the units that identify and separate the lexical items;

(b) the basic contrastive markers that identify and separate the units that constitute the patterns of grammatical structure;

(c) the basic contrastive arrangements of the patterns of grammatical structure that regularly elicit recognition responses of grammatical or structural meanings.

We cannot predict whether a certain person will speak at a given moment, or what he will say, or in what words and other linguistic forms he will say it. These are acts of *speech* (*la parole*). The sum of the speech acts of a community, however, does not constitute its *language*. The *language* (*la langue*) is the rigid system of patterns of contrastive features through which the individual speech acts of a speaker become effective substitute stimuli (signals) for a hearer. With this rigid system of patterns *we can predict* the patterns of the regular responses of the members of a linguistic community, when they are effectively stimulated by one of the patterns of the system. Descriptive structural analysis has as its goal such a descriptive statement of the patterns of a language system that we may "calculate" these regular patterns of responses to the patterned signals.

The field of linguistic science has been greatly enriched by the modern emphases upon "descriptive" linguistics. "Historical" linguistics has not been superseded by "description." The basic understanding of "structure" which developed at first primarily within the struggle to describe a great many widely diverse living languages is equally significant for both synchronic and for diachronic study.[49] The field of modern linguistic science has broadened greatly but it has been considerably unified by increasing "structural" insights.

For other materials that have surveyed the developments in linguistics from 1925 to 1950 see the following items:

(1) Robert A. Hall, "American Linguistics 1925–1950," *Archivum Linguisticum*, III (1951), 101–125, and IV (1952), 1–16.

(2) George S. Lane, "Changes of Emphasis in Linguistics with Particular Reference to Paul and Bloomfield," *Studies in Philology* XLII (1945), 465–483. See also *Studies in Philology* XLIII (1946), 461–464, for "Comment" by George L. Trager.

Throughout this chapter, attention has centered upon the growing understanding of certain features of the nature and functioning of human language, which has been achieved by the devoted labors of a host of linguistic scholars during the last 140 years. Primary attention has centered upon the results—especially the unexpected results—of these labors rather than upon the developing rigor with which new techniques, new tools, and new procedures have been employed. Some linguists have at times given the impression that, for them, the new techniques, procedures, and classificatory definitions alone constituted the substance of linguistic science. I do not want to belittle the scientific importance of sound techniques, rigorous procedures, and sharp classifications. I should like, however, to insist that one can achieve a sufficient mastery cf the tools, techniques, and procedures of linguistic analysis to be a good practitioner in analyzing and describing languages, without any real understanding of the important achievements which constitute the substance of linguistic science.

SUMMARIES

In each of the three periods in the development of modern linguistic science several important characteristics of human language have become clear and have become part of the assumptions upon which later linguistic work was built.

By 1875, the end of the first fifty years, the following views of language had become acceptable assumptions upon which to base procedures.

(1) Constant change is to be expected in all languages at every period of their history.

(2) These changes are not a succession of unrelated events in which anything can happen at random. In spite of what seemed to be many exceptions, they showed so much regularity that it was possible to grasp the correspondences of form in generalizations

upon which to determine language relationship and establish "families" of languages. The assumption of a basic regularity of change made possible scientific investigation.

(3) The changes of language could not have been the result of corruptions arising out of the mistakes of ignorant and careless speakers. Only by assuming that the regular usage of the speakers and writers of a language (community) furnish the only basis of correctness for that language (community) could such a dictionary as the *Oxford English Dictionary* have been conceived and produced.

By 1925, the end of the second fifty years, the following views of language had become for linguists common assumptions upon which to base their studies.

(1) The sound features of a language, even of unwritten languages, or of the language of the illiterate and uneducated, are its most stable features. Sound-changes operate in massive, uniform, and gradual alterations within a particular language or dialect, and within a particular period of time. Sound-changes are neither hindered nor helped by features of meaning, nor by the conscious choices of individuals. The regularity of these sound changes has made it possible to predict the precise forms of words in a dialect, or related language, before actual instances of them have been found.

(2) Multiple meanings for words is normal, not "queer." We must everywhere expect in language to find that the frequently used words have a surprising variety of meanings—not just one so-called literal meaning and a few figurative or transferred meanings.

(3) All the "mysterious" qualities of the sounds and "accents" of languages (and dialects) can be analyzed and described in terms of the physical movements by which they are produced, and also in terms of the specific kinds of vibrations that make up their acoustic characteristics.

(4) With the acceptance of the general assumption that the regular usage of the native speakers of a language constitutes the only basis for "correctness," as the basic principle upon which to carry out the work on historical dictionaries and the surveys of dialect areas which produced linguistic geography, there also

developed a greater understanding of the varieties of usage and the necessity for more and more rigorous controls, both in collecting the facts and in studying them. In order to have usage materials yield sound and significant results, these materials must not be mere chance observations. To provide the basis for any sound linguistic study, they must be consistently and systematically collected through an adequately controlled sampling process, and provide all the essential information of the historical, geographical, and social class circumstances in which the utterances occurred. They must contain the alternate forms with which they need to be compared and enough examples to make a quantitative evaluation significant. But even usage materials that provide all these necessary kinds of information in an adequate sampling, to be useful, must be handled rigorously with appropriate established techniques for linguistic analysis.

The years since 1925, the third period in the development of linguistic science, have again provided new insights into the nature and functioning of language—a basic reorientation which not only makes fruitful a restudy of the data formerly collected for descriptive and historical work, but also, when patiently explored, sheds new light on all the problems of communication and understanding.

Some of the new views which have resulted from or stimulated the linguistic activity of the past thirty-five years are the following.

(1) Language is structured. This structuring is a basic characteristic of every aspect of human language and has made it capable of more than the simple calls and commands. It has given human language the power to grasp and to communicate highly complicated reports. The languages of even the most "primitive" peoples have this basic structural characteristic, and are also capable of grasping and communicating similarly complicated reports. Such reports have made human language the storehouse of man's experience, built up and passed on from generation to generation. Through language, the knowledge and the wisdom won by the most intelligent and the most courageous individual of a group can become the knowledge and the wisdom of all those to whom he can talk. With language a man is no longer a puny individual learning only what he can from his own limited reactions to nature,

Through language he becomes a "group" man, receiving a tremendous inheritance from the accumulated experiences remembered and reported by those who lived before him.

(2) The basic material out of which a language is made consists of audible modifications of the breath-stream—vocal sounds. It has become clear, however, that that which is objectively the same uttered sound will be perceived and responded to very differently by those who speak different languages. In other words, the same phonetic differences usually have entirely different structural values from language to language.

(3) In general, there are no language sounds that are easy or difficult in themselves. Ease or difficulty of hearing or of pronunciation turns out to be a function of the way the phonetic material patterns in a person's native language. Native speakers of English produce and respond easily to the differences between /r/ and /l/ as structural units differentiating word-patterns: *race / lace; ram / lamb; river / liver; correction / collection; gentry / gently; pray / play.* Native Japanese speakers, in the early stages of learning English, find it difficult not only to produce these contrasts systematically; they cannot hear them well enough to differentiate these pairs of words when they are pronounced in immediate sequence, either in isolation or in minimum contrastive sentences. Japanese speakers would find it difficult to determine whether the following three sentences, given orally, are all alike *in meaning*, all different, or two alike and one different.

> They took the long road home.
> They took the wrong road home.
> They took the wrong load home.

(4) The child in learning his native language not only develops great facility and accuracy in responding to the limited number of contrastive units that identify the word-patterns and the grammatical structures of his particular language; he also, in developing this great skill, learns to ignore all those physical features that are not relevant to the identification of these word- and sentence-patterns. He thus, if limited to his native language and dialect, increasingly develops blind spots for a whole range of physical differences that constitute the contrastive, identifying units

of other languages. Thus the power or force in the structural arrangements of the first language (the native language) makes the
learning of a second language as an adult a very different matter
from the learning of the first language. The application of this
principle to other aspects of social behavior, especially as stimulated
by Edward Sapir, has given rise to significant results concerning the
social-cultural meanings of language in relation to the problems of
understanding across linguistic and cultural boundaries.

The fact of the matter is that the "real world" is to a large extent
unconsciously built upon the language habits of the group. No two
languages are ever sufficiently similar to be considered as representing
the same social reality. The worlds in which different societies live are
distinct worlds, not merely the same world with different labels attached.[50]

(5) The units which function in identifying the word-patterns
and the sentence-patterns of a language like English do not consist
of items of vocal sound features added together as building blocks.
These functioning units are bundles of contrastive differences—
contrastive differences of sound features, of sequences, of distribution, of pitch. They are abstractions. Physically, of course, each
speech act consists of a succession of sound waves, of varying
frequency, intensity, length, and so on. Broadly speaking, there
never is or can be an exact repetition of any particular succession
of sound waves as produced and heard. Precise measurements and
accurate recordings always reveal some differences. But in a linguistic community two or more physically different speech acts may
fit into a single functioning pattern and thus may be functionally
the "same." Basically, then, the material that constitutes language
must be recurring "sames" of speech acts. The sum of the speech
acts of a community does not, however, constitute its language.
Only as the sequences of a speech act are grasped or recognized as
fitting into recurring patterns of "sames" of vocal sounds do they
become the stuff out of which language is made. And only when
these patterns of vocal "sames" are correlated with recurring
"sames" of practical situations in man's experience, and thus become the means of eliciting "sames" of predictable responses, do
they become language itself. From this point of view the following
statement might serve as a definition of a *language*.

A language is a system of recurring sequences or patterns of "sames" of vocal sounds which correlate with recurring "sames" of stimulus-situation features, and which elicit recurring "sames" of response features.

A differently phrased definition is given by Sapir in his *Language*, 1921. "Language is a purely human and non-instinctive method of communicating ideas, emotions, and desires, by means of a system of voluntarily produced symbols."[51]

THE LAST TEN YEARS: 1950–1960

No survey of the growing insights into the nature and functioning of human language which have resulted, often unexpectedly, from the professional activities, during the last 140 years, of those devoted to linguistic science should stop short of at least a brief glance at the especially vigorous new linguistic activity of the last ten years.

Applications of Linguistic Knowledge

Of course there had been efforts to apply the developing linguistic knowledge even during the first period of Modern Linguistic Science. Whitney, in 1875, speaks of linguistic science as "bringing about a re-cast of the old methods of teaching even familiar and long-studied languages, like Latin and Greek," and says that it "has leavened all the connected branches of knowledge, and worked itself into the very structure of modern thought."[52] The *Oxford English Dictionary* (first named *A New English Dictionary on Historical Principles; Founded Mainly on the Materials Collected by the Philological Society*) was conceived and carried out as a practical tool for scholars, using in its construction the "methods and results of the new Philological science."

The linguistic science of the nineteenth century, especially the work in phonetics, lay back of the efforts to reform the teaching of languages in Europe, beginning in 1886 with Wilhelm Vietor's *Der Sprachunterricht muss umkehren*. Among the books of this time devoted to applying the results of linguistic science were, in English, Henry Sweet's *Practical Study of Languages: A Guide for Teachers and Learners*, 1900, and Otto Jespersen's *How to Teach a Foreign*

Language, 1903. This revolt from the older and widely used grammar-translation method of teaching language led to what was called "The Direct Method."

Early in the twentieth century also, Professor Thomas R. Lounsbury, of Yale University, attempted to bring to the attention of English teachers and the general reading public the practical significance of some aspects of the developing linguistic knowledge—*English Spelling and Spelling Reform,* 1902, *The Standard of Pronunciation in English,* 1904, and *The Standard of Usage in English,* 1907.

My own book *The Teaching of the English Language* (Thomas Nelson and Sons, 1927) is, as the Preface asserts, "an effort to interpret the modern scientific view of language in a practical way for teachers."[53] It deals with the problems of divided usage in grammar, pronunciation, and vocabulary, as well as those of the developing of language habits, attitudes, and tools, in terms of the knowledge won by linguistic science up to 1925. My *American English Grammar,* 1940, attempted to furnish the materials upon which to build the kind of school grammars indicated by the earlier book as necessary:

> We need a grammar that describes the forms and syntax of present-day American English accurately; a grammar that records the facts of the actual usage of those who are carrying on the affairs of English-speaking people and does not falsify the account in accord with a make-believe standard of "school-mastered" speech; a grammar that explains these facts in the light of their history, not by means of an *a priori* reasoning; and finally, a grammar that attempts to set forth the patterns or tendencies that have shown themselves in the drift of the English language.[54]

A later book, *The Structure of English,*[55] sought to provide some of the basic linguistic materials upon which to build a practical approach to sentence structure.

The specific application of the results of American linguistic science since 1925 to the problems of teaching English as a foreign language began in 1938 with the search for sound materials. *English Word Lists: A Study of Their Adaptability for Instruction*[56] was published in 1940, and Kenneth L. Pike's *Pronunciation,* 1942, contains not only exercises and explanations based upon a phonemic comparison of English and Spanish but also (pp. 25–97) *the* results of the first structural study of the intonation of American English.[57]

Beginning in 1941 the English Language Institute in its research, in its teaching of English as a foreign language, in its production of texts, tests, and other classroom and laboratory materials, and in its teacher training program, has devoted all its resources to the application of the results of modern linguistic science. The basic principles of the approach underlying the work of the English Language Institute are described in a volume entitled *Teaching and Learning English as a Foreign Language.*[58]

Language Learning: A Quarterly Journal of Applied Linguistics has, since beginning publication in January, 1948, served those of many countries who are interested in exploring modern linguistics for help in dealing with the problems of understanding between those of differing linguistic and cultural backgrounds.[59]

A recent book that develops more specifically the applications of linguistic science to the problems of teaching English as a foreign language is entitled *Foundations for English Teaching.*[60] It contains a more detailed discussion of the principles underlying the selection and organization of the English materials of structure and vocabulary, as well as a discussion of the use of dialogue form and the teaching procedures of the oral approach. It contains also a *programmed* set of basic structure-centered English materials with a near-minimum vocabulary in significant lexical sets, as a corpus upon which to base classroom texts and teachers guides.

For the efforts to apply modern linguistic knowledge to the teaching of foreign languages in the United States the article by William G. Moulton of Princeton University, entitled "Linguistics and Language Teaching in the United States 1940–1960"[61] presents the best over-all view.

The most significant application of linguistic knowledge to foreign language learning for the purposes not only of full communication and understanding but also of scientific description and precise and effective translation, has been undertaken and developed by the Summer Institute of Linguistics of the Wycliffe Bible Translators. This organization was founded in 1935 by a man of broad vision, W. Cameron Townsend, who believed that missionaries must thoroughly "understand" the people to whom they go, and to that end must understand and speak the languages of these people much more thoroughly than hitherto has been customary. But this thorough "understanding" was not an end in itself It was to be used especially in translating the Bible accurately and fully into such language as would make the meanings in the Bible attach to their thinking and experience.

In the sessions of the Summer Institute of Linguistics held each year at the University of Oklahoma, the University of Washington, and at the University of North Dakota, intensive courses in linguistics prepare the students to attack economically and master effectively, in contact with native speakers in the field, languages that are exceedingly complicated and structurally very different from any of the languages of the Indo-European family, to which English belongs. Under the direction of Kenneth L. Pike and his associates this language learning has been highly successful and a great number of descriptive structural analyses turned out by these workers are accepted and published in the best journals devoted to scientific linguistic studies.

Not only is the linguistic training of these workers highly productive, in their ability to learn to speak these exotic languages well, and to analyze and describe the language forms and processes with scientific acceptability, but this growing body of exact information concerning the nature and functioning of a tremendous range of very different languages has provided the basis for very significant advances in linguistic theory. Kenneth Pike's book, *Language in Relation to a Unified Theory of the Structure of Human Behavior,*[62] his "Dimensions of Grammatical Constructions,"[63] and especially his treatment of "Language as Particle, Wave, and Field"[64] plow new ground and offer new approaches to old problems.

Concerning the applications of linguistic knowledge to other fields the last chapter of Bloomfield's *Language,* 1933, presents some very brief comments.[65]

Psycholinguistics

The last quarter of a century or so has seen the development of at least two major approaches to the study of language: that represented by structural linguistics and that represented by behavioral psychology. The two have progressed more or less independently. . . . The kind of question the linguist asks is essentially one like "Does this as yet unobserved message conform to the rules of this code?" or more simply, "Can a speaker ever say this?" . . .

There are presumably some finite set of variables affecting the learning process, and the psychologist's question is something like "What factors are operating to cause this speaker to say this at this time?"

There is need for some exploration of the relationship of these two views, the structural, all-or-nothing, deterministic view on the one hand and the behavioral, more-or-less, probabilistic view on the other. It is not clear to what extent they are contradictory or merely complementary. However, it seems likely that there are gaps in each approach which make communication across disciplines not only desirable but necessary.[66]

The first formal efforts to set up "communication across" the disciplines, linguistics and psychology, resulted in the interuniversity summer research seminar held at Cornell University, June 18–August 10, 1951. The Social Science Research Council's Committee on Linguistics and Psychology was established in October 1952, with the purpose of bringing together "men trained in the various fields relating to the study of language with a view to planning and developing research on language behavior."[67] The second seminar was held at the University of Indiana in conjunction with the Linguistic Institute, during the summer of 1953. The results of the work of that seminar were published in the volume entitled *Psycholinguistics: A Survey of Theory and Research Problems,* edited by Charles E. Osgood and Thomas A. Sebeok.

Psycholinguistics is by no means a sharply defined field, but there has developed in it a great interest and vigorous activity. The selections brought together in the recent volume entitled *Psycholinguistics*[68] is a valuable and convenient collection of articles bearing upon language through which to stimulate and develop increasing communication between these disciplines.

Machine Translation

The discussion concerning the use of high-capacity general-purpose computers for the purpose of translating scientific reports has increased rapidly in volume since the suggestion was put forward in 1949.[69] By 1952 preliminary work on the problems involved was discussed both at Massachusetts Institute of Technology and at the Seventh International Congress of Linguists in London. The research in this field (referred to not only as "machine translation" but also as "mechanical translation" and "automatic

translation") was reported on and discussed at the Eighth International Congress of Linguists, in Oslo in 1957.[70]

A logical machine, in order to translate, has to perform the following sets of operations: it has to read the input text in the source language, it has to manipulate the input translationally, and it has to
furnish a usable output in the target language. . . .
A translation program, to be successful, has to accomplish more
than merely the one-by-one transfer of units from the source language
into the target language. It has to include some solution to the problems
of choice implicit in the fact that (a) a unit in the source language may
have more than one possible equivalent in the target language, and (b)
that the order of source-language units in the input may not be suitable
for the output in the target language. . . . the required selection and
arrangement decisions can be programmed only if the contextual conditions can be determined under which any given decision from among
several possible ones is to be implemented. The linguist's major contribution to MT research consists in the discovery of these conditions, and
in the formulation of a routine for basing a decision on it.
There appears to be a certain correlation, on the one hand between
lexical conditions and selection decisions, and on the other hand between syntactic conditions and arrangement decisions, but it is by no
means to be assumed that selection decisions are based on lexical conditions only, nor that arrangement decisions are based on syntactic—
or, more generally, grammatical—conditions only.[71]

The efforts to identify, describe, and program the linguistic
cues of a text so that a computer could perform the translating
operation have stimulated a variety of new approaches to linguistic
analysis[72]—especially those of a mathematical-logical character.
Warren Plath, of Harvard University, in his article "Mathematical
Linguistics,"[73] has furnished an up-to-date survey and bibliography
of the achievements in this new field of language study.

Transformations and a Generative Grammar

The linguistic approach frequently referred to as "transform
grammar" seems to have arisen out of one of the attempts to deal
with portions of discourse larger than the individual "sentence"—
that by Zellig Harris as set forth in his articles entitled "Discourse
Analysis" and "Discourse Analysis: A Sample Text."[74] The following quotations from the first article give a general statement of this
new approach.

Distributional or combinatorial analysis within one discourse at a time turns out to be relevant to both of these problems.

On the one hand, it carries us past the sentence limitation of descriptive linguistics. Although we cannot state the distribution of sentences (or, in general, any inter-sentence relation) when we are given an arbitrary conglomeration of sentences in a language, we can get quite definite results about certain relations across sentence boundaries when we consider just the sentences of a particular connected discourse—that is, the sentences spoken or written in succession by one or more persons in a single situation. This restriction to connected discourse does not detract from the usefulness of the analysis, since all language occurrences are internally connected. Language does not occur in stray words or sentences, but in connected discourse—from a one-word utterance to a ten-volume work, from a monolog to a Union Square argument. Arbitrary conglomerations of sentences are indeed of no interest except as a check on grammatical description; and it is not surprising that we cannot find interdependence among the sentences of such an aggregate. The successive sentences of a connected discourse, however, offer fertile soil for the methods of descriptive linguistics, since these methods study the relative distribution of elements within a connected stretch of speech.

On the other hand, distributional analysis within one discourse at a time yields information about certain correlations of language with other behavior. The reason is that each connected discourse occurs within a particular situation—whether of a person speaking, or of a conversation, or of someone sitting down occasionally over a period of months to write a particular kind of book in a particular literary or scientific tradition. To be sure, this concurrence between situation and discourse does not mean that discourses occurring in similar situations must necessarily have certain formal characteristics in common, while discourses occurring in different situations must have certain formal differences. The concurrence between situation and discourse only makes it understandable, or possible, that such formal correlation should exist.[75]

This method "seeks to provide statements of the elements, and in particular of the relative occurrence of all the elements of a discourse within the limits of that one discourse." That is,

Elements in identical environments
Elements in equivalent environments
Equivalence classes
Sentence order

Out of this work came the understanding of "equivalent sentences"—that

. . . two otherwise different sentences contain the same combination of equivalent classes even though they may contain different combinations of morphemes. . . . If we can show that two sequences are equivalent in any English sentences in which they occur, then they are equivalent in any text written in English.

But what is "equivalence"? *Two elements* are equivalent if they occur in the same environment within the sentence. *Two sentences* in a text are equivalent simply if they both occur in the text (unless we discover structural details fine enough to show that two sentences are equivalent only if they occur in similar structural positions in the text). Similarly, two sentences in a language are equivalent if they both occur in the language. In particular, we will say that sentences of the form A are equivalent to sentences of the form B, if for each sentence A we can find a sentence B containing the same morphemes except for differences due to the difference in form between A and B. For example, N_1 V N_2 is equivalent to N_2 *is* V-*en by* N_1 because for any sentence like *Casals plays the cello* we can find a sentence *The cello is played by Casals.*

We do not claim that two equivalent sentences necessarily mean exactly the same thing, or that they are stylistically indifferent. But we do claim that not all sentences are equivalent in this sense: the relation of equivalence is not useless, as it would be if it were true for all sentences.[76]

But for "equivalence" of this sort the grammatical forms of the two sentences need not be alike:

Grammatical equivalence can be investigated more systematically if we introduce a technique of experimental variation. Given a sentence in form A and a desired form B, we try to alter A by only the formal difference that exists between it and B, and see what happens then to our A. Given *The memorable concerts were recorded . . .* , suppose that we want to make this MNR sentence comparable in form to previous intervals beginning with N. To this end, we seek a variation of the sentence beginning *The concerts.* We may do this by putting an informant into a genuine social speech situation (not a linguistic discussion about speech) in which he would utter a sentence beginning *The concerts* and containing the words *memorable* and *recorded.* Or we may do it by the tedious job of observation, hunting for a sentence that begins with *The concerts* and contains *memorable* and *recorded.* By either method, we might get *The concerts were memorable and were recorded,* or something of the sort, whence we learn that when M (or any adjective) is shifted to the other side of N (its following noun) one inserts *is;* MN is equivalent to N *is* M. In this way we discover that when MNR is shifted to a form beginning with N, an *is* appears between N and the following M.

This technique of varying the grammatical form of a sentence while keeping its morphemes constant cannot be used within a text for there all we can do is to inspect the available material. But it can be used in the language outside the text, where we have the right, as speakers, to create any social situation which might favor another speaker's uttering one rather than another of the many sentences at his disposal. It is especially useful in a language like English, where so many morphemes occur in various grammatical classes.

The preceding paragraph indicates the basic safeguard in apply-- ing grammatical equivalence to extend our textual equivalence classes.[77]

Thus given the sentence "The memorable concerts were recorded," with the structure "the memorable concerts," with modifier preceding the noun, a change to the structure, "The concerts were memorable," with the modifier following the noun and the addition of the proper form of *is,* is a permitted grammatical equivalence, because of the evidence of "experimental variation."

The process of identifying permitted grammatical "transformations" has become a very useful tool in exploring the relationships between sentences. In fact, the "transform grammar" of Harris now seems to rest upon the assumption that *all the sentences* of a language are either *kernel* sentences or *transformations* of these kernel sentences.

The kernel is the set of elementary sentences and combiners, such that all sentences of the language are obtained from one or more kernel sentences (with combiners) by means of one or more transformations. Each kernel sentence is of course a particular construction of classes, with particular members of the classes co-occurring. If many different types of construction were exemplified by the various kernel sentences, the kernel would be of no great interest, especially not of any practical interest. But kernels generally contain very few constructions; and applying transformations to these few constructions suffices to yield all the many sentence constructions of the language.[78]

"Transform grammar" provides a new approach to the old task of decomposing the structures of sentences and describing or giving rules for the "elements" of which they are composed.

. . . the kernel (including the list of combiners) is finite; all the unbounded possibilities of language are properties of the transformational operations. This is of interest because it is in general impossible to set up a reasonable grammar or description of a language that provides for its being finite. Though the sample of the language out of which the grammar is derived is of course finite, the grammar which is made to generate all the sentences of that sample will be found to generate also many other sentences, and unboundedly many sentences of unbounded length. If we were to insist on a finite language, we would have to include in our grammar several highly arbitrary and numerical conditions—saying, for example, that in a given position there are not more than three occurrences of *and* between N. Since a grammar therefore cannot help generating an unbounded language, it is desirable to have the features which yield this unboundedness separate from the rest of the grammar.

Our picture of a language, then, includes a finite number of actual kernel sentences, all cast in a small number of sentence structures built out of a few morpheme classes by means of a few constructional rules; a set of combining and introducing elements; and a set of elementary transformations, such that one or more transformations may be applied to any kernel sentence or any sequence of kernel sentences, and such that any properly transformed sentences may be added sequentially by means of the combiners.[79]

A later statement by Zellig Harris of the "transform" approach is the following.

Transformational analysis decomposes each sentence of a language into (transformed) sentences (ultimately elementary sentences) and operators (unary and connective), without residue. This means that various sections are recognized as transforms of a sentence (or the original sentence as a whole is so recognized), and that there is no part of the original sentence which is not included in one of these transformed sentences and operators on them. The process can be repeated, each transformed sentence being itself decomposed into sections which are transformed sentences, until we obtain (transformed) elementary sentences with connectives.[80]

And another by Henry Hiż, a co-worker with Zellig Harris at the University of Pennsylvania:

I am dealing here with that branch of grammar which takes a body of sentences given empirically as its starting point, which compares sentences, which arranges them in grammatically connected sets and, by pointing out their similarities and differences arrives at structures of sentences and at smaller units into which sentences are analyzable. This procedure is manifestly the reverse of a constructive or generative path in grammar where one attempts to build up sentences from more elementary constituents.

There is an effort here to present grammatical studies of a language as something open, changing, progressing. There are infinitely many batteries of transformations for a language. We change our grammar, our global view of the language, by shifting our attention from one finite set of batteries to another.[81]

If then, as the quotations above indicate, "transform" grammar provides a grammatical apparatus for the decomposition of the sentences of a language and thus a means of establishing their mutual relationships structurally, it would seem that a "generative" grammar attempts to provide a set of procedures for just the opposite process.

The fundamental aim in the linguistic analysis of a language L is to separate the *grammatical* sequences which are the sentences of L from the *ungrammatical* sequences which are not sentences of L and to study the structure of the grammatical sequences. The grammar of L will thus be a device that generates all of the grammatical sequences of L and none of the ungrammatical ones. One way to test the adequacy of a grammar proposed for L is to determine whether or not the sentences that it generates are actually grammatical, i.e., acceptable to a native speaker, etc. We can take certain steps towards providing a behavioral criterion for grammaticalness so that this test of adequacy can be carried out. For the purposes of this discussion, however, suppose that we assume intuitive knowledge of the grammatical sentences of English and ask what sort of grammar will be able to do the job of producing these in some effective and illuminating way. We thus face a familiar task of explication of some intuitive concept, in this case, the concept "grammatical in English," and more generally, the concept "grammatical."[82]

The following quotation gives a later and more precise statement.

A *generative grammar,* in the sense of [SS] [*Syntactic Structures*], is not a large collection of neatly organized examples, supplemented with comments about these examples and hints as to how to construct similar ones. Nor is it a discussion of efficient and compact notations (e.g., inventories of phonemes, morphemes, categories or construction types) in terms of which the utterances of a corpus can be represented. A generative grammar is a system of explicit rules that assign to each sequence of phones, whether of the observed corpus or not, a structural description that contains all information about how this sequence of phones is represented on each of the several linguistic levels—in particular, information as to whether this sequence of phones is a properly formed or *grammatical* sentence and if not, in what respects it deviates from well-formedness. In particular, then, this grammar distinguishes a class of perfectly well-formed (fully grammatical) sentences. It is designed, in other words, to meet what Hockett has proposed as the basic test of significance for a grammar, namely, that it "generate any number of utterances in the language, above and beyond those observed in advance by the analyst—new utterances most, if not all of which will pass the test of casual acceptance by a native speaker." To Hockett's remark I should only like to add that a grammar must not merely specify an infinite class of properly formed utterances, but must also assign to each sequence of phones a structural description that provides a basis for explaining how this utterance is used and understood—that provides the structural information without which it is impossible to undertake this further task in a serious way [221]. . . .

The investigations of generative grammar described in [SS] [*Syntactic Structures*] were motivated in part by an interest in the problem of accounting for the ability of a speaker to produce and understand an indefinite number of new sentences (or for that matter, to recognize them as properly formed, or as deviating from well-formedness in one or another respect) ([SS], p. 15), a task that he performs regularly with great facility. A generative grammar can be regarded as an attempt to characterize certain aspects of this ability, and a particular theory of generative grammar is a proposal concerning its general and universal features [222]. . . .

The study of generative grammars is, however, a natural outgrowth of traditional descriptive linguistics. Modern linguistics has, typically, been concerned with the much narrower problem of constructing several inventories of elements in terms of which utterances can be represented, and has given little attention to the rules that generate utterances with structural descriptions [223].[83]

As shown earlier in this chapter, the advances made by linguistic science during the past 140 years have been marked by some specific evidence of a break-through into new ways of working and new understanding upon which later scholars have built. Certainly the last ten years, with the new linguistic syntheses of Kenneth L. Pike's "tagmemes," built upon an immense amount of new linguistic data and facts concerning the structures and processes of a very wide range of natural languages, and with the results of the new "decomposition" procedures of "kernels" and "transformations" developed by Zellig Harris; and with the "generative" grammar of Noam Chomsky—these ten years have produced new ways of attacking linguistic problems and some new views that have stimulated most vigorous discussion. Whether any of these new approaches or any combination of them will actually develop into another significant break-through as "structural linguistics" did from 1925 to 1935, and furnish the essentials of the theoretical base for the linguistic studies of the next generation, cannot now be predicted.

In the discussions of those who have tried to understand these new approaches a number of fundamental questions have been raised for which adequate answers do not seem to be available in the published materials. Valid criteria for the judgments of "grammaticality" as applied to sentences are essential for a "generative" grammar. The theoretical and practical principles upon which the criteria now used depend seem hard to find. It is also difficult to determine all the criteria to be used to judge the acceptability or permission of any particular type of "transformation."

Certainly a live linguistic science will continue to push out the boundaries not only of the verified information that constitutes our knowledge of language structure and processes, but also our understanding of the nature and functioning of human language itself.

We would then define linguistics, or linguistic science as a body of knowledge and understanding concerning the nature and functioning of human language, built up out of information about the structure, the operation, and the history of a wide range of very diverse human languages by means of those techniques and procedures that have proved most successful in establishing verifiable generalizations concerning relationships among linguistic phenomena.

In this much loaded and somewhat difficult definition there are five essential features that cannot be separated, for each succeeding feature is a qualifier of what has preceded. Perhaps the following arrangement of the parts of this definition may serve to give these important features their relative prominence:

Linguistic science is

(1) *a body of knowledge and understanding*
(2) (knowledge and understanding) concerning the *nature and functioning of human language*
(3) (this knowledge and understanding) built up out of *information* about the *structure,* the *operation,* and the *history* of a *wide range of very diverse human languages*
(4) (this knowledge and understanding built up) *by means of those techniques and procedures* that have proved *most successful* in *establishing verifiable generalizations*
(5) (verifiable generalizations) concerning *relationships among linguistic phenomena.*

CHAPTER THREE

Language Meanings and Language Signals

All those who have stood out in the discussion of reading problems from the sixteenth century to the present have stressed comprehension as a basic objective. The authors of the most widely used textbooks during all of the last three hundred years have consistently stressed the need to grasp, to comprehend, the meaning of what is read.[1] It is true that they have disagreed concerning the meaning of *comprehension*.

Some list a great many different comprehension skills, others only a few. Even the term "comprehension" has many different meanings as evidenced in the five changes of the title of the Society's Yearbook on *The Measurement of Understanding* while the yearbook committee was preparing that volume for publication.[2]

They have, however, insisted that the final measure of reading achievement must include an understanding of the meaning. Without, at this point, discussing the rather common assertion of some reading experts, "To say that reading is a 'thought-getting' process is to give it too restricted a description,"[3] let us accept *comprehension of the meaning* as our chief objective and attempt to analyze the problems of the sharing of meanings through language.

For the sake of centering the discussion upon essentials, two other matters should perhaps be specifically indicated and excluded from consideration.

(a) The meaning of the word *meaning* has been the subject of a tremendous amount of argument. From its first publication in 1923 Ogden and Richards' *The Meaning of Meaning*[4] has gone through ten editions. Leo Abraham's article entitled "What Is the Theory of Meaning About?"[5] presents more than fifty typical quotations from philosophical and psychological writers, in each of which the term *meaning* is used in a different sense.

We come then to the conclusion that meaning is practically everything. We always see the meaning as we look, think in meanings as we think, act in terms of meaning when we act. Apparently we are never directly conscious of anything but meanings.[6]

"Meaning" signifies any and all phases of sign-processes (the status of being a sign, the interpretant, the fact of denoting, the signification) and frequently suggests mental and valuational processes as well.[7]

Often "meanings" are grouped under two general headings: (1) the scientific, descriptive, representative, referential, denotive, conative kind of meaning, and (2) the emotive, expressive, non-conative kind of meaning.

This great diversity of statement seems to arise out of attempts to describe the specific content of the situations in which the word *meaning* occurs, and to classify and define the various kinds of meaning in terms of the meaning content of utterances in general. We shall not use this approach in our discussion of "language meanings" in relation to "language signals."

(b) There has developed a rather widespread impression (or myth) that modern linguistics, especially modern "structural linguistics," has no place for "meaning."' The two statements following are typical.

Certain leading linguists especially in America find it possible to exclude the study of what they call "meaning" from scientific linguistics, but only by deliberately excluding anything in the nature of mind, thought, idea, concept. "Mentalism" is taboo.[8]

A general characteristic of the methodology of descriptive linguistics, as practiced by American linguists today, is the effort to analyze linguistic structure without reference to meaning.[9]

One can indeed point to a variety of quotations from the writings of our American linguists that seem to substantiate the views that these linguists not only condemn the "use of meaning" in linguistic analysis (as indicated in the quotation from Carroll) but (as indicated in the quotation from Firth) even refuse to treat "meaning."

Concerning the supposed refusal to treat "meaning," quotations such as the following have sometimes been offered in evidence.

The situations which prompt people to utter speech include every object and happening in the universe. In order to give a scientifically accurate definition of meaning for every form of a language, we should have to have a scientifically accurate knowledge of everything in the speakers' world. The actual extent of human knowledge is very small, compared to this. . . .

The statement of meanings is therefore the weak point in language-study, and will remain so until human knowledge advances very far beyond its present state.[10]

Concerning the alleged condemnation of the "use of meaning" in linguistic analysis the evidence usually consists of quotations like the following.

Theoretically it would be possible to arrive at the phonemic system of a dialect entirely on the basis of phonetics and distribution, without any appeal to meaning—provided that in the utterances of the dialect not all the possible combinations of phonemes actually occurred . . . without knowing what any part of the sample meant, or even whether any two parts meant the same thing or different things. But he would need some kind of guarantee that every part of the sample meant something. . . . our approach differs in some respects from Bloomfield's— chiefly in that Bloomfield invokes meaning as a fundamental criterion.[11]

Some who are counted among our linguistic scholars have so vigorously condemned all "uses of meaning" that for many linguistic students the word *meaning* itself has almost become anathema.

On the other hand, those who oppose the recent developments in the methods of linguistic study nearly all assume, as a matter of course, that all use of every type of meaning has been rigidly excluded from the linguistic studies made in accord with these methods, and often make that assumed fact the basis of their opposition and criticism.

Sometimes it is insisted that the so-called "repudiation of meaning" in the work of American linguists stems from Leonard Bloomfield. This view rests not upon what Bloomfield has said about meaning (which seems to have been overlooked) but upon inferences drawn from a somewhat superficial reading of his discussions of mentalism and mechanism. Bloomfield's physicalism (mechanism, anti-mentalism), as it is expressed in his linguistic writings, was not a philosophy of the universe nor a psychological system, but solely, as he insisted over and over again, a matter of the method of *scientific descriptive statement:*

> An individual may base himself upon a purely practical, an artistic, a religious, or a scientific acceptance of the universe, and that aspect which he takes as basic will transcend and include the others. The choice, at the present state of our knowledge, can be made only by an act of faith, and with this the issue of mentalism should not be confounded. It is the belief of the present writer that the scientific *description* of the universe, whatever this description may be worth, requires none of the mentalistic terms, because the gaps which these terms are intended to bridge exist only so long as language is left out of account. [Italics mine][12]

Bloomfield strove vigorously to avoid mentalistic terms (*concept, idea,* and so forth) in the statement of his linguistic materials and believed that "Every scientific statement is made in physical terms."[13] But his efforts to achieve statements in physical rather than "mentalistic" terms do not lead to the conclusion that he "ignores meaning" or that "he takes no account of meaning." He and many of his followers have pointed to certain uses of meaning in linguistic analysis as constituting unscientific procedures, but they have constantly insisted that meaning cannot be ignored. Pertinent quotations from Bloomfield's *Language* are abundant:

> Man utters many kinds of vocal noise and makes use of the variety: under certain types of stimuli he produces certain vocal sounds, and his fellows, hearing these same sounds, make the appropriate response. To put it briefly, in human speech, different sounds have different meanings. *To study this coordination of certain sounds with certain meanings is to study language.* [Italics mine][14]

The following is from a private letter written by Bloomfield January 29, 1945:

It has become painfully common to say that I, or rather, a whole group of language students of whom I am one, pay no attention to meaning or neglect it, or even that we undertake to study language without meaning, simply as meaningless sound. . . . It is not just a personal affair that is involved in the statements to which I have referred, but something which, if allowed to develop, will injure the progress of our science by setting up a fictitious contrast between students who consider meaning and students who neglect or ignore it. The latter class, so far as I know, does not exist.

VARIOUS LAYERS OF LANGUAGE MEANINGS

All language, as we view it here, concerns itself with meanings. Or, perhaps, we should say rather that human beings are basically concerned with meanings and use language as their tool to grasp, to comprehend, and to share meanings. It is the linguist's business to turn the spotlight on the tool—language—itself in order to examine the physical material of which it is composed and to determine the ways this material has been selected and shaped to accomplish its function of mediating meaning. In performing this special task the linguist has become increasingly aware of the significance of language as the very basis without which human society could not exist.

It is certain that the actions of man involve some factor which is not present in the actions of plants and animals, just as these involve a factor which is not present in the actions of inanimate matter. It used to be thought that in plants and animals there was a "vital principle" which is wanting in lifeless things. That was animism; today we know that the peculiar factor in living organisms is a highly specialized, unstable chemical combination, the protoplasm. Let me now state my belief that the peculiar factor in man which forbids our explaining his actions upon the ordinary plane of biology, is a highly specialized and unstable biological complex, and that this factor is none other than language. . . .

By their common habits of speech the individuals of a human speech-community influence each other and work together with an accuracy of adjustment that makes of the speech-community something like a single biological organism. . . . (Speechless animal communities are either very loosely knit, or else, as among ants and bees, they are restricted to a few rigid schemes of operation.) It may be, now, the social value, the tremendous impact of his speech-forms when they are overtly uttered, that makes it possible for a man, even in the absence of significant outer events, to live most intensely and sometimes to bring forth from such an hour an enduring expression, which we call a work of art.[15]

Language has, however, been for man not only the means through which human individuals have been able to "work together with an accuracy of adjustment that makes the speech-community something like a single biological organism." It has been not only the means through which to procure the cooperation that puts at the service of the *group* all the knowledge and wisdom of the most intelligent and most courageous individuals. Language has also been the store-house of all the information and knowledge that man has been able to achieve throughout his many years of existence and has put into reports that his fellows could understand and remember. Language has furnished both the means of sharing meanings and also the means of storing up meanings.

It is the progressive passing on of various parts of this stored body of meanings that "domesticates" a child—that channels his behavior into the patterns that have significance for each of the various groups of which he becomes a member. Parents, with much "talk," develop for him the meanings of "toilet behavior," of eating with a spoon (or with chopsticks, or with the thumb and two fingers), of not eating "dirt," of "obeying" commands, of greetings and taking leave, of "ownership" or *his* and *theirs*, of "staying on the sidewalk" and "red and green lights," of putting on and taking off clothing, of toys, of birthdays and Christmas and Sunday and schooldays, of pictures and stories and games and songs. Through the "talk" of school companions and teachers he grasps the "meanings" that control the behavior of what is usually his first group outside the home. Later there are the behavior patterns of the members of a team—baseball, football, swimming, tennis; of a choir or chorus; of a "gang" or a club or a fraternity. Language, primarily in the form of oral tradition, furnishes both the store-house and the carrying agent of the common body of meanings that have special significance for each social group. To exist and to continue, a social group needs not only a body of common experience; it needs also a common body of "meanings" through which to achieve a common interpretation of that experience—

something of a common understanding of the significance of that experience. Each group has its own set of social-cultural meanings.

LANGUAGE SIGNALS

We have just insisted that all language is concerned with meanings—that language has provided the store-house for man's experience and the meanings that arise out of that experience; and it has provided the means of sharing those meanings. But *the language itself is not the meanings. A language is a code of signals.* A well-known diagram,[16] here somewhat modified, will furnish a simplified frame for some comments upon the nature of the signals which constitute a language code.

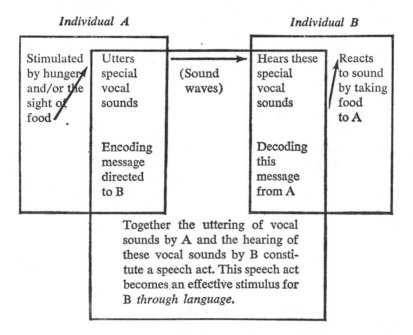

Individual A   *Individual B*

| Stimulated by hunger and/or the sight of food | Utters special vocal sounds | (Sound waves) | Hears these special vocal sounds | Reacts to sound by taking food to A |

| | Encoding message directed to B | | Decoding this message from A | |

Together the uttering of vocal sounds by A and the hearing of these vocal sounds by B constitute a speech act. This speech act becomes an effective stimulus for B *through language.*

The content of the message that A wants to send B is that he is hungry and would like to have some food. Of course A, like all animal life, stimulated by hunger, could react to such a stimulus by going himself to seek food, prepare it, and eat it. In such a case the practical stimulus and the practical response would be within the same organism, the same nervous system. But man has learned to use the sound waves as a means of physical connection between two individuals, two nervous systems, so that the individual having the hunger can, through a special use of these sound waves, procure the cooperation of another organism or individual to bring him the food to satisfy that hunger.

In this very simple example, several matters need particular comment.

(1) The "meaning" is the content of the *message* that A seeks to send to B. It arises out of the situation that affects A, and its purpose is to elicit a cooperative response from B.

(2) The particular sequences of sound waves, set up by A by means of special modifications of his breath stream, as that stream of breath passes from his lungs through his trachea, larynx, mouth, and/or nose, activates vibrations in the aural nerves of B. These sequences of "vocal sounds," made by A through the modifications of his breath stream, form the physical connection between A and B, and constitute a *speech act*. That is, the uttering of a sequence of vocal sounds by A, plus the hearing of this sequence of vocal sounds by B, constitute a speech act.

(3) Such a speech act—such a sequence of vocal sounds produced by A and heard by B—can be the physical means of conveying a message from A to B only when *the patterns of these vocal sounds fit the patterns of some* arbitrary *code of signals* agreed upon and familiar to both A and B. A *language* is such a code. The physical speech acts themselves are *not the message; nor* are they *the language*. The sum of the speech acts of a community does not constitute its language. Only as sequences of vocal sounds are grasped or recognized as fitting into recurring patterns do they become the stuff out of which a language can be made; and only when these patterns are correlated with recurring patterns of practical situations in man's experience and can thus be learned as a set of signals to elicit predictable responses do they become language itself.

(4) The language is not the meanings or the message; it is not the physical sequences of vocal sounds or the speech acts. A language is the *code of signals* through which various sequences of vocal sounds or speech acts get meaning; it is a code of signals by which messages can be sent from one individual to another.

To put the matter another way, we could say that the "speech act" corresponds to the series of "dots" and "dashes" produced by the telegraph key when a telegram is put on the wire. The physical sequences of dots and dashes is not the *message* of the telegram. Such sequences of dots and dashes have no significance in themselves. Only as they correspond to some one or more of the very limited contrastive patterns of dots and dashes which have been chosen for one of the telegraph codes[17] do they acquire any meaning.

For example, the sequence of three dots, three dashes, and three dots (· · · — — — · · ·) constitutes the distress call, *sos,* in the International code. In each of the telegraphic codes a pattern of dots alone (· · ·), or of dashes alone (— — —), or of dots and dashes (· — — ·) has been arbitrarily assigned to represent a letter of the Roman alphabet, or a digit of our numbering system. But the patterns of the International code do not have the same values in the Morse code. The pattern of three dots (· · ·) represents an *s* in both codes; but the pattern of three dashes (— — —), which represents the letter *o* in the International code, is the pattern to represent the numeral *5* in the Morse code. The sequence three dots, three dashes, three dots (· · · — — — · · ·) represents the distress call *sos* only in the International code; in the Morse code it is simply a meaningless sequence of *s5s.*

The International code uses as contrastive features only patterns of dots alone as the letter *s* (· · ·); dashes alone, as the letter *o* (— — —); or combinations of dots and dashes, as for the letter *p* (· — — ·). The Morse code, however, uses not only these contrastive features in patterns of dots and dashes but in addition the contrastive features of the length of the dashes and the length of the spaces between the dots. For example, in the Morse code a pattern of two dots separated by a short space represents an *i* (· ·); but a pattern of two dots separated by a longer space represents an *o* (· ·). A short single dash represents a *t* (—); a longer single dash represents an *l* (——). A series of three dots with equal spaces represents an *s* (· · ·); a series of three dots with greater space between the last two represents a *c* (· · ·); and a series of three dots with greater space between the first two represents an *r* (· · ·).

In a telegram, the substance of the message, the meaning, constitutes the matter of fundamental importance. But to be successful as a telegram, that message must travel from A to B. A telegraph system uses as its physical material to form the bridge from A to B sequences of dots and dashes which fit the patterns of one of the telegraphic codes.

We have, then, in respect to a telegram that goes from A to B, three matters that must be sharply distinguished:

(a) the message;
(b) the physical clicks, the dots and dashes of the telegraph instruments, that is, of the sending key and the receiving "sounder";
(c) the system of the contrastive patterns of dots and dashes that constitute the particular telegraphic code through which the particular sequences of these dots and dashes are given meaning.

The telegraph operator must achieve great skill both *in hearing the patterns* of the clicks—the dots and dashes—as they are produced at great speed, and also *in attaching to each of these patterns the precise meaning* given it by the telegraphic code.

Communication through language shows the same three features as does the process of a telegram.[18]

(a) The meaning is the message that is sent and received.
(b) The physical speech act—the actual sounds made by the vocal apparatus of A and carried by sound waves to activate the aural nerves of B—is comparable to the sequences of dots and dashes sent and received by the telegraph instruments.
(c) The language parallels the telegraphic code. The language, then, is not the message; nor is it the sequences of physical sounds which constitute the speech act. The language is the system of contrastive patterns through which sequences of specific speech acts get the power to function as signals of the meanings that constitute the message.

Any particular message can be put into any one of a variety of language codes. The number of messages that can be put into any one single language code is beyond our reckoning, infinite.

On the other hand, the number of different language codes that exist in the world probably does not exceed five thousand.

On the whole, practically all humans have learned one language code so well that, like the air they breathe, it has become part of the undifferentiated background of all their activity. They never realize its presence unless something interferes with its use. Except for the noises of the speech act, people are usually conscious only of the messages. They are not conscious of the *code* through which the messages come and go. We cannot remember when we learned to talk, or how, or even that we had to learn it.

And yet, in spite of the fact that all language codes are tremendously more complicated than any of the telegraphic codes, practically all humans do learn to use a highly intricate language code—often before the age of three, almost always before the age of five. They all learn a code that can grasp and communicate whatever meanings they have experienced. There are no records of underdeveloped or "primitive" languages *not* capable of dealing with the whole communicable experience of the natives. Of course, if any group has never seen a telephone, or a bicycle, or a telegraph system, there will be no words for these instruments. But given the experience, the speakers of any language are capable of forming adequate expressions within their own system. Two hundred years ago we ourselves had no such words as *bicycle* or *telephone* or *telegraph*. When the necessity arose we fashioned our words out of elements from classical Greek and Latin, languages which never had these particular words either.

Learning a language code is learning the signals by which meanings or messages are sent and received.

(a) Language signals, as do those of a telegraphic code, consist first of patterns of contrastive units of vocal sounds. These patterns, through an enormous amount of practice, are learned so thoroughly that their identification and recognition in the stream of speech is instantaneous and practically automatic.

(b) These language signalling patterns are, as are also those of a telegraphic code, arbitrarily assigned meanings. Learning the signals also includes learning the meanings connected with each pattern so completely that identification and recognition of the carrying physical patterns themselves sink below the threshold of attention, and only the instantaneous recognition of the signalled meanings remains.

In our language code, English, there are several important layers of signalling patterns. These layers can be separated for analysis and discussion but in the operation of our language code they supplement each other and constitute a system of signals.

(1) There is the layer of the signals of the meanings carried by the lexical items.

(a) These signals consist first of the contrastive patterns of the structural units that identify and separate the word-patterns.[19]

Given the same intonation patterns, the two sentences following differ solely in lexical meaning:

> The top of this *pen* was bent over.
> The top of this *pan* was bent over.

Pen and *pan* are different "words," representing different things. The fact that *pen* and *pan* are different "words" is signalled solely by the distinctive difference in their vowel sounds, /pɛn/ in contrast with /pæn/. And these two words are similarly separated from /pɪn/ *pin;* /pɔn/ *pun;* /pen/ *pane;* /paɪn/ *pine;* /pɔn/ *pawn.*

(b) These signals of the meanings carried by the lexical items consist also of the co-occurrence of other items of the lexical sets that identify the particular applicable meaning out of the total range of meanings that a "word" carries.

The lexical item *board* has a variety of different meanings, but in each of the following sentences, with the co-occurrence of the items in italics, there is no doubt concerning the particular applicable meaning.

> We found *a good* board *to cover the hole* in *the floor.*
> We found *good* board [without article] *and room* in a private home.
> We found it necessary *to* board *the ship* early.
> We found it necessary *to* board *up* all *the windows.*

The following quotations not only contain instances of the word *turn,* but each quotation contains items of the particular lexical set that identify the particular meaning to be attached to the word *turn* in that instance.

She made a sudden turn, as if to speak.
The rest of the party had vanished around a turn in the road.
We hesitated whether to go on or turn back.
They said they would take a turn around the garden before going in.
The manufacturers have had their turn; now we must consider the farmers.
It was only a dream but it gave me a terrible turn.

As native speakers of English we are not conscious of our use of these lexical sets in responding sharply to one single meaning out of the variety that a word often has. Such responses must be definitely learned, however, in the learning of a language. We are seldom aware that the co-occurrence with significant vocabulary items of such members of lexical sets constitute the signals that in the stream of speech identify the precise meanings that are applicable in a particular utterance.

(2) There is the layer of the signals of meanings carried by the grammatical structures.[20]

(a) These signals consist first of contrastive arrangements of form-classes.

The significant contrastive sequences that signal grammatical structures are not contrastive sequences of "words" as lexical items—"words" as they constitute the signals of the layer of meanings just indicated in 1, a and b above. The contrastive arrangements that constitute the signals of grammatical meanings are arrangements of large *classes* of words, or words as "parts of speech."[21] It is these *classes* of words, not the individual words themselves, that function as the structural units of the patterns that make up grammatical signals. In the context of live language in the actual process of signalling meanings, the "words" are formally marked as belonging to one of the form-classes. The "markers," not the meanings, signal the form-class, the "part of speech." And any word, when used in an utterance of a live English conversation, will become a member of one of the four major form-classes whenever in that utterance it is given the identifying markers of that form-class. Even a nonsense word so marked will automatically take on the *form-class meaning* of the particular "part-of-speech" class for which the markers identify it. The nonsense word-shape, *diggle,* for example, becomes "the name of a thing" when in an utterance it has such markers as *"A* diggle *was . . . ," "Two* diggle*s were . . . ."* Or it becomes an "action" word in "A woggle *diggled* another woggle"; or a "quality" word in "This woggle is *digglier* than . . ."; or a "manner" word in "This woggle uggled another woggle *diggly."*

Such parts of speech or form-classes, as arranged in patterns, constitute the signals of structures to which are attached the layer of grammatical meanings, as distinct from the layer of lexical meanings on the one hand, and the layer of social-cultural meanings on the other. Unless the "words" in these patterns have the markers to identify the form-classes, essential parts of the signals will be lacking and some kind of structural ambiguity will inevitably result. In English, the particular grammatical meaning of "kind of utterance"—whether it is a question, a request, or a statement—is signalled by contrastive arrangements of two major form-classes, Class 1 and Class 2. The utterance *Ship sails today* (as it might appear in a telegram) is ambiguous as it stands, because it lacks the essential part-of-speech markers for the words *ship* and *sails.* If a clear marker such as *the* occurred before the first word as in *The ship sails today,* there would be no ambiguity; the utterance would be a statement. If, however, the same marker were put before the second word, as in *Ship the sails today,* there would also be no ambiguity. This arrangement, however, would signal a different grammatical meaning. The utterance would now be a request or command. Other clear part-of-speech markers would also resolve the ambiguity but signal other grammatical meanings, as in *Shipped sails today,* or *Ship sailed today.* Other types of structural ambiguity arise when the markers to distinguish Class 3 words from Class 4 words do not appear in the utterance, as in *The dog looked longer than the cat.*[22]

(b) These signals of the meanings carried by the grammatical structures consist also of "function" words.

"Function"-words differ sharply from the almost limitless number of words that are or can be marked to fit into the four form-classes or "parts-of-speech," just discussed above. As here used, the essential difference does not lie in a contrast between empty and full words. The essential difference that sets off "function" words from those of the four large form-classes or parts-of-speech lies in the fact that *one must know the function words as items* in order to respond to certain structural signals. In the grammatical signals consisting of contrastive arrangements of form-classes, one does not need to know the lexical meanings of the words themselves. In fact these "words" may be entirely unfamiliar or they may be "nonsense" words with form-class markers. But in the grammatical signals consisting of function words the items themselves must be known and it is impossible to substitute for them any nonsense words. A comparison of the first four sentences below with the fifth sentence should help to illustrate this statement.

(1) *The boys* are coming tomorrow

(2) *A workman* is coming tomorrow

(3) *He* is coming tomorrow

(4) *Many* are coming tomorrow

(5) *Who* is coming tomorrow

(1) Are *the boys* coming tomorrow

(2) Is *a workman* coming tomorrow

(3) Is *he* coming tomorrow

(4) Are *many* coming tomorrow

In the first four sentences the pattern of the arrangement of the Class 1 (or Class 1 substitutes) and Class 2 words signals the meaning that these four are statements—1 + 2 (tied here by inflectional forms of number) for a statement, in contrast with 2 + 1 (tied by inflectional forms for number) for a question. But sentence (5) is a question. And the special signal of that grammatical meaning lies solely in the "word" *who*. In this sentence, *who* is a function word, which, in this arrangement alone signals the grammatical meaning "question."[23]

The following sentences contain examples of various kinds of function words.

There are several doctors in the next village
There are several doctors there
Are *there* any doctors there
Do the students work here every day
Now then what can I do for you
Have the boys done their work promptly
Have the boys do their work promptly
The students *had to have* their parents fill out a formal application
The boys *of* the leaders were invited to a reception
The boys *and* the leaders were invited to a reception

Compared with the thousands of "words" that can be given the markers of each of the four major form-classes, the number of the function words is very small. But to respond to the grammatical signals in which these words function as members of these form-classes, it is necessary only to have learned the identifying form-class markers and the patterns in which they appear; it is not necessary to know their lexical meanings. To respond to the signals of grammatical meaning in which function words constitute the signal, however, the separate function words must be learned as separate items—usually as items belonging to a list, each item of which signals the same structural meaning. There are no formal markers by which we can identify the words of these lists. They must be remembered as separate items.

(c) The signals of the meanings carried by the grammatical structures consist also of patterns of intonation.

The intonation patterns of English constitute a complex system, signalling a range of structural meanings and also a great variety of attitudes.[24] Some examples of intonation patterns that signal differences of structural meaning are the following.

> We may be able to get a shovel from the green house across the road
>
> We may be able to get a shovel from the green house across the road
>
> They are to come to the office directly // after the play
> They are to come to the office // directly after the play
>
> Will he be surprised
> Will he be surprised
>
> (A) Roosevelt usually wrote his own speeches
> (B) He wrote his own speeches
>
> The president of the university's committee on educational policies
> The president // of the university's committee on educational policies

Examples of intonation patterns signalling a difference in attitude are the following pairs.

He's a ⌐fine fa⌐ther

He's a fine father

Eggs ⌐again

Eggs again

All the sounds of language must inevitably be of some pitch and the stream of speech always creates sequences of pitch changes. Languages differ greatly, however, with respect to the use and significance of these sequences of pitch changes. Speakers of English employ a variety of patterns of contrasting pitch differences to mark some of the structures that signal grammatical meanings. These patterns at times furnish the minimum distinctive contrasts that separate and identify different signalling structures. They are thus a part of the signalling system of English structure.

But as the last two pairs of contrasting examples show, certain intonation patterns signal differences in the attitude of the speaker rather than differences in structure. In this respect intonation is significant for social-cultural meaning rather than for the meanings that attach to grammatical structures.

(3) Of the signals of meanings in English there are not only the layer of the signals of lexical meanings and also the layer of the signals of grammatical meanings but, in addition, the layer of the signals of social-cultural meanings.[25]

Here it is assumed that the meanings attaching to the lexical items as signals and to the grammatical structures as signals constitute only part of the meanings conveyed by the utterances that make up any stretch of talk. The meanings signalled by these replaceable parts of utterances constitute the *linguistic meanings,* not the *total meaning.* The total meaning of our utterances consists always of the linguistic meanings plus the social-cultural meanings. The following items will furnish a meager smattering of the great diversity of the kinds of meaning to be included.

(1) If I should say to you, "Today John Smith swam a hundred yards in forty seconds," the linguistic meaning of this statement would probably be perfectly clear. Knowing the meanings of the words you would know the type of movement represented by the word *swim,* the distance represented by "a hundred

yards," and the span of time represented by "forty seconds." You would recognize the utterance as an asserted report of an event that has already occurred. But is there any special significance in this statement? Why should anyone report this event? Is this fast or slow swimming? A hearer would miss the *social-cultural* meaning of this utterance unless he could fit the perfectly clear *linguistic meaning* of this sentence into a social frame of organized information—unless he should know, for example, that this time is more than five seconds better than the world record for this distance.

(2) You will remember that Rip Van Winkle, after his twenty years' sleep, returned to his village in the midst of an election. With his rusty gun and his ragged clothes he made his way to the inn at which the voting was taking place. There, one of his utterances almost caused a riot:

Alas! gentlemen, said Rip, I am a poor quiet man, a native of the place, and a loyal subject of the King, God bless him!
Here was a general burst from the bystanders—A tory! a tory! a spy! a refugee! hustle him! Away with him! It was with great difficulty that the self-important man in the cocked hat restored order. . . .

It was not the linguistic meaning of the utterance that produced the vigorous response. Twenty years before, when Rip started out on his tramp in the mountains, such a statement would have elicited no such reaction. It would have meant simply that he was a "good" citizen. But there had been twenty years of history, including the Revolutionary War. The linguistic meaning of the utterance was the same as it would have been twenty years earlier, but its "social" or "cultural" meaning had changed. Rip's statement now meant (in its social meaning) that he was an "enemy" of the newly established government. The reader of the story of Rip Van Winkle has missed its "meaning" unless he grasps at once the significance of the reaction of the group to Rip's words.

(3) What, for example, would be the special social-cultural meaning of the following statement? "Roger Maris got only 59 home runs in the first 152 games of the 1961 season." The significance of this statement (its social-cultural meaning) would be understood only by those having the organized information of the group who have the common experience of following the progress of professional baseball in the United States.

(4) A single deviation, or even a few deviations from the usual pronunciation of certain English sounds might have little or no social-cultural meaning. But certain consistent deviations from the norms could signal, in addition to the message that is intended, the social-cultural information that the speaker is a native of a particular part of the English-speaking world—New England, the deep South, Brooklyn. It could mark him as a foreigner of a particular native language background—French, German, Chinese. Or it could mean that the speaker is drunk, or furiously angry, or insincere, or deeply worried, or a womanish man, or a mannish woman.

These and various other types of social-cultural meanings arise out of the common experience of the members of a group of speakers. Each speaker of a linguistic community has been and continues to be a member of many separate groups, both those that are clearly identified as the members of the same family, fraternity, school, college class, choir, church, labor union, profession, neighborhood, and those that are temporary and more loosely identified as those who often commute on the same train, or who have crossed the Atlantic on the same boat, or are interested in the same sport, or in the same types of entertainment, or have had the same type of surgical operation, or who have read the same newspapers, same magazines, same books. For the members of these and similar groups (and all of us are members of many separate but overlapping groups), the utterances of our language acquire meanings beyond those that are signalled by the strictly linguistic units that constitute a formal language code. Social-cultural meanings include a large number of different varieties but these all have in common the fact that they attach to unique utterances as wholes rather than to the separable parts. Linguistic meaning alone, without the significance of a social-cultural meaning seems to constitute the "mere verbalism" so frequently condemned.

Lexical meaning consists of the recurrent "sames" of the stimulus-response features that regularly accompany recurrent "sames" of the arrangements of contrastive sound features that constitute the word-patterns.

Grammatical meaning consists of the recurrent "sames" of stimulus-response features that regularly accompany recurrent "sames" of the arrangements of form-classes, inflectional forms, and intonation sequences that constitute sentence structures.

Social-cultural meaning consists of the recurrent "sames" of stimulus-response features that (for separate but overlapping groups, including groups of the whole of a social culture) regularly accompany unique whole utterances or sequences of utterances.

All the meanings stored in language are communicated by the sets of language signals that constitute a language code. The process of learning to "talk" is the learning of the language signals of a particular code—a set of arbitrary signs in patterns correlating with portions of the meanings experience is building up. A child usually learns to "talk" his native language during his first two or three years. At this time, however, the content of the *messages* he can receive and those he can send by "talk" are limited by his own range of practical experience. This learning to "talk" is considered so easy a task that if a child does not achieve it by the age of four, worried parents often seek advice concerning his retarded development. On the other hand, learning to "read" is considered so difficult a task that it is urged that a child should not begin it before he has reached the age of six or seven; and then only after a period of careful preparation through a "readiness" program. As a matter of fact, learning to talk our first, our "native" language is perhaps the greatest intellectual feat most of us ever accomplish. (Even the most intelligent of animals other than man has never accomplished it after four or five years of devoted teaching by humans.) In comparison with a child's learning to "talk," the learning to "read" is a much simpler task and can be achieved well within a year after the child has learned to "talk" satisfactorily. What specifically, then must a child, who can talk satisfactorily, learn in addition, in order to read?

CHAPTER FOUR

The Nature of the Reading Process

The discussions of Chapters Two and Three have all dealt with *language*. An understanding of the nature and functioning of *language* must form the foundation upon which to build an understanding of the derived processes of writing and reading. Language must come first. As indicated above, so far as the evidence goes, all human beings "talk," and have talked from the beginnings of human society. Within our historical records there seems to be no evidence of any people without a structured language code fully capable of dealing with their whole experience. All have a "language" that functions not only as a means of sharing meanings but also as a storehouse for the meanings (the knowledge and the beliefs) that form the cumulative "education" of the succeeding generation.

   In comparison with the tremendously ancient activity of "talking" (the use of a language code made out of patterns of vocal noises, that is, of speech acts that acquire meaning through the signalling patterns of a particular language code) the processes of "writing" and "reading" are much later inventions. It is hard to realize that, even today, there are still more human languages that have no writing and reading by their native speakers than there are languages with such writing. Five hundred years ago only a very small percentage of the people in *any* country could read and write. Until the coming of radio and electrical loudspeakers, "town criers," with drums to call the people together at "street corners" and other public places, continued to announce important matters. This was true even in the small towns of France in 1939. Forty years ago, illiteracy in Russia amounted to more than 70 percent. Today in Pakistan it is 85 percent. In the United States, "Assuming . . . that adults who have not completed the fourth grade are functionally illiterate, approximately 11 percent of our adult population is illiterate. Furthermore, the percent of illiteracy varies for the various states from 3.9 percent to 28.7 percent."[1]

With the invention of writing the capacity of language as the storehouse of human experience has tremendously increased. Without writing, the storehouse of experience was limited to what was remembered by those living in the immediate circle of a group. Communication was limited by space and time. Only those who could hear a speaker could be told of the past. With the invention of writing, however, the necessity of the physical presence of the speaker was eliminated. One could, through writing, receive direct communication from those of other places and those of other times. Written communications could have the fullness and the accuracy of the original source of the wisdom or knowledge, rather than the fragments and inaccuracy of oral tradition.

As we approach our analysis and description of the nature of the "reading process," we must continually stress the views expressed in the paragraphs above. All the "writing" that concerns us here consists of graphic signs to represent human language. The storehouse of man's written communications is simply an extension —a tremendous extension—of the storehouse of meanings that has been provided by the language itself. Our task here is to explore the relations between the responses to the language signals of "talk" and those of "reading."

Ever since the publication in 1925 of the *Report of the National Committee on Reading,*[2] the statements by reading "experts" concerning the "nature of reading" have become more and more complex. In the *Second Report* in 1937,[3] W. S. Gray in "defining reading broadly" insisted:

A broader view of the nature of reading is that it involves the recognition of the important elements of meaning in their essential relations, including accuracy and thoroughness in comprehension. This definition, while implying a thorough mastery of word recognition, attaches major importance to thought-getting. Those who hold this view believe that reading involves both the recognition of the meaning of words and phrases and the fusing or organization of the various elements of meaning into a chain of ideas or an integrated system of thought. . . . The fact should be pointed out, however, that comprehension, as the term is used here, provides merely for a grasp of meaning in the form in which it is presented. It does not include the reader's reaction to the facts or view apprehended nor the discovery of their value or significance. It follows that a definition of reading limited to desirable habits of recognition and comprehension is inadequate to meet current needs. . . .

The Yearbook Committee believes that any conception of reading that fails to include reflection, critical evaluation, and the clarification of meaning is inadequate. It recognizes that this very broad use of the term implies that reading includes much that psychologists and educators have commonly called thinking. The Committee does not object if anyone wishes to make a distinction between securing ideas on the one hand and using them in thinking on the other. It takes the position, however, that since efficient readers do think about what they read while they are reading it, the teacher should provide needed stimulus and guidance both in securing ideas from the page and in dealing reflectively with them. . . .

But it is not sufficient that pupils merely recognize the words of a passage and comprehend and interpret their meaning. If they are aided through reading in acquiring adequate power of self-direction and ability to solve personal and social problems, they must learn to apply successfully the ideas gained from the printed page. . . . Desirable results are attained most economically when pupils make application of what they learn from the page while in the act of reading. It follows that reading, as here conceived, includes not only recognition, comprehension, and interpretation, but also the application of the facts apprehended in the study of personal and social problems. . . .

Inherent in the foregoing discussion is the conception that reading is also a form of experience that modifies personality. As pupils comprehend accurately, interpret broadly, and apply what they learn wisely, they acquire new understandings, broader interests, and deeper appreciations. Thus, personality is continually modified and enriched through reading. Furthermore, the fact is well known that reading, as well as other forms of experience, may produce various kinds of reaction—fear, ambition, appreciation, happiness, illness, action, critical thinking. Teachers should realize that such emotional responses are often aroused without adequate understanding on the part of the reader and that there may be decision and action without due consideration of all the facts involved. A properly conceived and intelligently directed reading program should reduce such responses to the minimum and should aid materially in developing a generation of citizens with social, stable, and enriched personalities. . . .

In adopting the broad conception of reading that has been discussed, the fact is recognized that many of the mental processes included are not confined to reading. In this report, therefore, reading is not conceived as a psychologically unique mental process but rather as a complex of mental activities having much in common with other complex operations and also some elements that are unique. The inclusion of the whole group of associated processes is justified by the fact that they make up an educationally coherent unit of organization.

In later statements Gray has repeatedly insisted upon this "broader concept of reading." In 1940 he phrased it as follows:

The concept of reading presented in this section is broad and comprehensive. It conceives reading as a purposeful activity which may alter the outlook of the individual, deepen his understanding, aid in the reconstruction of experience, stimulate intellectual and emotional growth, modify behavior and, in these various ways, promote the development of rich and stable personalities. It recognizes also that reading is a highly complex activity including various important aspects, such as recognizing symbols quickly and accurately, apprehending clearly and with discrimination the meanings implied by the author, reacting to and using the ideas secured through reading in harmony with the reader's purposes, and integrating them into definite thought and action patterns. Justification for including all these activities in a description of reading is found in the fact that they form a psychological unit which is dictated by the purpose that takes the reader to the printed page.[4]

In 1948 he develops these views at some length.[5] In 1956 he furnishes a condensed summary statement as follows:

In harmony with the foregoing statements, reading is conceived today as a complex activity of four dimensions: the perception of words, a clear grasp of meaning, thoughtful reaction, and integration. All four steps are essential in varying combinations if adults are to secure through reading an adequate understanding of the conflicting issues that current life presents, to choose wisely between alternatives, to find valid solutions to the challenging personal and social problems faced, and to develop richer and more stable personalities.[6]

Others have expressed similar views:

Reading is many-sided. It is a visual task involving sensation and perception. Reading is a psychological process; it involves fusing symbols with their meanings to comprehend an author's thought. Reading is a complex and unique experience involving the organism as a whole. It is a pattern of activities which varies with the reader's purpose and the kind of material which he is reading. Reading is one of several means of learning. It is an avenue of communication related to looking, talking, listening, and writing, which complement one another in many ways.[7]

Arthur I. Gates expressed his view as follows:

Reading is not a simple mechanical skill; nor is it a narrow scholastic tool. Properly cultivated, it is essentially a thoughtful process. However, to say that reading is a "thought-getting" process is to give it too restricted a description. It should be developed as a complex organization of patterns of higher mental processes. It can and should embrace all types of thinking, evaluating, judging, imagining, reasoning, and problem-solving. Indeed, it is believed that reading is one of the best media for cultivating many techniques of thinking and imagining. The reading program should, therefore, make careful provision for contributing as fully as possible to the cultivation of a whole array of techniques involved in understanding, thinking, reflecting, imagining, judging, evaluating, analyzing, and reasoning.

Another way of emphasizing the broad conception of reading that underlies this yearbook is to stress reading for use. The reading act is completed or nears completion as the child uses his reading in some practical way. He goes through steps of perception, understanding, and thinking in order that his reading may be put to work. Sometimes the content gives him facts he can use in a report; sometimes, directions for his construction activities; sometimes, material to be remembered or laughed over. But in every case the reading act includes application. Subsequent chapters illustrate the wide usefulness of reading in children's everyday activities.

Furthermore, reading is not to be regarded as limited to mental activities. The dynamic and emotional processes are also involved. In wholehearted reading activity the child does more than understand and contemplate; his emotions are stirred; his attitudes and purposes are modified; indeed, his innermost being is involved. That an individual's personality may be deeply affected by his reading is a basic assumption of the emerging practice of bibliotherapy—the treatment of personality maladjustment by means of reading and reflecting upon carefully selected materials. The reading program should, therefore, make provision for exerting an influence upon the development of the most wholesome dynamic and emotional adjustments.[8]

No one should quarrel with any of the assertions given by these reading experts concerning the need to make careful provision for "the cultivation of a whole array of techniques involved in understanding, thinking, reflecting, imagining, judging, evaluating, analyzing, . . . reasoning, and in making emotional and social judgments." Nor should he object to efforts to stimulate and strengthen any or all of these habits and abilities through the *use of reading*. But we certainly confuse the issue if we insist that this use of reading in stimulating and cultivating the techniques of thinking, evaluating, and so on *constitutes the reading process*. The abilities enumerated above are all abilities that are and must be developed through *the uses of language*. And it makes no essential difference whether the symbols employed in these uses of language are the sound features that come through hearing or graphic features that come through seeing. Every one of the abilities listed may be developed and has been achieved *by persons who could not read*. They are all matters of the uses of language and are not limited to the uses of reading.

In a basic analysis of the nature of the reading process itself and of the precise task of learning to read we must defer consideration of the uses to which reading may be put, as well as the abilities that may be developed through reading. To learn to walk the child must first achieve such muscular coordinations as will enable him to keep his upright balance by pushing with his feet upon something solid. To learn to swim he must first gain such muscular coordinations as will enable him to keep his balance while lying prone and pushing with his hands upon the water. In both situations, all consideration of the uses to be made of the skill of walking or that of swimming must be postponed until the first stages of the learning process have been mastered. For these first stages, it is necessary to discover exactly what must be learned.

We are concerned here with the process of reading as it applies to one's own native language. We have elsewhere considered briefly the problems of learning to read in a foreign language, and also the attempts to learn a foreign language through reading [see *Foundations for English Teaching* (1961), pp. 373–378].

For our purpose here, we assume an individual, a child, or an adult, who has not yet mastered reading of any kind, a total illiterate. For the sake of simplicity we assume a child of age four or five that has learned to "talk" his native language, English, satisfactorily. His pronunciation and vocabulary are without "baby-talk" deviations, he can report satisfactorily what he has consciously experienced and ask questions and make requests concerning that experience, and he can understand "talk" to him that uses only the materials that lie within the range of his linguistic and social-cultural experience. What precisely must such *a child learn*, in addition to his understanding and producing "talk," in order to "read" materials that also lie within the range of his linguistic and social-cultural experience?

The process of receiving a message through "talk" is a responding to the language signals of his native language code— language signals that make their contact with his nervous system by *sound vibrations through the ear*. The process of getting the same message (the same meanings) by "reading" is a responding to *the same set of language signals* of the same language code, but language signals that make their contact with his nervous system by *light vibrations through the eye*. The message is the same; the language code is the same; *the language signals are the same* for both "talking" and "reading." The only essential difference here is the fact that in "talk" the means of connection to the human nervous system consists of patterns of sound waves stimulating nerves in the ear, but in "reading" the means of connection to the human nervous system consists of patterns of graphic shapes stimulating nerves in the eye. All "writing" is the substituting of patterns of graphic shapes to represent the language signals of a code for the patterns of sound waves that have been learned as representing the same language signals. One can "read," insofar as he "can respond" to the language signals represented by patterns of graphic shapes as fully as he has already learned to respond to the same language signals of his code represented by patterns of auditory shapes.

In order to prevent any misunderstanding here let me insist that simply to respond to graphic signs by uttering certain sounds is *not* "reading." In similar fashion, a child's imitative repeating of the sound patterns in *da-dy* /dæ-di/ or *ba-by* /be-bi/ is *not* "talking." To be "talking," the sound patterns produced must have all the features of some language signal working through a language code to elicit a meaning response. To be "reading," the response to the graphic signs must also have all the features of some language signal operating in a language code, eliciting a meaning response. "Word-calling" (word pronouncing) without the meaning responses of the patterns that make the language signals of a code is neither reading nor talking.[9]

The process of learning to read in one's native language is *the process of transfer* from the auditory signs for language signals, which the child has already learned, to the new visual signs for the same signals. This process of transfer is not the learning of the language code or of a new language code; it is not the learning of a new or different set of language signals. It is not the learning of new "words," or of new grammatical structures, or of new meanings. These are all matters of the language signals which he has on the whole already learned so well that he is not conscious of their use. The child will continue, as he grows in experience, to develop his language capacity, especially in the variety and number of the lexical signals he can control. But this continued growth in meanings and in language signals must not take attention and effort away from the main business of the "transfer stage" of learning to read. During the "transfer stage," that is, during the period necessary to learn to respond rapidly to the patterns of graphic shapes and the correlating portions of the language signals they represent, the language materials available for use should be only those already well-controlled by the pupil. The "transfer stage" is not the time to push the development of additional language mastery. The "transfer stage" will have much less confusion for the pupil if the body of language meanings and language signals used is limited very strictly to those already within his linguistic experience.

Specifically, then, just what must be learned by children who are native speakers of English in order to accomplish this transfer from language signals *represented by auditory patterns* to these same language signals *represented by patterns of graphic shapes*? Some of the matters listed and discussed here should be learned prior to any systematic or formal approach to the particular activities that are usually considered to belong to the special procedures of reading teaching and learning. The order in which the specific items are discussed here is systematic rather than pedagogical. This order must not be taken as suggesting the sequence of the teaching; nor should the sets of materials discussed here together be taken as implying that all the items of each set should be taught at the same time or that the several items of one set should not be mixed with those of another. More than that, the explanations and the descriptions given here are for adults interested in discussing the reading process, and in understanding precisely all the kinds of responses the child must in some way learn in order to read efficiently. In many instances, we as adult readers now respond so unconsciously to these graphic features that it is extremely hard for us to realize that they are all *arbitrary, not natural,* and *had to be learned.* Our habits of unconscious response to them have been achieved only by thousands of hours of practice or use.

Learning to read, therefore, means developing a *considerable range of habitual responses* to a specific set of patterns of graphic shapes. Habits develop only out of practice. The *teaching* of beginning reading to children of four or five must be conceived, not in terms of the imparting of knowledge, but in terms of opportunities for practice. The descriptions and discussions given here, therefore, try to point out to adults the content that must become the burden of the habit responses. This content must in some way be embedded in the activities set up for children at home or in the classroom.

1. The Space-Direction Sequence

All the signals of language as represented by auditory patterns are produced in a sequence—*a sequence with a time dimension.* A time sequence is inevitable in speech. Writing—the patterns of graphic shapes—must in some way represent this sequence. Writing represents the time sequence of auditory patterns by means of a sequence of *direction* in *space,* within the surface limits of whatever material bears the writing. In English writing, the space-direction is a horizontal sequence of graphic shapes in parallel lines from left to right. In Arabic writing, the space-direction used is also a horizontal sequence in parallel lines, but from right to left.

Chinese writing uses a vertical sequence proceeding from top to bottom, in columns, beginning at the right, with each successive column to the left of the preceding one. The Chinese, in their more recent efforts to increase literacy among their people, have not only reduced the number of strokes necessary to make some of their written "characters," but have, in leading toward the use of an alphabet, encouraged the substitution of a horizontal line sequence from left to right for their old vertical sequence in columns. When the Turks changed from the use of Arabic script to Roman script to write their language (in 1929) they shifted from a right to left horizontal line sequence to a left to right sequence.[10]

The particular kind of space-direction sequence used to provide a substitute for the time sequence of speech is entirely arbitrary.[11] There seems to be no evidence that any of the possible directions in space has any advantage over the others. Any of the directional sequences can be mastered with equal ease and any one of them can serve the linguistic necessity of representing the order of "words" as uttered, by some sort of visual sequence for the graphic shapes. But whatever space-directional sequence is used it *must be learned*. There must be sufficient practice to develop an automatic habit of seeing and responding to all the graphic shapes in the substituted space-direction used. The habit of the substitution must be so complete that pupils automatically take the one for the other—that they respond as completely to the space-direction sequence as to the time sequence of speech.

This direction sequence has significance not only for the eye-movement habits from left to right horizontally in a line but also for the responses to the shapes of the letters. In English, all the letters, even the "capital letters" which are less complicated than those of the "lower case," must be "right-side up." An X or an H or an I or an O could be upside down but not lying horizontal on one side. An M upside down would represent another letter, W. The O, I, H, A, X, U, V, Y, M, W, T have no distinguishing directional features to the right and left; but C, G, Q, D, B, R, P, J, L, K, F, E have very distinctive right and left directional features. The right-left directional features of S, Z, N are not so prominent but they do make a difference, S—Ƨ, Z—Ƨ, N—И. These directional characteristics must be learned. For some of the lower case letters the contrasts of direction are structurally significant in that they form another letter, as, d—b, p—q, n—u, and b—p.

In most instances, the troubles pupils have in reversing the elements of letters or numbers (ɛ for 3) or the syllables of words /tarɡɪt/ (*target*) *for* /ɡɪtar/ (*guitar*) arise not from faulty seeing, or left-handedness, or any physical or psychological defect, but rather from insufficient learning of the significant features that depend upon the space-direction sequence of the written forms. Building up the habits of seeing written forms and parts of forms in the significant space-direction sequence the writing system uses is one of the first tasks of learning to read—one that should be accomplished in the "readiness" program.

2. The Identification of the Letters

The repudiation of the "alphabet method" as a way of learning or teaching reading in English began at least four hundred years ago. John Hart expressed it in 1570.

. . . for they [the letters] are misnamed much from their offices and natures, whereby the desirous are much the more hindered from learning to reade, though they were neuer so willing. . . . As for example. . . . For H. what reason is it to call it *ache*, which we speake when we would expresse the griefe of braine, flesh, or bone, and say and write heade ache, etc. whereas the nature and office of H. is to signifie the onely putting forth of the breath, before or after the pure voyces callde vowels. . . . It is a sophisticall maner of teaching when the letters apart must be named in one sort, and being put together, in another. . . .[12]

In using the "alphabet method" thus denounced throughout the later history of reading instruction

. . . the child first learns the names of the letters. He is then taught to read by pronouncing the letter names of the word. If the word is "cat," for example, the child says "c-a-t." The process is slow and laborious and it takes the child forever to make any progress in word recognition. The chief limiting condition of the alphabet method is that the sounds of the letter names alone have no meaning or associative connections.[13]

This almost unanimous rejection of the "alphabet method" of teaching reading has given rise to a variety of attitudes toward the alphabet itself. Statements such as the following appear frequently: "Children can learn to read without being able to identify a single letter by name"; "Learning the letter names serves no useful purpose before the child learns to read"; "It is not important that a child know the letters before he begins to read." Many teachers have come to believe that all teaching of the alphabet before the child begins to read is not only unnecessary but even harmful practice.

The discussions concerning the alphabet seldom specify exactly what "learning the letters" means. To learn the ABCs often means pronouncing the names of the letters in the conventional order. Learning the conventional sequence of these names certainly contributes little to the beginning stage of reading. It becomes a necessary tool, however, later on, in using a dictionary or the card catalog of a library.

To learn the "letters" often means pronouncing the names in order to "spell" words. This again contributes little in the beginning stage of reading.

But learning the letters may mean learning to identify and distinguish the graphic shapes that represent the written word-patterns. This ability to identify and distinguish the graphic shapes does not necessarily mean attaching the conventional names to these distinctive shapes, although the names are very useful as one means of checking the identification response. It is, however, *essential to reading at the very beginning* that pupils have already developed such an ability to *identify and distinguish the graphic shapes of the letters as can be shown by instant and automatic responses of recognition.* The developing of these habits of instant and automatic responses to the significant contrastive features of the letters of the alphabet is another matter that can well furnish the objective of many of the activities devoted to the "reading readiness" stage. At present some of these activities do already center about the distinguishing of a variety of shapes, but many teachers seem to feel that to introduce similar activities centering about the significant contrastive shapes of simple forms of the capital letters would in some way thwart progress toward reading.

Whether we like it or not, real reading that is efficient must rest upon habits of unconscious identification responses to the patterns of graphic shapes that represent the language signals of our language code. Just as the process of talking rests essentially upon responding to the significant bundles of contrastive sound features, so the process of reading rests essentially upon responding to the significant bundles of contrastive graphic features that represent those contrastive bundles of sound features.

The capital letters have the simplest forms and thus furnish the most efficient materials for learning the process of reading at the very beginning. Simple capital letters have only two basic elements of significant contrasts; lower case letters have four such basic elements; and cursive writing may have a variety of other complexities. The use, at the very beginning, of unadorned capital letters alone will simplify the set of graphic features that must be learned.[14]

ABCDEFGHIJKLMNOPQRSTUVWXYZ

Simple capital letters have only two basic formants: *circles* and *strokes*. The letters are made up of patterns of strokes, patterns of parts of circles, or patterns of parts of circles combined with strokes. Fifteen letters are *stroke* letters.

I, T, L, F, E, H, A, Z, V, Y, X, K, N, M, W

Five letters are *circle* letters.

O, C, G, Q, S

Six letters are *stroke and circle* letters.

J, U, D, B, R, P

For starting the reading process the beginner does not need to have a recognition control of the entire alphabet. Some of the letters occur much less frequently than others, as, for example, Q, Z, X, V, J. But the patterns of those that occur in the first materials to be read must be *recognized in contrast with one another* without hesitation. In fact, the child is not ready for the "reading process" itself until he automatically responds to the contrastive graphic patterns that identify a sufficient body of the letters to be used, as well as to the space-direction sequence of the materials to be read.

Thus, in the early "transfer stage" of learning to read, the number of the physical graphic shapes to be responded to automatically can and should be strictly limited, until after the child becomes aware of the fact that reading is a way of connecting patterns of writing-shapes with his own "talk." Even these limited letter shapes should be learned in sequences, not only in isolation. It is preferable that these sequences constitute words and not nonsense syllables, although at this time it is not desirable that these sequences be treated as words, or pronounced as words. The aim at this point is solely to build up automatic responses to a limited number of contrastive shapes within patterns consisting of three letters each.

For example, the following twelve letters can form the sequences of at least thirty-five words, most of which will be found in the talk of five-year-old children.

A, T, H, M, F, C, S, B, R, P, D, N

A, AT, HAT, MAT, FAT, CAT, BAT, PAT, RAT, SAT, AN, CAN, DAN, FAN, MAN, MAP, PAN, RAN, TAN, NAP, AM, DAM, HAM, MAM, RAM, SAM, TAM, BAD, DAD, HAD, MAD, PAD, SAD, TAD, TAP

The prereading use of these sequences centers attention at first upon two at a time, with the question "Are they alike or different?" Some pairs should be alike and others different.

A—AT,   AT—HAT,   HAT—MAT,   BAT—RAT,
PAN—PAD,   PAN—NAP

Later the game should use three patterns each time, in which all three may be alike, two alike with one different, or all three different.

MAT—MAP—NAP
TAP—PAT—FAT

This learning to respond rapidly and accurately to the contrastive shapes of a limited number of letters should constitute a part of the program to make the child ready for the reading process. As indicated above, he masters the reading process only insofar as he learns to respond to the patterns of graphic shapes as they represent the range of language signals he has already learned to use in "talk." For this purpose he will later need to learn a variety of other significant graphic shapes.

3. Other Graphic Shapes

The physical basis of reading, of course, consists of graphic shapes in recurrent contrastive patterns. The first step toward reading must always be learning to notice the contrastive identifying features of the graphic shapes and to recognize the patterns as they recur. The next step, which is the reading process itself, must always be establishing the connection between these recurrent contrastive patterns of graphic shapes and portions of the language signals.

Most of these graphic shapes are the letters of the present-day English alphabet, which appear as "capital" letters, "lower-case" or "small" letters, and "cursive" letters. There is a one-for-one correspondence between the members of each of these sets, but the "capital" letters have the least complicated shapes. The next chapter will treat in some detail the connection between these sets of graphic shapes that we call "letters" and the language signals of English, and thus provide an answer to the question, "Just what part of the language signals of English do the letters of the alphabet represent?"

In the rest of this chapter, we shall call attention to some of the graphic shapes other than "letters" that must be read.

(a) The graphic shapes we call "numerals" are not alphabet signs but "word" signs. There are two commonly used sets of these "numerals," again with a one-for-one correspondence between the items of the two sets. Both sets of graphic shapes must be learned, for both must be "read," but the Arabic numerals occur much more frequently, and their shapes thus have a higher priority. The graphic shapes for the Arabic numerals form a system of recurring items in repeated short series. In order to be read, contrastive shapes of each item must be learned, as well as the sequence in each series, and the fixed order of the various series in the system. Correlating with each item of each of the series is a "word," a "number word" or a "number phrase"; and it is these *number words* and *number phrases* which *must be learned in their fixed order* before the learning of the graphic signs should be attempted. In other words, the child must be "able to count" first. That is, he must be able to "say" the number words of English in their fixed order. He must learn *the order of these words* so well that he can without hesitation "count" backward as well as forward, at any part of the system. It is this "saying" of the number words in the various series, and in the order of the system, that constitutes the *linguistic* or *language features* of the English numbering system.

The graphic shapes of the "numerals" do not in any way represent the parts of the number words as do the letters of the alphabet. Each graphic numeral sign represents a complete number word in a one-for-one correspondence.

The number
   words— one, two, three, four, five, six, seven, eight, nine, ten.
The graphic
   numerals— 1   2   3   4   5   6   7   8   9   10

In learning his language the child learns to "count,"—to say the number words in their fixed order. These number words, as words, are represented graphically by sequences of letters of the alphabet, and the child will learn to read them as he learns to read any other words in his language. But these number words are also represented by the graphic numeral signs—1, 2, 3, 4, 5, 6, 7, 10, 21, and so forth. These numeral signs he will have to learn to read in an entirely different way. With these he will need to attach a whole word-pattern to each sign. Because of this basic difference, the reading of the graphic numeral signs should be postponed until *after the child has mastered the reading process with the use of the alphabet.*

The same should be said concerning all the other graphic signs that do not consist of alphabetic patterns. The following list calls attention to a few examples of other sets of similar "word" signs.

(b) The graphic signs for mathematical processes are also "word" signs like the numerals.

+	plus	—	minus	=	equals
	add		subtract		are
	and		less		

×	times	÷	divided by	∴	therefore
	multiplied by				

(c) Abbreviations of various sorts represent words or sequences of words.

i.e.	*that is, id est*
e.g.	*for example, exempli gratia*
etc.	*and so forth, and others, et cetera*
Co.	*company*
Dr.	*doctor*
Mr.	*mister, master*
Mrs.	*missis, mistress* (for a married woman)
Miss	*mistress* (for an unmarried woman)
A.M.	*before noon, ante meridiem*
A.M.	*Master of Arts, Artium Magister*
U.S.A.	*United States of America*
USSR	*Union of Soviet Socialist Republics*
UNESCO	*United Nations Educational, Scientific, and Cultural Organization*

4. Graphic Signs for Meanings Not in Language Signals

In some respects, graphic contrasts convey meanings not carried by the language signals. Some features of punctuation signal such additional meanings. For example, the sentence units marked at the beginning with a capital letter and at the end by one of the "sentence stoppers" are *rhetorical* sentence units rather than *grammatical* sentence units. Frequently such a rhetorical sentence unit pulls together, by means of these graphic marks of beginning and end, the material of several grammatical sentence units. As a matter of fact, one can find, in the written material marked off graphically as single "sentences" units consisting not only of single words, and single phrases, but also combinations of many elements brought together into one unit of considerable length. The 1943 report of the President of Columbia University contains one word-group, punctuated as a single sentence, which fills eleven pages and consists of 4284 words.[15]

The graphic marks of punctuation can thus create "written sentences" that give a unity to blocks of material that do not regularly fit the patterns of "sentences" marked by the usual language signals.

Paragraphs are essentially matters of graphic signalling. The physical sign of a paragraph is the indentation of written material on a new line. The "paragraph" itself consists of the written material standing between two such indentations. There are neither lines[16] nor indentations among the language signals of "talk." The graphic contrast of "indented lines" can be used by a writer to signal certain groupings of his utterances.

Both the graphic marks of paragraphing and those of written sentence beginnings and endings furnish signals of grouping beyond those of the language signals of "talk." This is also largely true of the marks of internal punctuation within the written sentences—the comma, the semicolon, and the colon. Quotation marks, as indications of a repetition of the exact words of a former utterance, also signal meanings for which "talk" has only lexical items.

5. Language Signals Not Represented in Writing

On the whole, contrary to the belief of many, *written materials contain less of the language signals than does talk.* In the graphic representations of language there are left out such language signals as intonation and stress and pause. These are important features of the signals of meanings, especially of social-cultural meanings. If one is to read with comprehension the graphic representations of the language signals, *he must learn to supply those portions of the signals which* are not in the graphic representations themselves. He must supply the significant stresses, pauses, and intonation sequences. A large part of learning to read is a process of learning to supply rapidly and automatically the portions of the oral signals that are not represented in the graphic signs. It is not simply a matter of speed and fluency. It shows itself in oral reading in what has been called reading "with expression." This oral reading "with expression" consists, not only of avoiding a "monotone" in pronunciation, and an oral production of the sound patterns that make up the separate words, but also of supplying the tone sequences, the stresses, and the pauses that in talk mark the word groupings that signal the total range of meanings. Real reading is not solely a passive process of receiving meanings, and just saying words. Real reading is *productive reading*—an active responding to all the sets of signals represented in the graphic patterns as they build up, and the carrying forward of such a complete cumulative comprehension as makes it possible to fill in the intonation sequences, the special stresses, and the grouping pauses that the written text requires to fill out its full range of signals. The simple question *When did he come?* can have the major stress upon any one of the four syllables, within a single intonation sequence.

When did he come

When did he come

When did he come

When did he come

Each of these stresses would signal a particular different meaning. Nothing in the graphic shapes of the written representation of the question utterance itself provides the clue. Significant intonation sequences cannot be determined for single detached written sentences. Only the full cumulative understanding of the utterances in succession can furnish the clues to the social-cultural meanings which dictate the intonation and stress pattern.

The reading process then is by no means a simple process, although it can be summed up in one simple statement.

One can "read" insofar as he can respond to the language signals represented by patterns of graphic shapes as fully as he has learned to respond to the same language signals of his code represented by patterns of auditory shapes.

A repeating here of four sentences that appeared earlier in this chapter will perhaps help to give this statement more surface.

All "writing" is the substituting of patterns of graphic shapes to represent the language signals of a code for the patterns of sound waves that have been learned as representing the same language signals. The process of receiving a message through "talk" is a responding to the language signals of his native language code—language signals that make their contact with his nervous system by *sound vibrations through the ear*. The process of getting the same message (the same meanings) through the "reading" of "writing" is a responding to *the same set of language signals* of the same language code, but language signals that make their contact with his nervous system by *light vibrations through the eye.* The message is the same; the language code is the same; *the language signals are the same* for both "talking" and "reading." The only essential difference here is the fact that in "talk" the means of connection to the human nervous system consists of patterns of sound waves stimulating nerves in the ear, but in "reading" the means of connection to the human nervous system consists of patterns of graphic shapes stimulating nerves in the eye.

The first stage in learning the reading process is the "transfer" stage. It is the period during which the child is learning to transfer from the auditory signs for language signals, which he has already learned, to a set of visual signs for the same signals. This process of transfer is not the learning of the language code or of a new language code; it is not the learning of a new or different set of language signals. It is not the learning of new "words," or of new grammatical structures, or of new meanings. These are all matters of the language signals which he has on the whole already learned so well that he is not conscious of their use. This first stage is complete when within his narrow linguistic experience the child can respond rapidly and accurately to the visual patterns that represent the language signals in this limited field, as he does to the auditory patterns that they replace.

The second stage covers the period during which the responses to the visual patterns become habits so automatic that the graphic shapes themselves sink below the threshold of attention, and the cumulative comprehension of the meanings signalled enables the reader to supply those portions of the signals which are not in the graphic representation themselves.

The third stage begins when the reading process itself is so automatic that the reading is used equally with or even more than live language in the acquiring and developing of experience—when reading stimulates the vivid imaginative realization of vicarious experience.

CHAPTER FIVE

Phonics, Phonetics, Phonemics, and the Alphabet

The discussion in Chapter One ended with the following sentence: It is perhaps not overstating the situation to say that the most important deficiency of the studies devoted to reading problems arises out of a misunderstanding or an ignoring of

(a) the nature of the various types of signals which constitute language in general and the English language in particular; and,

(b) the actual structural significance of the alphabet in comparison with other writing systems.

We now seek specifically to answer the question "Precisely what do the letters of the alphabet represent?" In the preceding chapter, we have stressed the necessity of learning to respond automatically to the contrastive graphic shapes of the letters. But to learn the alphabet as part of a signalling device demands more than this responding to the significant contrasts in the shapes of the letters which comprise the English alphabet. Children must also learn to respond automatically to whatever it is that these contrastive letter shapes represent. As in the example used above, one who wants to use a telegraphic code must first develop habits of hearing the specific contrastive patterns of dots and dashes that constitute the physical units, and then he must develop also habits of automatically connecting each of these patterns of dots and dashes with the letter or numeral or punctuation mark for which each stands. High skill in making both kinds of response must be achieved.

Part of the problems of discussing this mastery of the English alphabet arise out of difficulties of communication. The discussions of various approaches to reading have long used the words *phonics* and *phonetics*. Some of the more recent discussions use also the newer word *phonemics*. If we can first clarify the sets of meanings that cling to the words *phonics* and *phonetics,* and then later distinguish the meanings of *phonetics* and *phonetic* from those of *phonemics* and *phonemic,* we may shed some light upon these problems of communication and make some progress in establishing a meeting of minds.

PHONICS

Linguistics has much more to offer than a simple "back to phonics" proposal. Unfortunately, this seems to be all that Rudolf Flesch and a number of others have found in the reading materials of Leonard Bloomfield.[1] Flesch comments as follows:

> Several years later, Bloomfield took time out to prepare an alphabetic-phonetic primer, based on strictly scientific principles. It was an excellent piece of work, carefully designed to teach children quickly and painlessly. . . .
>
> The introduction to this Bloomfield primer was published as an article in the *Elementary English Review* in April and May, 1942. I ran across that article eight or ten years ago and that's what started me on this whole business. Taking the ideas of that article and applying them in homemade fashion, I taught my eldest daughter Anne to read when she was five years old.[2]

He then quotes the following portions from Bloomfield.

Here is what Bloomfield told the country's elementary English teachers twelve years ago: "The most serious drawback of all the English reading instruction known to me . . . is the drawback of the word-method. . . . The child who fails to grasp the content of what he reads is usually a poor reader in the mechanical sense. . . . If you want to play the piano with feeling and expression, you must master the keyboard and learn to use your fingers on it. The chief source of difficulty in getting the content of reading is imperfect mastery of the mechanics of reading. . . . We must train the child to respond vocally to the sight of letters. . . ."[3]

Flesch seems to take these particular statements as evidence that Bloomfield supports "phonics" as *the* approach to learning to read. And he expresses his own program in the following vigorous fashion.

We mean phonics as a way to learn reading. We mean phonics that is taught to the child letter by letter and sound by sound until he knows it—and when he knows it he knows how to read. We mean phonics as a complete, systematic subject—the sum total of information about the phonetic rules by which English is spelled. We mean phonics as it was taught in this country until some thirty years ago, and as it is taught all over the world today. There is no room for misunderstanding, is there? We say, and we cannot be budged, that when you learn phonics, in our sense of the word, you learn how to read. We want our children taught this particular set of facts and rules, because we know that this and only this will do the job. . . .

Let's understand each other. Systematic phonics is one thing, unsystematic phonics is another. Systematic phonics is *the* way to teach reading, unsystematic phonics is nothing—an occasional excursion into something that has nothing whatever to do with the method used to fix words in the child's mind. Either you tell a child that the word is *trip* because the letter sounds add up to "trip" and nothing else—or you tell him, "Don't you remember, we had the word last week, in the story about the trip to the woods." Phonics is *not* "one of many techniques the child can use to unlock the meaning of words . . ."— phonics is simply the knowledge of the way spoken English is put on paper.[3]

Flesch, in his reading of the Bloomfield article from which he drew the widely scattered five sentences quoted above (the first from page 130-a, the second from 184-a, the third and fourth from 185-b, the fifth from 130-b), seems to have overlooked or disregarded Bloomfield's critical comments on the "phonic" methods. The following three consecutive paragraphs come from page 129 of the same article.

The letters of the alphabet are signs which direct us to produce sounds of our language. A confused and vague appreciation of this fact has given rise to the so-called "phonic" methods of teaching children to read. These methods suffer from several serious faults.

The inventors of these methods confuse writing with speech. They plan the work as though the child were being taught to pronounce—that is, as if the child were being taught to speak. They give advice about phonetics, about clear utterance, and other matters of this sort. This confuses the issue. Alphabetic writing merely directs the reader to produce certain speech-sounds. A person who cannot produce these sounds, cannot get the message of a piece of alphabetic writing. If a child has not learned to utter the speech-sounds of our language, the only sensible course is to postpone reading until he has learned to speak. As a matter of fact, nearly all six-year-old children have long ago learned to speak their native language; they have no need whatever of the drill which is given by phonic methods.

The second error of the phonic method is that of isolating the speech-sounds. The authors of these methods tell us to show the child a letter, say *t,* and to make him react by uttering the (*t*) sound. This sound is to be uttered either all by itself or else with an obscure vowel sound after it. Now, English-speaking people, children or adults, are not accustomed to make that kind of a noise. The sound (*t*) does not occur alone in English utterances; neither does the sound (*t*) followed by an obscure vowel sound. If we insist on making the child perform unaccustomed feats with his vocal organs, we are bound to confuse his response to the printed signs. In any language, most phonemes do not occur by themselves, in isolated utterance, and even most of the successions of phonemes which one could theoretically devise, are never so uttered. We must not complicate our task by unusual demands on the child's power of pronouncing. To be sure, we intend to apply phonetics to our reading instruction, but this does not mean that we are going to try to teach phonetics to young children. In the absurdity of trying this we see the greatest fault of the so-called phonic methods.[4]

In the statement here quoted, Bloomfield uses the expression *phonic methods* as well as the word *phonetics.* He condemns the *phonic methods;* he approves the application of *phonetics* to reading instruction, but not the teaching of *phonetics* to young children.

PHONIC(S) AND PHONETIC(S)

Rudolf Flesch, as do also most of those who write professionally about the teaching of reading, seems to make no distinction
between *phonics* and *phonetics, phonic* and *phonetic*. He·reports as
follows. [Italics mine.]

I also learned that the *phonetic* method developed by the late
Professor Leonard Bloomfield was and is used experimentally in some
Roman Catholic parochial schools in Chicago. In March 1954, . . .
I went to Chicago to see for myself.

There are no "non-readers" at St. Roman. If a child is slow in
catching on to reading, his teacher pays a little special attention to his
work in *phonics,* and that's that.

The materials used in those schools are those originally developed by Dr. Bloomfield, printed and adapted for class-room use by
the Sisters of St. Joseph. (I studied the materials later and found
them practically identical with Bloomfield's own unpublished manuscript.) . . .

And here ends my eyewitness report. What does it prove? I think
it proves conclusively three things:

1. If you teach reading with phonics (regardless of the particular
   method used), student achievement in all subjects will be, on the
   average, one grade higher than the national norm.
2. If you teach reading with phonics, you will have no cases of
   "non-readers."
3. If you teach reading with phonics, you will produce students with
   a habit of wide reading.[5]

It is also difficult to establish any distinction in the meanings
of *phonics* and *phonetics* or *phonic* and *phonetic* from their use
in the following paragraph. [Italics mine.]

It is the so-called natural or intrinsic method of teaching *phonics,*
as opposed to direct, sounding *phonics,* which is the traditional *phonetic method*. In any case it is not a question of whether *phonics* shall
or shall not be taught, but at what stage it should be introduced.
Should *phonics* and word analysis come before a basic sight vocabulary
has been acquired? Tate found that children read more fluently and
with better comprehension if not taught *phonics* from the start. Gar-
rison and Heard obtained similar results and also reported that a
nonphonetic group lost less during the summer vacation following the

first grade than a *phonetic* group. Mosher and Newhall and Sexton and Herron were unable to demonstrate that including *phonetics* in the first grade had any advantage. Gates studied the relative merits of a *phonetic* and *nonphonetic* method and selected the *nonphonetic* training as his preference. All these investigators are inclined to agree that the start is best with the "look-and-say" method. Winch, in England, demurs, but the bulk of the evidence is against him. Another English authority, Schonell, sides with the majority. Research has shown that children are not likely to derive much profit from *phonics* instruction before they have a mental age of at least seven years. For that reason alone it seems unwise to give more than passing attention to *phonics* at the start. In the modern school, less emphasis is placed on *phonics* in the first grade than in grades two and three. Sexton and Herron found that *phonics* instruction begins to show a positive influence on reading achievement for the first time in the second grade.[6]

In this paragraph I can find very little significant difference in the meanings of the two words in the following pairs of expressions.

[a.1] . . . were unable to demonstrate that including *phonetics* in the first grade had any advantage.

[a.2] . . . less emphasis is placed on *phonics* in the first grade than in grades two and three.

[b.1] . . . studied the relative merits of a *phonetic* and *nonphonetic method* and selected the *nonphonetic training* as his preference.

[b.2] . . . has shown that children are not likely to derive much profit from *phonics instruction* before they have a mental age of at least seven years.

[c.1] . . . the so-called natural or intrinsic *method of teaching phonics,* as opposed to direct, sounding phonics, which is the *traditional phonetic method.*

Paul Witty, in his article "Phonic Study and Word Analysis,"[7] uses the words *phonic* and *phonics* seventy-nine times, and the words *phonetic* and *phonetics* fifty-nine times—a 57 percent to a 43 percent frequency. In Part I of this article, however, 68.9 percent of the instances are of the words *phonic* and *phonics,* 31.1 percent are of the words *phonetic* and *phonetics.* In Part II only 43.25 percent are the words *phonic* and *phonics,* and 56.75 percent the words *phonetic* and *phonetics.* The following pairs of quotations seem to show no significant differences in their use and meanings.

[a.1] For some time, teachers have introduced games and contests to motivate *phonetic* instruction.

[a.2] [At the end of the same paragraph] For use by the primary teacher, the ———— Publishing Company has recently designed a set of puzzles to teach *phonics*.

[b.1] My *Workbook in Phonics, Part One,* is devoted largely to the
[b.2] beginning *phonetic elements:* while *My Workbook in Phonics, Part Two,* presents the long and short vowels. . . .

————, ————, and ———— have prepared a series of workbooks entitled

[b.1] *Phonics We Use.* Initial consonants are presented first, then final and medial sounds.

[c.1] Apparently only *if* the *phonics teaching* is part and parcel of the thought getting activity,

[c.2] only *if* the *phonetic analysis* is an immediate means to an immediate end, is it helpful to children in the intricate kind of growth demanded of their meager powers of generalization.

In much of the writing concerning methods of teaching beginning reading the words *phonic* and *phonics* overlap in their uses and meanings with the words *phonetic* and *phonetics.* For some, the words seem completely interchangeable in such expressions as *the phonic (phonetic) method, to teach phonics (phonetics), to use phonics (phonetics) in word analysis, to motivate phonic (phonetic) instruction, must use his phonic (phonetic) training.* When, then, those who use these words as interchangeable items read such materials as Bloomfield's article "Linguistics and Reading," they inevitably misunderstand. For Bloomfield, as for all those who deal with *linguistics* as *the scientific study of language, phonetics* is concerned with such matters as the nature of the sounds of language, their differences, the articulatory movements by which the differences are produced, the vibrations that account for their acoustic effect. *Phonetics as a science is not concerned with the ways these sounds are conventionally spelled,* nor with the process of reading. In order to discuss, in writing, the sounds of a language, linguists usually use some type of "phonetic alphabet" as set forth in the section entitled "Phonetics" in Chapter Two. But the use of such an alphabet is not "phonetics." A "phonetic alphabet" is simply a tool that is useful in identifying roughly the language sounds. Phonetics itself is an internationally respected science dealing with the descriptive analysis of speech sounds.[8]

On the other hand, linguists, who constantly use "phonetics" in many aspects of their work, often object violently to the utterances in which reading specialists freely use these words *phonetic* and *phonetics*. This is not only true for those equating *phonetics* with *phonics* as shown above, but especially for the statements about English as a non-phonetic language.

The thing about the phonetic method which is likely to perplex the child is the non-phonetic nature of the English language.[9]

. . . the phonetic method suffers the limitation that English does not hew to the line phonetically. . . .
Because of the non-phonetic characteristics of the English language. . . .[10]

. . . teachers say the children are hopelessly discouraged because they discover immediately that the common words of English are not phonetic.[11]

Any teacher of reading must take into account two classes of non-phonetic words.[12]

. . . the problem of applying phonetic principles to a language made up chiefly of unphonetic polysyllabic words. But even the monosyllabic words in American-English are often unphonetic. . . .
Thus one sees that American-English is neither a monosyllabic language, nor a highly phonetic one. It is not surprising, therefore, that phonetic systems slavishly followed leave the pupil confused and bewildered concerning the pronunciation of many words. . . .
English words are so unphonetic that a pupil must acquire a variety of approaches and develop flexibility in dealing with word forms.[13]

Nor is the phonic method practicable in all languages. . . . in the languages of India which are highly phonetic it can be applied readily. But in those which are only partly phonetic, the sounds of the letters must be supplemented by other aids to word recognition, such as meaning, word-form clues, structural analysis of words and the dictionary.[14]

TEACHING PRACTICES IN "PHONICS"

In order to avoid misunderstanding and confusion, we shall, in our discussion of reading, distinguish sharply between the words *phonics (phonic)* and *phonetics (phonetic)*.

We shall use the word *phonics* to represent the various sets of teaching practices that aim to develop the pupil's ability to "sound out a word." The following quotations give something of the variety of specific practices covered by the name *phonics* from 1925 to the present.

While there are only 26 letters in our language, these letters represent more than 40 sounds. With these few sounds we are able to speak all of the words we use. In order to pronounce words correctly and to learn to pronounce new words, it is necessary to learn what these sounds are and how they are represented in print. . . .

A study of phonetic sounds will be of very little assistance at first in word recognition. Failure to recognize this fact causes many teachers to lose faith in phonetic work and abandon it before it is developed far enough to be of distinct value. The ears of the pupils must first be trained to recognize sounds, and their minds must be trained to connect these separate sounds into words. This development of the ear and mental habit requires under normal conditions about six weeks.

Ask the pupils to listen to see if they can tell what word you have in mind; then pronounce slowly by sound a few familiar words, such as m-a-n, r-a-t, d-o-g, s-l-e-d, and other simple words found in the lists in this course.

At first it will be necessary almost to speak the word before most of the pupils will recognize it. If, however, the practice is continued for a few minutes each day, the pupils will soon become very skillful at interpreting words when their sounds are given aloud by the teacher.

Next, ask the pupils to listen to the sounds of a word given by the teacher. Have them repeat the sounds heard, and pronounce the word. Continue this practice a few minutes each day for a week.

The pupils are now ready to begin learning the letter symbols. Sound aloud the word man. Write it on the board thus: m a n. Sound it, pointing to the sounds, and have the pupils sound the word. Point out the separate sounds and have the pupils associate the symbols with their appropriate sounds. Test the pupils to see if they can recognize the sound for which each letter stands when it is written alone.

In the same manner teach s, c, l, r, f, g, and t by sounding them in words, like sat, cat, lad, rat, fat, and glad. Give much practice in sounding the letters from the board, both in complete words and in isolation. In a very few days the pupils should be able to recognize the sound for which any of these letters stand when the letter is written on the board.

Require the pupils to use their knowledge of phonics in the reading class and in their study. The practice of pronouncing words for pupils who hesitate at the sight of an unfamiliar word will render useless any system of phonics which is being taught. Pupils must form the habit of sounding words they do not recognize. This habit is formed by requiring the pupils to use their knowledge of phonics to determine unfamiliar words.[15]

These activities [attention to initial and final letters of phonograms, noticing common parts of words—syllables, double letters, and so forth, finding little words in bigger ones, having each pupil build up his own groupings or families based on some common element, and contrasting reversed words—*was* and *saw* for example] differ from conventional phonics in which the main procedure is to study isolated letters and phonograms, build upwards from these, and train diligently on translating letters into letter sounds after having studied the sound equivalents of letters.[16]

This little book [*Sounds the Letters Make*] offers rhymes and pictures that make it easy to identify the sounds of speech and the letters that represent them. . . . Through the repetition of the rhymes and the emphasis on the recurring sounds the child hitherto *auditionally unobservant* often becomes sound conscious, and consequently learns to speak, read, and spell more easily. . . .

> First we'll learn one sound of A.
> Can you hear it as you say,
> "Abie has the tummy ache,
> Too much ice-cream, too much cake,
> Abie has a pain inside;
> Stayed away from school and cried."
> Read this rhyme and find each way
> You can write this sound of A. . . .

> The teacher said to little Ben
> "Remember *ng* is not *n*.
> The sound of *ng* sings a song.
> It's very clear in ding, dong, dong.
> Let's make it clear in coming, going,
> In something, nothing, raining, snowing." . . .

> "Sh! Sh!" says Mother to Joe,
> "Don't wake the baby; he's sleeping you know.
> Sh! Be careful! He'll open his eyes!"
> I know that old *sh,* but I had a surprise
> This morning at school, when my teacher showed me
> I could hear it in *ship* and *shadow* and *she!*[17]

This method differs basically from other phonic methods in that it does not start with reading, which is, in phonics, the translating of printed letters or words into the sounds of spoken words. Instead it first teaches the child the writing of the sounds by using the letters which say the sounds. This direct approach from the *sounds* of the words the child knows and uses in speaking into the *written characters* which represent the sounds is a direct, simple, logical explanation to him of the whole writing and reading process. . . . As soon as he can write a word he can usually read it, often at a glance wherever he sees it. In fact, reading as such need not be taught to many children, but training in the *blending* of the sounds in a syllable is needed for some. When a child has once mastered the phonic tools, he is able to decipher and pronounce and understand any printed words which come within his speaking vocabulary.[18]

The child breaks down the word into initial, terminal, and first vowel sounds. The consonant sounds are whispered or voiced so as to avoid the vowel appendage as much as possible. The vowel is found by breaking down the initial sound plus the vowel. Then he proceeds to initial blends, the vowel with *r*, and diphthongs. By these four steps he learns sounds related to letters and begins to see and hear familiar parts in words. . . . There comes a time when telling a child the word becomes ridiculous, particularly when, with a little help, he can build up knowledge of phonetics and learn to attack a word for himself.[19]

A common fallacy is the assumption that sounding for beginning reading is nothing more than a process of learning the sounds corresponding to separate letters and letter groups, a hundred or more phonograms, then blending these elements to form words. This was the time-honored method beginning with the introduction of the alphabet in ancient times, down through Noah Webster's day and even beyond. . . . Since about 1925 in American schools the older method of learning phonics by a synthetic process has given way to a more effective method which begins with common words the children understand and enjoy using. The more common sounds that recur in words are first met within the framework of the total word, then through a generalizing process the children learn to identify common recurring sounds in unfamiliar words met in reading. . . .

This intrinsic method of learning sounding becomes an integral part of learning to read instead of a separate skill which may fail in application when the pupil meets an unfamiliar word, or which may later have to be retaught as a skill for reading. The analytic method avoids blending problems, the chief stumbling block with other methods. The older concept of sounding persists in the popular mind because starting with the smallest elements seems more logical than the more subtle process of learning the elements through first becoming familiar with word wholes.[20]

Phonics thus has been a name used in English, since the first quarter of the nineteenth century, for those practices in the teaching of reading that have aimed at matching the individual letters of the alphabet with specific sounds of English pronunciation. The word *phonics* itself was used in English as early as the seventeenth century. At that time, however, it was applied to "the science of sound in general," to acoustics—in such forms as Phonicks, Diaphonicks, Cataphonicks as synonymous with Acousticks, Diacousticks, and Catacousticks. In the early nineteenth century its meaning was extended to include specifically the science of spoken sounds, somewhat equivalent to *phonetics,* as the linguist now uses that term.

The general use of the term *phonetics,* as interchangeable with *phonics* to represent the practices of "sounding" seems to have been a rather recent development. Linguists have not so far as I know used the word *phonetics* in this way. There did develop, however, in the nineteenth century a *phonetic* approach to reading, using a "phonetic" alphabet, which was discussed rather widely and was tried out in a considerable number of schools. The Massachusetts Teachers Association in 1851, appointed a committee "to take into consideration the subject of Phonetics." This committee reported to the Association in November 1852, recommending "that teachers in different parts of Massachusetts . . . test the merits of the Phonetic system for themselves by actual trial in their schools." The report itself sets forth the situation, first describing the *Phonography* invented by Isaac Pitman, of Bath, England, in the year 1837 as "a system of short-hand writing based upon a philosophical representation of the forty sounds of the language," and then "the system called *Phonotopy* or printing by sound," which was developed five years later by Isaac Pitman with the assistance of Alexander John Ellis[21] of Bristol, England.

In Phonotopy all the letters of the Romanic alphabet were preserved which could be used to advantage. . . . The remaining letters of the Romanic alphabet are made in the Phonetic print, uniformly to represent those sounds for which they most frequently stand in the usual print. The seventeen new letters, which it was necessary to introduce for those sounds of the English which were generally designated by combinations of letters in the Romanic print, were made so much in harmony with the remainder of the alphabet, that a person previously unacquainted with the Phonetic print, can read the most of the words without assistance.

It is thought that the principal object in securing this resemblance of the Phonetic print to the Romanic, was originally to induce the public to adopt the former as a *substitute* for the latter. But it has been found, without taking a radical step, that a wonderful gain may be made in teaching the reading, spelling, and enunciation of the common orthography, by the primary use of the Phonetic alphabet, and the Phonetic books. Not only should the child be taught to read by the means of the sounds of the language, which has been a favorite idea of many prominent friends of education, but he should have a fixed character for every sound, or else, in the outset, he will be likely to have a natural tendency to dislike his book; a tendency sometimes, to be sure, overcome by a skilful teacher, but often irremediable.

For the common orthography has such a variety of changes, not only in the sounds attached to each letter of the Romanic alphabet, but also in the number of combinations attached to each sound, that the child is liable to become so confused at the commencement of his educational career, as to render it extremely difficult, if not impossible, for him to progress with any degree of rapidity satisfactory to the teacher. . . .

The Phonetic system of instruction, thus beneficial in its effects, has been introduced in 119 public and five private schools of Massachusetts.

A Committee of the American Academy of Arts and Sciences, a Committee of the American Association of the Friends of Education, a Committee of the American Institute of Instruction, two Joint Committees of the Massachusetts Legislature on Education, a Sub-Committee of the Boston Primary School Committee, a Committee of the Ohio State Teachers' Association, a Sub-Committee of the School Committee of Cincinnati, and various committees of divers associations in different parts of this country, as well as in England, have reported in favor of this system of Phonetic instruction.[22]

This was a "phonetic teaching method" using "a pronouncing or sounding orthography," or what has been called more commonly, a "phonetic spelling." When then the term "phonetic method" is applied to textbooks after the middle of the nineteenth century it is not always easy to determine whether the actual practices used were the ones described above as those of "phonics," or those of the "phonetics" given here.[23]

This advocating of a "phonetic" approach to reading using a "phonetic alphabet" was certainly not new in the nineteenth century. John Hart, in his book of 1570, proposed a type of "phonetic alphabet" for the teaching of reading.[24] Benjamin Franklin made a similar proposal in 1768 in setting forth his *Scheme for a New Alphabet and Reformed Mode of Spelling*.[25]

The teaching practices that have been especially characteristic of "phonics" are *not* those advocated by Bloomfield in his
article "Linguistics and Reading"; *nor* are they the teaching practices which we shall stress in this book. Our approach does rest
upon *the relation between the sound patterns of the words and
the letter symbols of our alphabet* but this relation is *not* such as
to lead us to seek to match specific letters with each of the physical "sounds" of our language. Nor does it assume that the pronunciation of a word is a *fusion* or *blending* of the sounds represented
by the individual letters by which the word is spelled. The relation of the sound patterns of the "words" to the letter symbols of
our alphabet is *not a one-for-one correspondence between the isolated individual letters of the spelling and specific separate phonetic features of the sound pattern*. The "phonics" approach of
(a) isolating and in many instances trying to pronounce the individual "sounds" of a word, and (b) seeking to learn the "sounds
each letter makes" has had some merit, for it served to turn attention to the fact that our language sounds and alphabet spellings are indeed related. Because of that fact, "phonics," in spite
of all the critical discussion and all the evidence brought against
its assumptions and practices, has persisted. We shall return to
some linguistic considerations of "phonics" later, after we discuss English spelling in the next chapter. Here we need to turn
again to the linguists' interest in "phonetics" as the science of
speech sounds.[26]

PHONETICS AND PHONEMICS

A very few quotations, out of the abundance available, were
given above to show something of the widespread assertion that
"English is not a phonetic language." This or a somewhat equivalent statement appears in nearly every discussion of the problems
of teaching phonics.

There is not a series of basic materials on the market today that
does not include instruction in phonics, but it is functional phonics,
not a superimposed system of reading. It is closely integrated with
meaningful reading, and taught in close conjunction with other procedures such as context clues, structural clues, and word-form clues.
The basis for this practice rests in the following assumptions:

English is a language that follows no lawful pattern of pronunciation as German or Spanish. Consequently, no single method of word attack can be depended upon. This becomes increasingly obvious as the reader meets more involved polysyllabic words.

Whereas one can sound out simple three- and four-letter words with only a minimum loss of time, one's rate of perception is slowed down materially as he attempts to use a highly synthetic approach on more involved words.[27]

English is an experimental rather than a phonetic language anyway.[28]

In a purely phonetic language there are as many letters in the alphabet as there are elementary sounds. Having twenty-six letters in our alphabet we would expect to have twenty-six elementary sounds.

Actually there are forty-four elementary sounds in English and only twenty-three alphabet letters with which to indicate them because c, q, and x are superfluous. . . .

The authors' studies reveal, also, that our langauge is not purely phonetic. Thirteen percent of all English syllables are not phonetic. Eighty-seven percent of all syllables in our language are purely phonetic and the words in which unphonetic syllables occur are in part phonetic. Knowing the phonetic facts about our language, therefore, provides the tool with which pupils may recognize instantly nearly all of our English words.[29]

Underlying statements such as these, and underlying also most of the practices of the phonics approach, is the assumption that *writing is the language* and that *the pronunciation is simply making sounds as directed by the spelling:* "Unfortunately, we have with us a large class of persons who speak without thinking how our words are spelled, and who, therefore, squeeze all the juice out of our speech by refusing to enunciate carefully all the niceties of sound that the words contain."[30]

From this point of view it is insisted that the word *usually* must have four syllables and *every* must have three; that there must be no *p* in *warmth,* or in *something;* that the word *Arctic* has a *c* in the first syllable and must be pronounced [arktɪk]; that in the words *hundred* and *children* the *r* precedes the *e* in the final syllable and therefore these words must not be pronounced [həndərd] and [čɪldərn].

This assumption also underlies the usual instructions for pronunciation given in elementary textbooks of a foreign language.

These instructions, for the most part, deal with the pronunciation of the letters: "Since no letter of the Spanish alphabet is pronounced exactly like the corresponding English letter, it will be understood that the equivalents given in Lessons I–III are only approximate. . . . *qu* (*u* silent) pronounced like *k*. Occurs only with *e* and *i* (que, qui)."[31]

With this assumption of the primacy of the written word, whenever the regular pronunciation of very common words does not follow the spelling, the "word" is said to be unphonetic: "The children [in the stories to be read] always 'run' but seldom 'walk,' because 'run' is phonetic and 'walk' is not."[32]

A linguist, however, would insist that the vocal sounds are the primary material out of which a language code is made. These vocal sounds are *the phonetic features,* and their systematic analysis and description constitute the *phonetics* of the language. All the "syllables" and other sequences of "talk" consist of phonetic features—that is, of audible modifications of the breath stream that can be analyzed and described in terms of the muscular movements used to produce them.[33] All sequences of vocal sounds whether the "words" of a philosopher or the "babbling" of an infant child are "phonetic." Graphic representations of the English language use, for the most part, the Roman alphabet. The "words" are "spelled" by writing sequences of the letters of this alphabet, or by naming orally the letters that constitute each sequence. This spelling of English words is not always consistent and regular.

When, then, in the quotations given above, "words" like *walk* or *laugh* are said to be "unphonetic" it is not that English "follows no lawful pattern of pronunciation" but simply that the *spelling* in these instances is at fault. The extent of such "irregular" spellings for English words and the historical circumstances through which these irregularities developed will be treated in Chapter Six.

English, then, like all other human languages, is and must be "phonetic." The pronunciation of English, like the pronunciation of all other languages has its own "lawful patterns." That pronunciation is one of its most stable features—so stable in fact that "phonetic laws" have furnished the basis for a soundly scientific approach to the study of its history and that of the language family to which it belongs.

Phonetics applied to English as to other languages has furnished an increasingly intricate and generally accepted set of techniques by which to identify, isolate, and describe the specific sound features. As a subject for study, "phonetics" has attempted to set up the criteria or the frames through which to grasp the complete range of sound differences producible by the human vocal apparatus. "Phonetics" also has provided the practical approach through which to learn to hear and to make whichever of these vocal differences occur in any particular language. Phonetic descriptions are in absolute terms—the same physical criteria apply to all languages. The phonetic approach has revealed something of the tremendous number of sound differences humans can and do make. A fully adequate *phonetic alphabet,* having a separate graphic sign for every different sound feature of all the various languages that exist, would need thousands of separate signs. For indicating the differences of English pronunciation in the northeastern section of the United States, the *Linguistic Atlas of New England* used a phonetic alphabet of 121 graphic units, 32 for vowels and 89 for consonants, plus sets of shift signs and double shift signs for each of the 32 vowel units and sets of diacritics for each of the 89 consonant units.[34]

"Phonetics" has thus centered attention upon the physical differences that characterize each of the vocal sounds and has found the number of these differences far beyond our realization and belief. We are concerned here, however, not with items of vocal sound as items, but rather with those bundles of sound contrasts that function in identifying the word-patterns of a particular language.[35] To know that two items of vocal sound are different is not enough; we want to know whether the differences between these two items constitute one of the functioning contrasts that a particular language (English) uses to separate and identify word-patterns. The difference between the voiceless hiss [s] and the voiced buzz [z] is a phonetic difference, in whatever language it occurs. We can hear it in English and we can hear it in the Spanish of Mexico, as well as in the Portuguese of Brazil. In English this phonetic difference is used in contrast, to separate and identify many word-patterns: /raɪs/ *(rice)*—/raɪz/ *(rise)*; /aɪs/ *(ice)*—/aɪz/ *(eyes)*; /sil/ *(seal)*—/zil/ *(zeal)*; /yus/ *(use* as in "a use")—/yuz/ *(use* as in "to use"). In the Spanish of Mexico this phonetic difference is *never used* in contrast to separate and identify any word-patterns. In the Portuguese of Brazil it *is used* in contrast to separate and identify word-patterns. In all three languages it is a *phonetic difference.* In the Spanish of Mexico it is *only a phonetic difference;* but in both English and Portuguese, because of its use in contrast to identify word-patterns, it is also a *phonemic* difference.

Phonetics is a set of techniques by which to identify and describe, in absolute terms, all the differences of sound features that occur in any language. *Phonemics* is a set of techniques by which to determine for a *particular language* which phonetic features form bundles of functioning contrasts to identify the word-patterns of that language. Phonetics can deal at the same time with the sound features of a single language or all or any number of languages. Phonemics can deal with only one language at a time. It is the *phonemes* of English that identify the various English word-patterns. The number of phonetic differences describable in any language runs into thousands; the number of phonemes identifiable in a language is by comparison very few—from twenty to sixty.

To repeat a statement made earlier (Chapter Two): The habits of pronunciation that the child develops in learning his native language are not habits of producing and hearing the separate sounds as isolatable items in individual words but rather habits of patterns of functioning contrasts in the unique structured system of a particular language.

To bring all this to bear upon the problems of reading we must now consider the structural significance of the alphabet.

THE ENGLISH ALPHABET

During the preceding discussions we have used the terms "alphabet," "Roman alphabet," "Greek alphabet." In the preceding chapter it was the forms of the letters as used "in English writing," and now the heading of this section appears as "The English Alphabet." The matter may not be of very great importance, for we are concerned here primarily with "the alphabetic principle" in writing systems as opposed to other types of graphic representation. On the other hand because the various alphabets (Greek, Roman, Cyrillic, Runic, and so forth) do show a variety of differences in shapes, in number of letters, in order, and in use, I shall here use specific names in order to avoid possible confusions. By "English Alphabet" I mean simply the sets of letters usually used to represent graphically the English language in print and in writing.

Much has been added by discovery and research, to our knowledge and understanding of the writing systems of the world within the last fifty years and even within the last twenty-five years.[36]

This knowledge has served not only to push farther back into the past the histories of the individual writing systems themselves but also to provide the evidence through which to work upon the problems of connection and relationships among the various systems.

Earlier in this book we made a point of stressing the antiquity of human language. There seems to be no evidence of any primitive human society without a language competent to grasp and to share the complete experience of its members. In comparison with this antiquity of language, writing systems must have developed much later. The history of writing systems, however, is by no means short. With the evidence now available, competent scholars agree that a large number of the Sumerian cuneiform tablets go back to the fourth millennium before the Christian era— to 3100 B.C., to a period 5000 years ago: ". . . the Sumerians— that gifted and practical people who, as far as is known today, were the first to invent and develop a usable and effective system of writing."[37]

These tablets, mostly from excavations at Nippur, an ancient Sumerian site about a hundred miles from Baghdad, have been copied, pieced together, studied, and only in part translated and interpreted within the last twenty-five years. They antedate the oldest Egyptian as well as the earliest Chinese writing systems.

The deciphering of Mycenean Linear B, now established as the oldest piece of Greek writing in existence, was achieved by Michael Ventris only ten years ago.[38] It pushed back the history of Greek writing from about 800 B.C. to about 1400 B.C. The "alphabet⸱ (syllabary) of Linear B equals in antiquity the Phoenician "alphabet⸱ (syllabary) which also arose about the middle of the second millennium B.C.

But more important than any changes in the relative chronology or history of various individual writing systems—of Greece, or Egypt, or China, or Sumer—is the beginning of a new type of study directed to the connections and relationships between the structures of the various systems. I. J. Gelb's book of 1952 is such a study.

The aim of this study is to lay a foundation for a new science of writing which might be called grammatology. While the general histories of writing treat individual writings mainly from a descriptive-historical point of view, the new science attempts to establish general principles governing the use and evolution of writing on a comparative-typological basis. The importance of this study lies in its being the first systematic presentation of the history and evolution of writing as based on these principles.[39]

This recently developing "structure" approach to the nature of the writing systems of the world has served to clarify and to emphasize a variety of matters that those who are concerned with the "reading" of any of these systems must consider. The basic "structure" of each particular writing system will necessarily determine what must be learned as the first steps to the reading of materials written in that system. Writing systems differ most significantly not in respect to the differences in the variety of graphic shapes used, but in respect to what features of the language are represented by those shapes. From this point of view the history of the various writing systems is the history of man's earliest struggles to understand the elements that constitute his language. These struggles do not begin with the early nineteenth century—the date given above for the first steps in the modern "scientific" view of language. They reach back several thousands of years to the first efforts to invent a means of giving graphic expression to the meanings he could grasp and communicate through his language.

The first type of that graphic expression was through pictures—not pictures that represented his linguistic expression of these meanings, but pictures that represented directly the meanings themselves—pictures that showed the shapes of things, or the actions of the hunt or a battle, or of fighters swimming a river. There were series of pictures showing a sequence of events. Pictures of this kind often served as mnemonic devices to recall the occurrences of a legend. But although these pictures could and did record events and situations they were not the pictographs of *picture writing*. *Picture writing* requires the use, in the representation, of a "strict order of the signs following the order of the spoken words." On the other hand, pictures in which "the meaning is conveyed by the totality of little drawings without any convention as to the beginning of the message or the order in which it should be interpreted" are *not picture writing*.

On the whole, *pictographs* representing the meaning of the linguistic expression constitute the *forerunners* of writing, not *real* writing—that is, the graphic devices tied to the order of the linguistic signals as they come out in speech—*phonography*.

After the efforts to represent graphically the meaning of the linguistic whole, came the attention to the separate "words" as the first linguistic units to be symbolized in writing. This type of writing provided separate signs for each word. It was *logographic*. This is the kind of writing we use for our numerals. The graphic sign 7 stands in our English writing for the word pronounced /sɛvən/ (spelled *seven*). The single sign 7 stands for the whole sound-pattern which constitutes this word in English, not for the separate parts of this sound-pattern. Thus as a representation for the total *sound-pattern* which constitutes the word it is phonographic; and as a graphic representation of a total word-pattern, it is logographic. The sign 7 is thus a phonographic *logogram*. It is *not* an *ideogram*,[40] a representation of an "idea" or a "meaning"—of "seven-ness." It is strictly a word sign, as is 75 for /sɛvəntɪ faɪv/ (*seventy-five*), or 57 for /fɪftɪ-sɛvən/ (*fifty-seven*), or 777 for /sɛvən həndrəd ənd sɛvəntɪ sɛvən/ (*seven hundred and seventy-seven*). Other languages use this graphic shape (often slightly modified as 7) as a representation of their own words: *sieben* (German), *sept* (French), *shichi* (Japanese), *siete* (Spanish), *sette* (Italian). Most of Chinese writing consists of logograms and thus requires an immense number of separate graphic signs. Large Chinese dictionaries have forty to fifty thousand logographic "characters." A typewriter may have 5500.

The next linguistic unit that was symbolized in writing was the syllable. Many of the languages of the world have used and still do use syllabaries for their system. In a syllabary the separate signs do not represent the words as wholes except, of course, when the whole word consists of a single syllable, as do many of the words in Chinese. Nor do the signs of a syllabary represent the separate phonetic units which constitute the syllable. Japanese writing uses a large number of word-signs (Chinese characters, called by the Japanese *kanji*) and two types of syllabary, the *katakana* with only 47 basic signs, and *hiragana* with more variant forms of its basic syllabary shapes. The syllabary of Linear B used at least 69 signs.[41] According to I. J. Gelb there were only 22 to 30 signs in the Semitic syllabaries, 56 in the Cypriotic syllabary, 100 to 130 in the Sumerian cuneiform syllabaries.[42] As with the Japanese writing, some of these syllabaries were used together with a rather large number of word-signs (logograms). Sumerian writing, for example, in addition to its syllabic signs used some 600 other signs.

The next linguistic features to be symbolized by writing were the separate phonetic units of syllables—the writing that constitutes an *alphabet*. A syllabary as well as an alphabet symbolizes the sounds of a language, but in a different way. We are familiar with the way the letters of our alphabet represent the sound units of a word-pattern. It may help to stress the difference between an alphabet and a syllabary if, for illustration, here, we use some of these same letters as syllabary signs.

Each of our letters has a name which consists of a separate syllable. Examples are the following.

Letter	Name
D	dee /di/
T	tee /ti/
J	jay /ǰe/
K	kay /ke/
L	ell /ɛl/
M	em /ɛm/
N	en /ɛn/
U	yu /yu/
S	es /ɛs/

If then we use each of our letters to represent its full name as it sounds, each letter will stand for a *syllable* rather than the single phonetic units it usually represents when used as a letter in our alphabet. As syllabary signs then the following letters I C U symbolize the single syllable words *I see you*. The following, as syllable signs represent a few more words in context.

```
O  A  B  C  D  2  B  S
L  M  N  O  B  S
O  S  A  R,    1  S⁴³
```

The chief difficulty of using our letters as syllabary signs arises out of the great limitation of signs for syllables with other vowels than /i/ and /e/ in open syllables, as B, D, C, with /i/, and J, K, with /e/, and only /ɛ/ in closed syllables, as F, L, M, N, S with /ɛ/.

Alphabetic writing is not phonetic writing—with each letter representing one *phone* in the pronunciation of a word. As indicated in Chapters Two and Three and earlier in this chapter, the bundles of sound contrasts that constitute the functioning units to identify our word-patterns are the *phonemes. Alphabetic writing is basically phonemic.* Just as the habits of pronunciation that a child develops in learning his native language are not habits of producing and hearing the separate sounds as isolatable items, so the habits of reading alphabetic writing are not habits of responding to the individual letters as representative of isolatable phones. Just as he responds to the phonemic patterns that identify the word-patterns in speech he must learn to respond to the graphic representations of these phonemic patterns in reading.

But practically none of the writing systems in actual use are "pure" systems using only one of the types of linguistic units for graphic representation—words, syllables, phonemes. Logographic systems often contain syllable and alphabet representations. Our own alphabetic system contains also a variety of examples of word-writings. All the systems have some advantages. For our own language with its fairly large number of vowel phonemes our alphabetic representation has special advantages.

The great advantage of the Greco-Russian–Greco-Roman type of alphabet is not that it specifies phonemic features incapable of specification by all other alphabet types, but rather that it is the only type which has alphabetic resources which permit a writer to distinguish between *consonant clusters* and *vowel clusters* and *consonant-vowel* sequences without extra work.[44]

SUMMARY

At this point it may be useful to bring together in brief statements the particular features that differentiate the four terms we have discussed.

Phonics has been and continues to be a way of teaching beginning reading. It consists primarily in attempting to match the individual letters by which a word is spelled with the specific "sounds" which these letters "say." *Phonics* is used by some teachers as one of the methods of helping pupils, who have acquired a "sight-vocabulary" of approximately 200 words, to solve the problems presented by "new" words by "sounding" the letters.

Phonetics is *not* the same set of materials and activities as *phonics. Phonetics* is a set of techniques by which to identify and describe, in absolute terms, all the differences of sound features that occur in any language. *Phonetics* is not concerned with the ways in which words are spelled in English by the traditional alphabet. "Phonetic" alphabets have been constructed to serve as tools to represent graphically the actual pronunciations of linguistic forms, and these alphabets have been tried from time to time in the efforts to achieve a more effective way of teaching beginning reading.

Phonemics is a set of techniques by which to identify and to describe, especially in terms of distribution, the bundles of sound contrasts that constitute the structural units that mark the word-patterns. It is the *phonemes* of the language that alphabetic writing represents.

An *alphabet* is a set of graphic shapes that can represent the separate vowel and consonant phonemes of the language. All *alphabets* are phonemically based, and the procedures of teaching the process of reading alphabetic writing must take into account this essential fact of the structural base of alphabetic writing.

ORIGIN OF THE ALPHABET

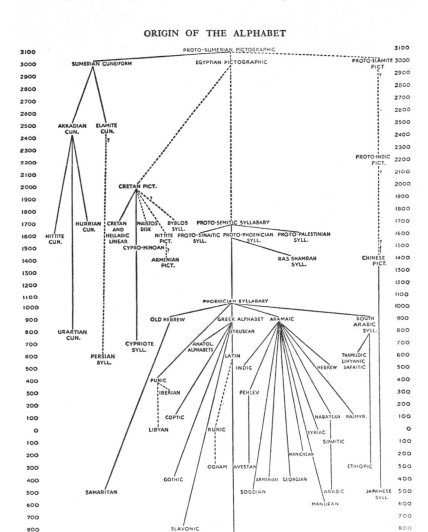

ORIGIN OF THE ALPHABET   MEDIEVAL DEVELOPMENTS

Source: I. J. Gelb, *A Study of Writing: The Foundations of Grammatology,* Chicago, University of Chicago Press. Copyright 1952 by The University of Chicago. Chart is the front endpaper of the book.

But an alphabet is always adjusted to the requirements of each separate language that uses it. The Greek-Roman alphabet has thus been applied to the writing of English and thus shaped by the uses of English. The special uses of this English alphabet will furnish the material for the next chapter, entitled "English Spelling."

CHAPTER SIX

English Spelling: Background and Present Patterns

The chart entitled "Origin of the Alphabet" shows the fact that all "alphabets" stem from the ancient Greek alphabet. The Greek alphabet, although it is phonemically based in accord with "the alphabet principle," is not, in the modern sense of the term, a "phonemic alphabet" for each of the languages to which it has been applied.

A strictly "phonemic" alphabet would have one symbol for each of the separate phonemes of *a particular language,* that is, for each of the bundles of sound contrasts that function in identifying the word-patterns of that language. These phonemes are not separate *sounds,* but *bundles* of sound contrasts that are phonetically actualized differently in various environments. One cannot pronounce the English phoneme /t/. He can pronounce the phonetic realization of this phoneme as it occurs initially in the word *top,* or as it occurs finally in the word *pot,* or as it occurs in the initial cluster of the word *stop.* And these three pronunciations would all be different. He couldn't pronounce all these three phonetic realizations of /t/ at a single time. The phoneme /t/ is not a single physical unit. It is a single abstract structural unit. Similarly a "strike" in the game of baseball is an abstract structural unit actualized in a variety of different physical actions. All "strikes" in baseball have the same functional value in one of the patterns of an "out"; but the "called strike," the "swinging-strike," the "foul-strike," the "foul-tip-strike" are all physically different. One cannot define "the strike" in any simple statement; one can only describe the various contrastive features that mark each of the behavior patterns that identify one of the three "strikes" that constitute an "out."

The English Alphabet is phonemically based but it is not, as used for English, a "phonemic alphabet" in the sense that there is only one letter symbol for each phoneme and only one phoneme for each letter symbol. *We cannot expect, therefore, to be able to match each letter of the English alphabet, as it occurs in the graphic representation of English word-patterns,* with an English phoneme. Although phonemically based, the individual letters of the alphabet with which we write do not stand in a one for one correspondence with the separate phonemes of our language.

Nor is the English alphabet, or any of the national alphabets that stemmed from the ancient Greek alphabet, a "phonetic" alphabet. It was this very fact that stimulated the active development in the nineteenth century of phonetic alphabets like that of the International Phonetic Association.

Phonetic alphabets were designed with the hope that it would be possible to represent the individual sounds so precisely that the full details of the pronunciation of any language could be revealed by the writing alone. In the struggle to achieve this goal a succession of additional signs have been added to the International Phonetic Alphabet. But even the most extended set of phonetic symbols devised for practical use falls far short of the number of sound differences that can be perceived in a single language.[1] Practical alphabets for the general reading of languages cannot hope to be "phonetic." The Greek alphabet arose out of the Phoenician syllabary[2] in the efforts to provide an adequate writing for the Greek vowels (which were greater in number than those of the Semitic languages for which that syllabary was fashioned) and for the various vowel-consonant and consonant-consonant clusters of the Greek language. This Greek alphabet was the writing system through which the people who spoke many different languages were made literate—Etruscans, Romans, Old Irish, Goths, English, Norse, Poles, Russians, Bulgarians, Finns, and others. The attempts to use it as a spelling system to represent the phonemes of a succession of different languages, by men who did not understand the phonemic principle of alphabetic writing, accounted for some of the inconsistencies or lack of "fit" in the traditional alphabets as used for the diverse sound systems of differing languages. The pronunciation systems of many languages have also undergone a great variety of changes after their particular modification of the Greek alphabet was adopted. Usually spelling changes have accompanied sound changes, but not always consistently. Sometimes the spelling changes have been delayed so long as to necessitate "spelling reforms" of considerable extent. Sometimes spelling changes have been arbitrarily introduced for some small portion of the vocabulary in accord with principles quite inconsistent with the basic patterns for the vocabulary as a whole. In other words some of the languages using an alphabetic graphic representation for their writing are very well spelled, many are less well spelled, and some are at present rather poorly spelled. Finnish seems to be very well spelled. Spanish has some inconsistencies but on the whole is well spelled. English is very distinctly less well spelled than most of the languages using the Greco-Roman alphabet. But the view that English spelling is completely erratic or that it is so erratic that we must forego all the advantage of an alphabetic system is entirely without foundation.

To stress the inconsistencies of English spelling, critics practically always point to the variety of sounds represented by the letter combination *-ough,* and the variety of ways in which our spelling represents the sound [i]:

dough, (al)*though*		*through,*
bough, slough (of despond)		*cough, trough*
tough, rough, enough		*hiccough*
we, me	*key*	*meet, speed, feel*
mete, cede	*meat, lead, real*	*field, yield, believe*
seize, receive	*machine, caprice*	*people, amoeba*

But after all, although such spectacular groups of inconsistent spellings do occur, the list of *-ough* spellings is a very small one and most of the spellings for the vowel sounds fit into a very few patterns. A brief sketch of the background of present-day English spelling[3] should help us to understand the nature and extent of some of the problems involved, and furnish a basis for an evaluation of some of the methods used in learning to read this kind of spelling.

BACKGROUNDS OF MODERN ENGLISH SPELLING

Today, many scholars seem to agree that the Greek alphabet came into being as early as the tenth century B.C., and probably even in the eleventh century. The earliest inscriptions in this alphabet were written from right to left as were the Semitic syllabaries. Later appeared the *boustrophedon* direction of writing—in lines, alternately from right to left and from left to right, "as the ox draws the plough." Not all of the early writing proceeded from top to bottom; some of it started at the bottom and went up. After 500 B.C. Greek writing practically always went from left to right and from top to bottom.

Before the official adoption of the "classical" Greek alphabet a variety of local Greek alphabets were spread throughout the areas where Greek was spoken. It was one of the eastern group— those of Asia Minor and the adjacent islands—that was officially adopted in Athens in 403 B.C. This was the Ionic alphabet, that of the Ionians of Miletus, and used by them from a very early period. During the hundred years after the adoption of the Ionic alphabet in Athens, practically all the other local alphabets had disappeared.[4]

But even the classical Greek alphabet was not a strictly consistent phonemic alphabet for Attic Greek. Of the seven vowel letters, four (two pairs) were separate signs to distinguish vowel length. *Epsilon* (E, ε) was "short" in contrast with Eta (H, η) "long"; *Omicron* (O, o) was "short" in contrast with *Omega* (Ω, ω), "long." The other three vowel letters, *Alpha, Iota, Upsilon,* stood for both the long and the short features of these vowels. *Xi* and *Psi* each represented consonant clusters rather than single consonants.

The Old English[5] (Anglo-Saxon) alphabet, however, did not come directly from the classical Greek alphabet. It was an adaptation of the Latin alphabet, which in its turn stems from the Greek alphabets, but probably from the western rather than the eastern group of these alphabets, and probably also through the Etruscan alphabet as the link connecting it to the Greek forms.

To represent the Old English pronunciation system, that is, to spell the words of Old English with the letters formerly used for the spelling of Latin words, required again considerable adaptation to make the Latin alphabet "fit."

The Latin alphabet had only five vowel letters, with phonetic values approximately like those given for the symbols of the transcription alphabet used above—*a, e, i, o, u.* Old English needed not only both short and long markers for these signs but there were also other vowel qualities for which were used the combination letter *æ* (for a sound like that of Modern English *bat* /bæt/ and *bad* /bæd/) and *y* (for a rounded high front vowel).

For consonant values, Old English used two "runic" letters, *Wen* for *w* and *Thorn,* þ, with *Eth,* a crossed Ð, đ, for what later became *th* spellings. The letter *c* was used not only for the value [k], Old English *cōc,* Modern English *cook,* but also before front vowels for the value [č], Old English *cild,* Modern English *child.* The letter *g* represented not only the value of [g], Old English *gōd,* Modern English *good,* but also the value [y], Old English *ġeoc,* Modern English *yoke.* The spelling combination *sc* had the value [š], Old English *scip,* Modern English *ship,* Old English *scinan,* Modern English *shine.*

In Old English, the phonetic difference between the sounds [s] and [z] was not phonemic. The letter *s* thus represented the voiceless value [s] at the beginnings and ends of words, and the voiced value [z] between vowels: Old English preterit singular *rās,* with voiceless sound [s], but Old English preterit plural *rison,* with voiced sound [z]. In similar fashion, the difference between the sounds [f] and [v] was not phonemic in Old English. The letter *f,* therefore, represented the voiceless value [f] at the beginnings and ends of words, and the voiced value [v] between vowels:

Old English *hrōf,* Modern English *roof,* and Old English *ofer,* Modern English *over;* Old English *līf* with voiceless sound [f], Modern English *life;* Old English *on life* with voiced sound [v], Modern English *alive.*

Although there was considerable variety in the spelling of Old English words, the patterns of that spelling were fairly consistent in their relation to the phonemes of the language.

As one passes from the Old English period to Middle English he finds changes in the spelling, but these spelling changes reflect, rather consistently, changes in the language.

Perhaps the most significant language change that shows itself in Early Middle English is the "leveling" of the vowels in the unstressed inflectional endings. In Old English, practically all dative plurals ended with *-um;* most of the case forms of "weak" nouns and "weak" adjectives ended with *-an,* the preterit plurals of verbs with *-on;* the nominative and accusative plurals of one large class of nouns ended with *-as,* genitive plurals with *-a.* By 1100 only 16½ percent of these endings were still spelled with their historical vowel letters; 73 percent were spelled with *e;* and 11½ percent had *a, o,* or *u,* but not the letter with which they had formerly been spelled. From all the evidence we should conclude that the pronunciation of these inflectional endings had changed from one in which the separate vowels were kept distinct to one in which these vowels were all leveled to the sound [ə], and rather regularly spelled with *e.* The spelling followed but lagged behind the sound change. There were still, within the writing of a single author, some instances of the older historical forms and of a confusion of the older patterns. A hundred years later the newer spelling with *e* was practically complete; only a very infrequent historical spelling appeared and none of the "confused" forms.

By the end of the thirteenth century, the English language had taken into its vocabulary an immense number of French words and Anglo-French scribes had done much to respell the language. The letter *c,* before *e* and *i,* was used for the sound of [s], as in *cell, cellar, circle, city.* The letters *qu* replaced *cw* in such words as *queen, quoth,* and *quick.* The letters *th* replaced *þ* and *ð* in *thin, thikke.* The letters *u* and *y* were used as consonants as in *euere* (*ever*) and *ye.* The letters *gh* replaced the Old English *h* in such words as *riht* (*right*), *broht* (*brought*), *rūh* (*rough*).

Beginning in Middle English and influenced somewhat by the conscious spelling changes of the *Ormulum*, there arose the practice of doubling vowel letters to mark the length of the vowel, and the doubling of consonant letters after a short vowel.[6]

These practices produced such spellings of the long vowels as *hoom* for Early Modern English *hōm* from Old English *hām, stoon* for Early Modern English *ston* from Old English *stān, blood* from Old English *blōd, roof* from Old English *hrōf.* The doubling of consonants appears in such words as *bitter* (Old English *biter*), *copper* (Old English *coper*). The *Ormulum* has such spellings as *messe, spellenn, fillenn, unnderrstanndenn, Ennglisch, hellpenn, itt, iss, hiss, þiss, shall, himm.*

Three matters of special importance for present-day English spelling need comment as we pass from late Middle English to Early Modern English—from the time of Chaucer to that of Shakspere.

First, there was in the pronunciation of English the so-called "loss of *e*" in the unstressed inflectional syllables. These inflectional syllables, with the distinct vowels spelled with *a, o,* or *u,* had been all leveled to an [ə] sound, spelled with *e,* as English developed from Old English to Middle English. But the syllables themselves still persisted—Old English Nominative Plural *stānas* became Middle English /stɔn-əs/; Old English participle *lufod* became Middle English /luv-əd/. Now in the fifteenth century with the "loss of *e,*" the inflectional syllable was eliminated. But the *e* remained in the spelling. The spelling-pattern continued *stones,* with the phonemic word-pattern /stonz/; the spelling pattern *loved,* with the phonemic word-pattern /ləvd/; the spelling-pattern *walked,* with the phonemic word-pattern /wɔkt/. The spelling-pattern with *e* in words like *stones* continued as a sign of the quality of the vowel in the stem of the word, but loss of the [ə] vowel sound eliminated the second syllable and produced approximately a hundred *new* consonant clusters at the ends of words.[7]

Second, there was in the pronunciation of English the "great vowel shift" that developed primarily during the fifteenth century. This shift affected six of the vowel phonemes and two of the phonemic diphthongs. It amounted to a redistribution of these phonemes in the word-patterns of English, without any shift in the spelling patterns of these words. It was this development that put the English use of these vowel letters entirely out of line with the spelling practice of the continental European languages and the earlier spelling of English through the time of Chaucer.

The following examples will furnish a much simplified statement of what developed over a period of a hundred years from the first half of the fifteenth century. For one vowel series there were the following:

Spelling				Spelling
name	/na:mə/	>	/nem/	*name*
swete	/swe:tə/	>	/swit/	*sweet*
ride	/ri:də/	>	/raɪd/	*ride*
waye	/waɪə/	>	/we/	*way*
lay	/laɪ/	>	/le/	*lay*
gay	/gaɪ/	>	/ge/	*gay*

A second vowel series is represented by the following:

hom	/hɔm/	>	/hom/	*home*
roote	/rotə/	>	/rut/	*root*
hus	/hus/	>	/haʊs/	*house*
foughte	/faʊxtə/	>	/fɔt/	*fought*

In the case of these changes of the vowel sounds the earlier spelling, on the whole, remained and from this time these vowel letters represented the changed sounds rather than the sounds they represented in fourteenth century English, and the ones they represent in the spelling of other European languages.

Third, there was the attempt to have the spelling represent the "etymology." This "etymological spelling" seems to have arisen during the sixteenth century in connection with words borrowed from Latin or Greek, or supposed to have come into English from those languages. It was an attempt to maintain in the spelling a letter "silent to the ear," "which visibly connects a word with the past, which tells its history, and indicates the quarter from which it has been derived." Thus, for example, the *g* in *deign, feign, reign, impugn* is said to be "most eloquent to the eye . . . telling as it does of *dignor, fingo, regno, impugno.*" But this use of spelling to show the "etymology" of a word—its connection with the past—was confined to showing a connection with Greek or Latin. It ignored all the other sources of English words, and was thus applied to a comparatively small portion of the English vocabulary.

Those who thus introduced these letters as "etymological" signs did not possess a linguistic knowledge sufficient for even the beginnings of their task and thus created many false forms. Of the Latinate words in the English language of the sixteenth century, the majority had come through Old French, not directly from classical Latin. They had already gone through a number of sound-changes and, therefore, from the point of view of a sound etymology, should not contain any of the "silent letters" put in to show a connection with classical Latin. The *b* in *debt* and in *doubt,* put in to make a connection with Latin *debitum* and *dubitum,* never represented a feature of pronunciation of English and has falsely represented the etymology. Chaucer spells these words without a *b,* as *dette, det, detteles,* and *doute, douteles;* Coverdale uses *detter* and *dowtles.*

The *g* inserted in *sovereign* and the *s* inserted in *island* have not the slightest basis in "etymology." The *g* in *sovereign* to connect the word with Latin *regno* is wrong. *Sovereign* is not even remotely derived from *regno.* It comes from Old French *soverain, souverein,* which in turn comes from Popular Latin *superānus,* from *super,* meaning *above.* It was spelled *soverein* as late as 1741. The word *island* is not at all Latinate but an English compound of *īg-land* or *ēa-land,* meaning *water* or *stream land.* It was confused with *isle,* which is related to Latin *insula.*

Altogether the principle of "etymological" spelling—the continuing or the putting in of "silent" letters to indicate a connection with some form from which the word is supposed to have been derived—is a false principle to be applied to spelling. In English it was never consistently applied even to the Latinate vocabulary, and the ignorance of those who attempted to apply it has resulted in many forms which are not only false etymologically but also forms which interfere most seriously with the basic spelling patterns of Modern English.

For the late sixteenth and the seventeenth centuries, two matters must be brought into attention before turning to the spelling patterns of the present.

(a) During the late sixteenth and seventeenth centuries a tremendous number of new "words" increased the vocabulary of English. A second mass of French words came into English with different types of pronunciation and spelling from those assimilated during the thirteenth and fourteenth centuries. Examples are *caprice, routine, intrigue, coquet (coquette), group, sabre.* But there were many others from a great variety of sources—the musical terms from Italian, the scientific terms made from Greek and Latin forms, the many names for strange goods imported from the Indies, Russia, and the New World, as the voyages of discovery and settlement changed the central focus of geographical thinking from the Mediterranean to the Atlantic. If the numbers of the vocabulary entry cards for the *Middle English Dictionary* and the *Early Modern English Dictionary* can be accepted as valid evidence then during the two hundred years from 1475 to 1700 the vocabulary of English increased approximately 275 percent—from about 45,000 entries to 125,000 entries.

(b) With the developing of printing, beginning in England at the end of the fifteenth century, the determination of the spelling became more and more the province of the printers and their "correctors."

If therefore a Corrector suspects Copy to want revising, he is not to postpone it, but to make his emendations in the Manuscript before it is wanted by the Compositor, that he may not be hindered in the pursuit of his business; or prejudiced by alterations in the proof, especially if they are of no real signification; such as far-fetched spelling of Words, changing and thrusting in Points, Capitals, or anything else that has nothing but fancy and humour for its authority and foundation.[8]

Under the influence of the printer, the ideal for spelling became "regularity"—that the "same" word be spelled always in the same way wherever it occurred. "Correctness" of spelling gradually came to mean uniformity, and the diversities in the practice of authors were eventually almost completely eliminated by the rules set up and applied by the editors and proofreaders.

By the end of the seventeenth century the patterns of modern English spelling were fairly well set. In spite of the many inconsistencies that appear when one attempts to match the items of the word-sounds with individual letters, and the many gross violations of spelling patterns arising from the arbitrary changes aimed at producing "etymological" spellings, modern English spelling is not hopelessly chaotic. Most of that spelling is patterned. It is basically phonemic in its representation, with *patterns of letters,* rather than *single letters,* as the *functioning units* of the representation. It is this fact that makes the *phonics* approach to reading and to spelling considerably less than satisfactory. It is this fact too, that accounts for what slight success the *word-method* attack has had in spite of its use of wholly inadequate criteria of identification.

PRESENT PATTERNS OF ENGLISH SPELLING

For English spelling then we must emphasize the fact that *throughout its history single letters have never matched single sound features.* There have always been patterns of letter sequences which *represented* (but not necessarily duplicated) those patterns of contrastive differences of sound that identify word-patterns. In other words, in English as spoken, the lexical units, "words," are identified by word-patterns consisting of "unique" sequences[9] of phonemes. In English as written, these word-patterns (identified by unique sequences of phonemes) are represented by spelling-patterns consisting of sequences of letters. The spelling-patterns *represent* the word-patterns; but the individual letters in the sequence of a spelling pattern do not necessarily duplicate the sequence of the phonemes in the word-pattern for which the spelling-pattern stands.

In the word spelled *h a t* with the sequence of phonemes /h æ t/, the letters *h* and *a* and *t* do stand in the sequence of the phonemes /h/ /æ/ /t/. But in the word spelled *h a t e,* the sequence of phonemes is /h/ /e/ /t/. Each of these two word-patterns consists of three phonemes in the sequence indicated /hæt/ and /het/. The spelling-patterns which represent these two words both use the vowel letter *a*. It is the difference in the spelling-patterns (the total sequence of all the letters in the spelling-pattern) that signals that the *a* in *hat* represents a different phoneme from that represented by the *a* in *hate*. That the phoneme sequence /h/ /æ/ /t/ is a different word-pattern from the phoneme sequence /h/ /e/ /t/[10] is signalled by the difference between the vowels /æ/ and /e/. The *spelling-patterns* represent this difference by using the simple sequence *h a t* for the first and the same sequence plus an *e, h a t e,* for the second.

We are concerned here with showing how, in the writing of present-day English, our conventional *spelling-patterns* represent the *word-patterns* of the language. As indicated above[11] one large part of learning to read means learning to respond to the conventional spelling-patterns as representations of the word-patterns. *In learning to talk, a child has had to learn to respond to the patterns of phonemes which identify the word-patterns.* These language responses have included both a high-speed recognition of the physical patterns of phonemes that mark off and identify the word-patterns he uses, and an equally high-speed recognition of the portions of his experience that his "community" attaches to these word-patterns as meanings. Now, *in learning to read he must develop similar habits of high-speed recognition response to the identification features of the spelling-patterns that represent the word-patterns that he knows.* We cannot here describe all the identification features of all the spelling-patterns a mature reader must know. That task can only be satisfactorily accomplished through a series of textbooks.[12] Here we shall try to describe, with a representative number of examples, enough of the spelling-patterns to provide an understanding of the nature of the materials which textbooks to guide a sound approach to reading should include.

Let me first point out that in this description of spelling-patterns we are concerned with the spelling-patterns to which *readers* must learn to respond. We are *not* now concerned with the kind of description of spelling-patterns necessary for *writers*—those who must learn to produce the spelling-patterns. To describe the patterns of English spelling to which readers must learn to make high-speed recognition responses constitutes a very different, and much simpler, problem from that of describing these same patterns in order to furnish a complete and trustworthy guide for the writer—the one who must learn to produce (at less speed, perhaps) the spelling sequences for each individual word. Of course, the two descriptions overlap to some extent, and the skill developed for recognition responses will support the learning of the habits of accurate spelling in writing. But a reader's habits of accurate recognition at high speed will not necessarily make him an excellent speller; nor will well-developed spelling skills necessarily make one a highly efficient reader.[13]

For the reader, the following spelling-patterns form the identifying features of a large part of the word-patterns of English.[14] Throughout this description we must remember that we are using the term *word-patterns* for the sequences of phonemes that identify "words" as *spoken,* and the term *spelling-patterns* for the sequences of graphic shapes (the letters) that identify in *writing* for the *reader* these word-patterns of speech. We must remember too that, like the word-patterns of speech, the spelling-patterns of writing acquire significance through contrast. There are contrasts of detail within the sets of smaller patterns that constitute the larger patterns, and contrasts of the larger patterns themselves.

(1) The first and perhaps most significant set of spelling patterns are those for one-syllable words with the general shape of (consonant-)vowel-consonant.

(a) The most productive of this set of spelling patterns is in accord with the following example.

hat, hit, het (nonstandard), *hot, hut*

Hundreds of words fit into this particular set of spelling-patterns.

at	it	(et)	——	——
bat	bit	bet	——	but
cat	——	——	cot	cut
——	——	——	dot	——
fat	fit	——	——	——
gat	(git)	get	got	gut
hat	hit	(het)	hot	hut
——	——	jet	jot	jut
——	lit	let	lot	——[15]
mat	mit	met	——	——
(Nat)	nit	net	not	nut
pat	pit	pet	pot	——[15]
rat	——	——	rot	rut
sat	sit	set	sot	——
tat	tit	——	tot	——
vat	——	——	——	——

(b) In the list just given we have used the same final consonant letter with a contrast showing first only in initial consonant letters. There are, however, many items with the same initial consonant letter and having a contrast in the final consonant letter.[16]

bat	bad, bag, ban;
cat	cad, cam, can, cap;
fat	fad, fag, fan;
gat	gab, gad, gag, gal, gap, gas;
hat	had, hag, (Hal), ham, has;
mat	mad, mam, man, map, (Max);
(Nat)	nab, nag, (Nan), nap;
pat	pad, pal, pan, pap;
rat	rag, ram, ran, rap;
sat	sad, sag, (Sam), sap;
tat	tab, tag, tam, tan, tap, tax;
vat	van
(da-)	dab, dad, dam, (Dan);
(ja-)	jab, jag, jam;
(la-)	lab, lad, lag, lam, lap, lax;
(ya-)	yam

(c) As a third possibility for this particular set of spelling-patterns there are the many items with the initial and last consonants the same as those just given, but with the contrasting feature of the pattern the vowel letter in between. Examples are the following.

bad	bid	bed	——	bud
bag	big	beg	bog	bug
ban	bin	(Ben)	——	bun
cad	——	——	cod	cud
can	——	——	con	——
cap	——	——	cop	cup
dab	——	——	——	dub
dad	did	——	——	dud
dam	dim	——	——	——
(Dan)	din	den	don	dun
fad	——	fed	——	——
fag	fig	——	fog	——
fan	fin	fen	——	fun

had	hid	——	hod	——
hag	——	——	hog	hug
ham	him	hem	——	hum
has	his	——	——	——
mad	mid	——	——	mud
mam	(mim-)	(-mem)	mom	mum
map	——	——	mop	——
mat	mit	met	——	——
nab	nib	neb	nob	nub
nap	nip	——	——	——
pan	pin	pen	——	pun
pap	pip	pep	pop	pup
pat	pit	pet	pot	——
rag	rig	——	——	rug
sad	——	——	sod	——
sap	sip	——	sop	sup
sat	sit	set	sot	——
tab	——	——	——	tub
tag	——	——	——	tug
tam	(Tim)	——	(Tom)	——
tan	tin	ten	ton	tun
tap	tip	——	top	tup
——	vim	——	——	——
van	——	——	——	——

(d) In all the patterns of these particular sets there are also many words with the initial consonant phoneme represented by two letters (digraph):

than	then	them	this	
shad	sham	shed	shin	ship
chap	chat	chin	chip	chit

and many with the final consonant phoneme represented by two letters:

bath, hath, lath, path, pith, with;   wish;

ash, bash, dash, gash, lash, mash, sash;

gush, lush, rush;   much, such.

bang, fang, gang, hang, rang, sang, tang;
ding, king, ping, ring, sing, ting, wing, zing;
long, song;   bung, hung, lung, rung.

(e) In all the patterns of these particular sets there are also many words with initial consonant clusters, many words with final consonant clusters, and many words with consonant clusters both at the beginning and at the end.

span	spin	——	——	spun
spat	spit	——	spot	——
asp	gasp	hasp	rasp	
lisp	wisp			

stab, stag, stem, step, sting, stop, stub, stud;

best, jest, lest, pest, test, vest, west, zest;
fist, list,   bust, dust, gust, just, lust, must;
chest

skeg,   skid, skim, skin, skip, skit;

ask, bask, cask, mask, task;   desk;
disk, risk;   dusk, husk, musk, tusk.

Out of the more than 150 consonant clusters that appear in modern English spelling only these three—*sp, st, sk,*—occur both initially and finally in words.

(f) Some of the other consonant clusters of two phonemes, of three phonemes, and even of four phonemes are the following. These are all in what has been called, under (1) above, the "first and most significant set of spelling patterns" for modern English.

blab, bled, blob, blot, blur, blush,
blast, blend, blond, blunt;

bran, brash, brat, bred, brig, brim, bring, brush,
brand, branch, brink, brisk, brunt;

clam, clan, clap, clang, clash, cling, clip, clod, clog, club, clung,
clamp, clank, clasp, cleft, clench, clink, clump;

cram, crap, crash, crib, crop, crud, crush,
cramp, crank, craps, crest, crimp, crisp, croft, crunch, crust;

drab, drag, dram, drip, drop, drug, drum,
draft, drank, drench, drift, drink, drunk;

flag, flan, flap, flash, flat, flax, fled, flesh, flip, flit, flog, flop, flush,
flask, flinch, flint, flunk;

fresh, fret, frog, from,
frank, French, frisk, front, frump;

glad, glen, glib, glob, glut,
gland, glint;

grab, graf, gram, grid, grig, grim, grip, grin, grog, grub,
graft, grand, grant, grasp, grind, grist, grits, grunt;

slab, slag, slam, slap, slash, slat, Slav, sled, slid, slim, sling,
slip, slit, slop, slug, slum, slush,
slant, slink, slump, slung;

smash, smog, smug, smut,
smelt;

snag, snap, snip, snob, snub, snug,

splash, split, sprig, spring,
splint, sprint;

string, strap, strip, strum, strut,
strand;

helps, gulfs, gulps, milks, tufts, sinks, belts, desks, asks, twelfths.

(g) In this same set of patterns must be included also the single syllable word-patterns ending in the consonant phonemes /k/, /f/, /s/, /l/. The spelling-patterns of these words differ somewhat from those of the others above in that the final consonant letter is "doubled." For /k/ the letters used are not two *k*'s but *ck*.

back	——	beck	bock	buck
——	Dick	deck	dock	duck
hack	hick	heck	hock	huck
jack	——	——	jock	——
lack	lick	——	lock	luck
——	——	——	mock	muck
——[17]	nick	neck	——[17]	——
pack	pick	peck	pock	puck
rack	rick	reck	rock	ruck
sack	sick	——	sock	suck
tack	tick	——	tock	tuck

	(biff)			buff
——	——	——	——	cuff
——	(diff)	——	doff	duff
gaff	——	——	——	(guff)
——	——	——	——	huff
——	——	——	——	luff
——	miff	——	——	muff
——	——	——	——	puff
raff	riff	——	——	ruff
——	tiff	——	toff	tuff

chaff, quaff, staff, whiff, skiff, cliff, sniff, stiff, scoff, bluff, fluff, snuff, scruff, gruff, stuff.

bass, lass, mass, pass, cess, chess, less, ness, (guess), hiss, kiss, miss, buss, cuss, fuss, muss.[18]

class, glass, brass, crass, grass, bless, cress, dress, press, tress, stress, truss.

all[19]	ill	ell	——	——
ball	bill	bell	——	——
call	——	——	——	cull
——	dill	dell	doll	dull
fall	fill	fell	——	——
gall	gill	——	——	gull
hall	hill	hell	——	hull
——	kill	——	——	——
——	——	——	loll	lull
mall	mill	mell	moll	mull
pall	pill	pell	poll	——
tall	till	tell	——	——
——	rill	——	——	——
——	sill	sell	——	——
wall	will	well	——	——

small, spall, thrall, stall, squall, shell, spell, quell; chill, skill, spill, drill, frill, grill, shrill, thrill, trill, still, quill, swill, twill; scull, skull, trull.

All of the various types of spelling-patterns included under the section just finished (marked (1) a-g) belong to the same set. They all use one of the five vowel letters of our alphabet with a single consonant letter (*t a p, p a t; t i p, p i t*), or two consonant letters representing one consonant phoneme (*sh, ch, th, ng*), or two to five consonant letters representing a cluster of two to four consonant phonemes (*s t -a- n d, s t r -a- n d s, t w -e- l f t h s*). As used throughout this set of spelling-patterns each of the five vowel letters represents a single vowel phoneme. The word-patterns represented by this very large set of spelling patterns are all single syllable words. But these syllables occur very frequently as parts of multisyllable words. The number of the examples listed here, which is only a very small part of the total items included in this large set of spelling-patterns, is slightly over 500. This set of spelling-patterns is basic for all English spelling and must be responded to at high speed with practically no errors by those who would read with high efficiency. This kind of habitual response is, of course, not the only requirement for efficient reading but it is a basic necessity for which there is no substitute.

And perhaps it is well to insist again, in order to avoid misunderstanding, that these recognition responses which must be learned through much practice do not remain conscious responses. As great skill develops they become automatic habits and the recognition response itself sinks below the threshold of attention. The principles and some of the details of the practice through which to develop these effective but finally unconscious recognition responses will be discussed in the next chapter, entitled "Materials and Methods: The Essentials of a Linguistically Sound Approach."

The large set of spelling-patterns illustrated above (under (1)a-g) constitutes, however, only one of the spelling-patterns to be mastered by *readers*. Nor should one conclude that these basic spelling-patterns can or should be described and dealt with in absolute terms. I would insist again that it is *the contrast of one set of spelling-patterns with other sets of spelling-patterns* that signals the connection of the graphemes with the phonemes; it is not the single grapheme, the single letter, that can be matched in any absolute terms with the individual phonemes. We need, therefore, to show now some of the other sets of spelling-patterns in contrast with the one just discussed.

(2) The second set of spelling-patterns, and a highly productive set, are those that use the final letter *e* to differentiate them

from the patterns just described in (1) a-g. The following are some examples.

bad	*bad* e
fad	*fad* e
mad	*mad* e
cam	*cam* e
dam	*dam* e
lam	*lam* e
Sam	*sam* e
tam	*tam* e
ban	*ban* e
can	*can* e
Dan	*dan* e
man	*man* e
pan	*pan* e
van	*van* e
cap	*cap* e
gap	*gap* e
nap	*nap* e
rap	*rap* e
tap	*tap* e
bid	*bid* e
hid	*hid* e
jib	*jib* e
rid	*rid* e
dim	*dim* e
lim	*lim* e
Tim	*tim* e
din	*din* e
fin	*fin* e
pin	*pin* e
tin	*tin* e
win	*win* e
chin	*chin* e
pip	*pip* e
rip	*rip* e

bit	*bit* e
kit	*kit* e
mit	*mit* e
rit	*rit* e
sit	*sit* e
lob	*lob* e
rob	*rob* e
cod	*cod* e
rod	*rod* e
ton	*ton* e
cop	*cop* e
hop	*hop* e
mop	*mop* e
pop	*pop* e
cot	*cot* e
dot	*dot* e
not	*not* e
rot	*rot* e
tot	*tot* e
rub	*rub* e
tub	*tub* e
dud	*dud* e
dun	*dun* e
run	*run* e
tun	*tun* e
cut	*cut* e

This type of contrast also occurs with spelling-patterns having initial consonant clusters.

grad	*grad* e	*grip*	*grip* e	*slim*	*slim* e	*sprit*	*sprit* e
spat	*spat* e	*slid*	*slid* e	*slop*	*slop* e	*strip*	*strip* e

The same kind of contrast is significant with the spelling-patterns listed in (1) g.

back	*bak* e
jack	(*Jak* e)
lack	*lak* e
(*Mack*)	*mak* e
rack	*rak* e
sack	*sak* e
tack	*tak* e
quack	*quak* e
all	*al* e[20]
ball	*bal* e
gall	*gal* e
hall	*hal* e
(*Dick*)	*dik* e
hick	*hik* e
lick	*lik* e
pick	*pik* e
tick	*tik* e
mall	*mal* e
pall	*pal* e
tall	*tal* e
wall	*wal* e
cock	*cok* e
jock	*jok* e
block	*blok* e
smock	*smok* e
pock	*pok* e
duck	*duk* e

(3) In addition to the two major sets of spelling-patterns that, in contrast, cover a large part of the active practices of English spelling, there are a number of important spelling-patterns of much more limited application.

(a) There are two sets of spelling-patterns that represent more fully the phoneme /i/ in single syllable words, in contrast with those having the phoneme /ɛ/.

bet	beat	pet	peat	best	beast	den	dean
(het)	heat	set	seat	led	lead	(Len)	lean
met	meat	(Chet)	cheat	red	read	men	mean
net	neat	whet	wheat	(Ben)	bean	hep	heap[21]

fed	feed	wed	weed	bet	beet	step	steep
bled	bleed	sped	speed	met	meet	(Ken)	keen
red	reed	bred	breed	pep	peep	ten	teen

(b) There is a minor set of spelling-pattern contrasts for words with the vowel phoneme /e/.

bat	bait	man	main	brad	braid	swan	swain
gat	gait	fan	fain	clam	claim	char	chair
lad	laid	pan	pain	plan	plain	far	fair[22]
mad	maid	ran	rain	bran	brain	par	pair
pad	paid	van	vain				

ball	bail	fly	flay	fry	fray
fall	fail	ply	play	pry	pray
hall	hail	sly	slay	spry	spray
mall	mail	shy	shay	sty	stay
pall	pail				
wall	wail				

(c) There are also minor sets of spelling-pattern contrasts for words with the vowel phoneme /o/ and for those with the diphthong /aʊ/.

God	goad	got	goat
rod	road	cox	coax
Tod	toad	blot	bloat
(Lon)	loan	sock	soak
(Ron)	roan	clock	cloak
sop	soap		
cot	coat		

bond	bound	prod	proud
pond	pound	trot	trout
shot	shout	Scot	scout
		spot	spout

As a matter of fact, the three major sets of spelling-patterns discussed here form the basis of the modern English spelling that most of us really learn. There are, of course, some other minor patterns than those noted here[23] but for the beginning stages of reading it is the major sets of contrastive spelling-patterns that require the kind of practice that leads to high-speed recognition responses. That these three major sets of patterns do constitute the basis of our practical spelling habits seems to be shown by the following facts.

(a) Small groups of ten or more educated adults, including some professional writers, were asked to write, first, ten one-syllable "nonsense" words; then, afterward, ten two-syllable "nonsense" words; and finally, ten three-syllable "nonsense" words. The nonsense words produced were all within the three major sets of spelling patterns illustrated above, and more than 90 percent within the two sets (1) and (2). Only one nonsense word appeared with a consonant cluster not given in the lists of those common for English—*srig*.

(b) All these and other "nonsense" words I have collected simply fill in the slots in the patterns not taken by any actual words of the language. In the examples given above of some of the simple patterns short lines indicate such slots.

(jat)	(jit)	jet	jot	jut
tag	(tig)	(teg)	tog	tug
(paff)	(piff)	(peff)	(poff)	puff

(c) Native speakers of English who are able readers, pronounce "nonsense" words without hesitation in accordance with these major patterns of English spelling. Native speakers of English who read English satisfactorily but who know no foreign language whatever similarly pronounce foreign words, with which they are confronted, in accord with these major spelling-patterns.

Now, after the discussion that has attempted to list and illustrate with a considerable number of examples the major contrastive sets of the spelling-patterns of English, it may be helpful to bring together into a single view what seem to me the most significant conclusions of this chapter.

(1) Modern English spelling is not so thoroughly chaotic that we must abandon its use in teaching the beginning stages of reading and start with the learning of one or two hundred "sight" words, with no attention to the sequences of letters by which these words are graphically represented. Nor is Modern English spelling such that we can start the teaching of reading by trying to match

the separate "sounds" which constitute the "word" as spoken, with the individual letters which make up the "word" as written. English spelling has never been "phonetic" in the sense that there has been a separate letter sign for each difference of vocal sound, and in the sense that the pronunciation of a word is simply the fusion of the separate sounds for which each of the letters stand. Although English spelling has been and is now phonemically based, and although most of the spelling representation of English is phonemically "regular," there is not now nor has there ever been a one for one correspondence between the separate phonemes as actualized in the pronunciation of a word and the individual letters of the spelling of that word. Thus neither the practices of the usual "word-method" approach of building up first a "sight vocabulary" of approximately 200 words, nor the practices of the usual "phonics-method" approach of "word-analysis," or of "sounding out" words, build upon and use to advantage the basic features of Modern English spelling.

(2) Modern English spelling is fundamentally a system of a comparatively few arbitrary contrastive sets of spelling-patterns, to which readers, to be efficient, must, through much practice, develop high-speed recognition responses. These recognition responses must include not only the automatic (habitual and "unconscious") high-speed recognition of the spelling-pattern itself in its contrastive set but also an automatic (habitual but somewhat more "conscious") connecting of the contrastive spelling-patterns with the language word-patterns which they represent. The signals of the "meanings" conveyed are the language signals of English. For readers, the language signals they must respond to are carried by (represented graphically by) the contrastive spelling-patterns.

(3) The high-speed automatic recognition responses which readers must acquire differ quite clearly both in kind and in quantity from the productive skills which writers must achieve. This difference seems especially clear in respect to the spelling of unstressed syllables. For example, the unstressed final syllables of multiple syllable words seldom contain significant identifying vowel phonemes. Throughout the last seven centuries, at least, the vowel sounds within these final unstressed syllables have rather consistently been actualized as [ə] (or in some situations as [ɪ]):

"In modern English speech, vowels are regularly obscured in syllables that have neither primary nor secondary stress, especially in those that follow the main stress; they then approach, or fall into, the sound of the mid-mixed vowel or [ə]."[24]

The number of different spellings for these unstressed syllables is large. Examples are: sof*a*, orph*a*n, silk*e*n, vict*i*m, shog*u*n, hand*some*, pest*le*, pist*o*l, pist*i*l, tins*e*l; mett*le*, met*a*l, hand*le*, sand*a*l, drag*o*n, dung*eo*n, reg*io*n, mount*ai*n, vill*ei*n, influ*e*nce, endur*a*nce, renew*a*ble, corrupt*i*ble, syn*o*d, want*e*d, lett*u*ce.

For the *writer* the use of any such words as these presents a difficult problem. He must learn the particular vowel letter required by each word in order to produce it. As a *speaker* he has learned to produce and to respond to the sound-patterns which identify them, but these sound-patterns all have the same vowel phoneme in the final syllable: /sofə/, /ɔrfən/, /sɪlkən/, /vɪktəm/, /šogən/, /hænsəm/, /pɛsəl/, /pɪstəl/, /tɪnsəl/, /mɛtəl/, /hændəl/, /sændəl/, /drægən/, /dənǰən/, and so on. There are hundreds of words with this vowel /ə/ in the unstressed syllables. The *writer* must learn, however, the particular sequence of letters used to spell the unstressed syllables of each individual word. The *reader* has no such problem. He needs to learn only to realize that the spoken words in his vocabulary that have /ə/ in the unstressed syllables may be written with any of the five vowel letters. For the *reader* the spelling-pattern must be identified as produced by some writer; the *writer* must learn to do the producing of each individual sequence of letters.

(4) The basic spelling-patterns of English are those listed in the first set above. These consist of one syllable words spelled regularly in accord with a very simple pattern. In this set of patterns there is always one of the five vowel letters and a final consonant letter or letters, as in *at, it, an, in, on, as, is, up, ash, ant.* In most instances there is also an initial consonant letter or letters: *mat, sit, man, ton, but, sash, shad, spend.* The vowel letters in this set of patterns do have a one for one correspondence with vowel phonemes: *a* as in *hat, i* as in *hit, e* as in *bet, o* as in *hot, u* as in *hut.* Thousands of English words appear with this set of spelling-patterns. It is with this set of spelling-patterns, and this set only, that the ordinary phonics approach really applies. The following chapter will contain a discussion of the linguistic signifi-

cance of some of the methods of teaching the basic sets of spelling-patterns. Here it is sufficient to point out that with this first set of spelling-patterns the contrastive features to be mastered lie within the set itself. In approaching the other basic sets of spelling-patterns the fundamental contrastive features to be mastered are those of contrast between the sets.

CHAPTER SEVEN

Materials and Methods: The Essentials of a Linguistically Sound Approach

Learning to read is learning *to do* something. Progress and achievement in learning to read must, therefore, be evaluated *not* in terms of knowledge *about* something, but in terms of the completeness and the efficiency of performance. Only the amount and kind of practice that develops firm habits can lead to the skills of efficient performance. A major part of learning to read, therefore, must consist of habit-forming practice. Reading is a type of linguistic performance. It is a type of linguistic response that depends first of all upon the language control achieved by each particular individual reader. Learning to read must begin with and build upon the habits of that precise language control. Of course one can postpone learning to read until a greater measure of language control has been achieved; but, whenever learning to read begins, it must start with and build upon whatever habits of language responses exist for the learner at that time. The process of learning to read (or that of teaching a child to read) becomes confused and inefficient if it is mixed with a variety of efforts to develop, at the same time, and with the same material, an increased language control.

From the evidence available, we believe that we can assume that *any* child *can* learn to read within a year after he has learned to "talk" his native language satisfactorily. This degree of language control means that the child's pronunciation and vocabulary must be without "baby-talk" deviations, that he can report what he has consciously experienced, and that he can understand "talk" to him which uses only the materials that lie within the range of his linguistic and social-cultural experience. But learning to "talk" must come first. We have, therefore, in the discussion above (Chapter Four) described the "process of reading" in relation to the language control already mastered by the child before he begins to learn to read. And we would always measure the child's *reading perform-ance* against the background of that language control. In other words, one can "read" in so far as he "can respond" to the language signals, now represented by contrastive spelling-patterns, as completely and as efficiently as he has learned to respond to *the same language signals* formerly represented by contrastive sound-patterns.

We are concerned here with the processes—the uses of the materials described above, especially in Chapters Three, Four, and Six—through which learning to read can be accomplished. We seek thus to find not only more efficient procedures and activities through which to build up the basic habits of high-speed recognition responses necessary for reading, but also ways to achieve more complete and efficient total reading performance as an end product.

THE BEGINNING: THE "TRANSFER" STAGE

In the discussions above we have constantly tried to define sharply the materials that must be thoroughly mastered by the child if he is *to add the ability to read to his already achieved ability to talk*. We have thus tried to exclude everything that is not essential in order that the maximum of thought and practice may be concentrated upon the one task—establishing the necessary recognition responses as habits. If we would have the child make steady and sound progress in learning to read well, we must not confuse that task with any of the other objectives of elementary education. In learning to read, the immediate objective for the child is *not* the learning of "new words," or of "new grammatical structures," or of "new meanings." He has already achieved the language control with which we must start. If the only materials immediately available for teaching reading contain any considerable body of language forms outside of those already well controlled by the pupil—new word shapes and new word meanings, new grammatical structures—then the reading should be postponed until either the language control of the pupil includes firm habit responses to these forms or the materials can be produced for which the pupil is ready. Confusion and frustration in the "transfer" stage makes "remedial" reading necessary.

At the end of Chapter Four—"The Nature of the Reading Process"—we marked out three stages in the development of reading ability. Each of these stages needs comment. The first stage has been given the name *the transfer stage* in order to stress as heavily as possible the one single and simple distinguishing feature of the reading process. Learning to read in one's native language is learning to shift, to transfer, from auditory signs for the language signals, which the child has already learned, to visual or graphic signs for the same signals. Both reading and talking have the same set of language signals for language *reception*. In talking, contrastive bundles of sound features represent these signals; in reading, contrastive patterns of spelling represent these same signals. For *language reception through talk,* the child of four has developed, by means of more than 5000 hours of *practice,* great skill in making high-speed recognition responses to the patterns of sound features that represent the language signals; *for a similar language reception through reading* the child needs to develop, by means of from one tenth to one fifth as many hours of practice, a similar but new skill in making high-speed recognition responses to the spelling-patterns that also represent the same language signals.

Building up this new skill does not require any more intelligence on the part of the pupil than that necessary for him to learn to talk. And if the essential materials for practice are properly selected and arranged in a series of small steps, each of which is thoroughly learned in its sequence, the adding of a skill in language reception through reading to an already acquired skill in language reception through talk, should not be difficult nor give rise to any confusion or frustration. Freedom to read, like other types of physical and intellectual freedom, will, however, require effort and work on the part of the pupil.

The following listing attempts to furnish help to those guiding the activities of pupils through the "transfer" stage of learning to read.

Two Matters of Exclusion

We are concerned here with *reading only, not* with *writing*. It is true that reading and writing together constitute literacy. And certainly there can be no reading except of that which has first been written. But the two abilities are not the same, and few of us are called upon to produce written material of wide extent. On the other hand, we live in an age of an education based primarily upon reading and a society that requires reading of some sort for most of its activities. There are, however, those who believe that the most effective way to learn to read is through writing.[1] We are *not* here concerned with the *productive spelling habits* necessary *for the writer*. Our approach here centers upon developing the habits of high speed recognition responses to English spelling-patterns, that constitute the process of reading. We can expect, of course, that the developing of recognition responses to certain English spelling-patterns will contribute to the productive skill of the reader as a writer. But the selection of the materials to be used, the sequence of their groupings and the methods of their practice will be determined solely by the needs of the pupils learning to read.

The recognition responses to be developed in the reader of the transfer stage are those of spelling-patterns consisting of sequences of letters of the present-day English alphabet. It is alphabetic writing. Inasmuch as the graphic shapes which constitute our numerals (both Arabic and Roman) are *not alphabetic writing* but logographic or "word" writing, the "reading" of all numerals is postponed until after *the principle of our alphabetic writing has been fully grasped*. Of course, the words by which the numeral signs are read are alphabetically written, as:

Number Words		Numerals	
One	for the numeral sign	1	I
Two	for the numeral sign	2	II
Three	for the numeral sign	3	III
Four	for the numeral sign	4	IV
Five	for the numeral sign	5	V
Six	for the numeral sign	6	VI
Seven	for the numeral sign	7	VII
Eight	for the numeral sign	8	VIII
Nine	for the numeral sign	9	IX
Ten	for the compound numeral sign	10	X
Eleven	for the compound numeral sign	11	XI
Twelve	for the compound numeral sign	12	XII
Thirteen	for the compound numeral sign	13	XIII
Thirty	for the compound numeral sign	30	XXX

But the spelling-patterns for these number words are not (except the word *ten*) those of the first large set of spelling-patterns to be used here in the beginning reading exercises of the transfer stage. To introduce for reading either the numeral signs or the number words at the beginning of the transfer stage would make no progress whatever toward our immediate goal at this time (the reading of alphabetically written materials) and would run the risk of causing considerable confusion and delay in the habit responses we seek to develop as the first step.

To "Learn" the Letters

The first set of recognition responses to be developed are those for the letters of our alphabet. The letters that appear in our spelling-patterns must be identified as contrasting shapes. And this identification must be practiced until the child's recognition reactions to the significant features that separate each letter from all of the others are automatic. The goal here should be high-speed identification with 100 percent accuracy. Insufficient mastery of this first step will inevitably cause delay and confusion later.

For the practice activities to develop the kind of thorough mastery demanded here, there are five guiding principles.

(1) For the first steps, and until *after* the principle of our alphabetic writing has been fully grasped, the letter shapes should

be strictly limited to those of unadorned capitals like the following:

ABCDEFGHIJKLMNOPQRSTUVWXYZ

Telegrams for delivery have for years been typed in such capital letters only. The child will of course eventually need to learn to respond also to "lower-case" or "small" letters, and to the letter shapes of "cursive" or "hand" writing. But the capitals, if made with the simplest strokes, have the fewest significant contrastive features, and make a much easier first step for the child who wants to read. Children have learned and can learn to read using each of the various sets of letter shapes, but, because simple-line capitals have given rise to significantly fewer confusions at the beginning, we have postponed the use of "lower-case" letters and of "cursive" letters until the "process of reading" is well under way.

(2) It is not absolutely necessary for the child to learn to identify *all* the capital letters at the beginning and before he starts the actual reading. He must, however, have established correct automatic recognition responses to those letters that will be used in the materials of the transfer stage. On the other hand, no delay or confusion will result from using all the letters in the practices of identification. Even the form of the infrequent Q, for example, can well be used to sharpen the contrasts of O, G, C. For the nineteen letter shapes that must be learned thoroughly the following sequence has proved most free from confusions: first the "stroke" letters; then those of combinations of "strokes" and parts of "circles"; then those of "circles" or parts of circles.

Thorough "learning of the letters" means such a learning as will produce instant "recognition" of the particular pattern of "strokes" that separates or distinguishes each of the following letters not only from the "circle" and "combination stroke and circle" letters, but also and especially from every other "stroke" letter.

I T L F E H
A N M K Z
V W X Y

Such a learning will produce the instant recognition of the particular pattern of "combination of stroke and circle" that separates and distinguishes each of the following letters not only from the all "stroke" letters and from the all "circle" letters but also and especially from every other "combination stroke and circle" letter,

D   B   P   R
U   J

and, in similar fashion, it will produce the instant recognition of the particular pattern of each of the "circle" letters that serves as its identification in contrast with every one of the other letters of the two groups above, as well as of those of its own group of "circle" letters.

O   Q   G   C
S

(3) The significant or identifying features of the particular shape of each of the letters are always features in *contrast*. The teaching and learning practices to build up the necessary automatic recognition responses must, therefore, in order to be effective, always deal with the contrasts of two or more letters at a time, not with single individual letters. The important question is always "Are the two letters, or the two sets of two or more letters, alike or different?"

(A)		(B)		(C)	
I	T	IF	IT	FIT	TIF
T	T	TF	TF	FIF	FIE
I	I	TF	FT	IFT	IFF
T	I	TT	FF	IEF	IFE
F	T	IT	TI	FEI	FEI
F	F	FT	TF	EFT	TFE
E	F	EF	FE	EIE	ETE

Each new letter should be introduced as contrasted with each of the letters already used as shown in Column A, above; then worked into the contrasts of pairs of letters of Column B; and afterward into the groups of three letters in Column C.

(A)		(B)		(C)	
T	T	FT	TF	FIT	FIF
T	F	EE	FE	FIE	FEE
F	T	HE	EH	HEH	EHE
F	E	AH	AH	AHA	AHE
E	H	EA	AE	FAN	HAN
E	A	EA	AE	MAN	MEN
H	A	AN	NN	MAM	MAM
A	N	NM	MN	HAM	HEM
N	N	MM	NN	MET	TEM
N	M	HM	MH	HIM	HIN
M	M	AM	EM	FAT	FET

The introduction of each new item should provide the occasion for a review of all those previously practiced. Practices such as these should continue day after day and produce an ever increasing number of items for which the correct response of "alike" or "different" becomes easy and rapid. The materials for these practices if put on flash cards can be made a game for groups that have approximately the same ability. If properly programmed they can provide for individual silent practice through which each child can progress at his own pace. The responses need require only the simplest single indication for "alike" or for "different," and can be adjusted to activities for five-year-old children. At the beginning, the practices should include only the minimum two items with but one contrastive feature. Until the children begin, *through their own activity,* to understand what is required, progress will properly remain very slow. Their *ability to see* the significant contrastive features of the separate letters will come primarily as a result of their own guided activities, rather than from any explanations by the teacher. This ability to identify the difference between three-letter groups is so important a basic skill at this stage that the variety of practices necessary for its full development should become the chief activity of the pre-reading child.

(4) The contrasts themselves will consist of such matters as the number of strokes; the position of the strokes—whether

vertical or horizontal or slanting; the relative size of the circle portions and position as combined with strokes. But even more important than the types of contrast just indicated are *the contrasts of the order or sequence of the individual letters in groups.* Sensitiveness to differences of the arrangement of the two or three letters in groups separated by spaces must be developed from the very beginning. The difference between IF and IT will probably come first; but the differences between IF and FI and between IT and TI must follow immediately. Thorough training in responding to these differences of two and three letter sequences, from the beginning, will prepare the pupils for responding to the many significant matters of direction sequence that characterize our English writing system. Pupils must not only develop high-speed recognition responses to the contrasts of shape and position that identify the patterns of the individual letters, they must have similar high-speed recognition responses to the sequences in which these letter patterns appear.

(5) The habit-forming practices to develop all these high-speed recognition responses do not necessarily require that the pupils know the "names" of the letters of the alphabet. Learning those names, however, during the process of building up the habits of recognition of the contrastive shapes, need not interfere with the progress of the pupils toward the immediate goal for these practices. And these names can provide the basis of certain exercises for checking the recognition habits.[2] But we must here insist vigorously that in these practices to develop automatic habits of recognition for the letter shapes, *there must be no attempt to connect the letters themselves with sounds.* Nor should the groups of letters used in the practices of "alike" or "different," which happen to form "words" for us who can read, such as IT, IF, FIT, HIT, AT, HAT, be treated at this preliminary stage *as words to be pronounced and connected with meanings.* Any such *attempts now to relate letters to sounds and sequences of letters to words will cause much confusion for the pupils and delay their progress not only at this stage but especially later.*

To "Learn" the Spelling Patterns

The second set of automatic recognition responses to be developed are those for the major spelling-patterns of English.

Superficial observers who seek to find simple one for one correspondences between the individual letters of our alphabet and the separate "sounds" of our pronunciation often conclude that English spelling is a "mess." And not infrequently good research scholars do not spell well as they write. But it is still true that no one ever learns to read widely and well in English without in some way developing automatic recognition responses to our major spelling-patterns. He may learn to read holding the book upside down as Henry Bradley did,[3] but even in that position the sequences of letter shapes constituted the same spelling-patterns that we must all learn in order to read efficiently.

For the practice activities to build up clear-cut but high-speed recognition responses to the major spelling-patterns there are the following guiding principles.

(1) In order to avoid confusions and frustration on the part of the pupils the procedures aimed at developing recognition responses to the spelling-patterns must wait until the habits of response to the contrasts of letter shapes (the capital letters) and the contrasts of letter sequences have become firmly fixed. During the practices necessary to build up automatic responses to the distinctive features of the letters of our alphabet in contrast with each other and in contrastive sequences, there must be no attempt to connect these letters with sounds, nor to connect any of the sequences of the letters with "words" as having meaning. Building a clear understanding of the connections of spelling-patterns with the word-patterns of the language is the most important step in learning to read. It can be most effectively and thoroughly accomplished if the pupils who approach this step have already mastered the alphabet as indicated in the immediately preceding discussion. Uncertainty in the pupil's recognition responses to alphabet forms and sequences at this point inevitably gives rise to confusion and delays in grasping the fundamentals of reading.

(2) The heart of the practical spelling-problem for English lies primarily in the representations of the vowel phonemes. (See Chapter Two, the section entitled "Structural Units and Word Patterns.") On the whole, each consonant letter does regularly represent a single consonant phoneme.

B   /bɪn/ *bin,* /rəb/ *rub,* /rubi/ *ruby*

D   /dɛn/ *den,* /nad/ *nod,* /odər/ *odor*

F   /fæn/ *fan,* /stæf/ *staff,* /kɔfɪ/ *coffee*

K   /kɪn/ *kin,* /pik/ *peek,* /brekɪj̆/ *breakage*

L   /lɪp/ *lip,* /pil/ *peal,* /pɛlət/ *pellet*

M   /mæn/ *man,* /ræm/ *ram,* /momənt/ *moment*

N   /nɛt/ *net,* /tɛn/ *ten,* /ponɪ/ *pony*

P   /pɪn/ *pin,* /spɪn/ *spin,* /nɪp/ *nip,* /kapɛr/ *copper*

T   /tɪn/ *tin,* /stɛm/ *stem,* /nɛt/ *net,* /wetər/ *waiter*

V   /vaɪn/ *vine,* /laɪv/ *live,* /nɛvər/ *never*

Z   /zon/ *zone,* /bəz/ *buzz,* /rezər/ *razor*

R   /ræt/ *rat,* /tar/ *tar,* /vɛrɪ/ *very,* /baro/ *borrow*

H   /hɛn/ *hen,* /ho/ *hoe* (Initially only, the letter *h* represents
       this phoneme—except for a very few words—*herb, heir,
       honor, hour,* and, for some dialects, *humble.*)

W   /wɪn/ *win,* /wo/ *woe,* /wu/ *woo* (Initially only, the letter *W*
       regularly represents this phoneme.)

J   /j̆ɛst/ *jest,* /prej̆ədɪs/ *prejudice* (Initially primarily, the letter
       J represents this phoneme.)

Y   /yɛs/ *yes,* /yu/ *yew* (Initially, the letter *y* regularly repre-
       sents this phoneme.)

S   /sil/ *seal,* /mæs/ *mass,* /besɪk/ *basic* (Initially the letter *S*
       regularly represents this phoneme; also finally especially
       in clusters with voiceless consonant phonemes. This letter
       frequently represents the voiced spirant after voiced sounds
       and between vowels as in /čozən/ *chosen,* and sometimes
       finally /raɪz/ *rise.*)

G   /get/ *gate,* /go/ *go,* /bæg/ *bag,* /gagəlz/ *goggles* (This letter
       also represents the phoneme /j̆/, especially before /ɛ/;
       /aɪ/; /ɪ/, as in /j̆ɛm/ *gem,* /j̆aɪənt/ *giant,* /j̆ɪnj̆ər/ *ginger.*)

C   /kæt/ *cat,* /kəp/ *cup,* /kek/ *cake,* /kot/ *coat* (This letter
       also represents the phoneme /s/, especially before /ɛ/ as
       in /sɛntər/ *center;* before /ɪ/ as in /sɪtɪ/ *city;* and some-
       times before /aɪ/ as in /saɪprəs/ *cypress;* /saɪfər/ *cypher.*)

X   /baks/ *box,* /tæks/ *tax,* /fɪks/ *fix* (This letter in final or
       medial position regularly represents the consonant cluster
       /ks/.)

Q   /kwin/ *queen,* /kwɪk/ *quick* (This letter regularly followed
       by the letter *u* represents the consonant cluster /kw/.)

As the preceding list shows, of the twenty-one consonant
letters thirteen have practically complete regularity in representing

single phonemes. These are *B, D, F, K, L, M, N, P, T, V, J, R, Q*.

Five consonant letters, *H, W, Y, S, Z*, when they occur initially also represent single phonemes with practically complete regularity. The letter *S* usually represents the voiceless spirant /s/ in all situations, but between vowels and at the ends of words after voiced sounds it can represent the voiced phoneme /z/. The letters *S* and *Z* both sometimes represent the very infrequent /ž/ in such words as *measure, treasure, azure*. The letter *Y* when it is not initial regularly represents a vowel phoneme.

Two consonant letters, *C* and *G*, each represent two phonemes. *C* regularly represents /k/ in most situations, but it usually represents the phoneme /s/ before /i/, /ɪ/, and /ɛ/ as in *cedar, city*, and *cell*. *G* regularly represents the phoneme /g/ in most situations, but it often represents the phoneme /ǰ/ before /ɛ/, /ɪ/, and /aɪ/ as in *gem, gin, gist, giant*.

The letter *X* practically always represents the consonant cluster /ks/ as in *box, fix, appendix*. Initially, for a very few words it represents /z/, as in *xylophone, Xerxes*.

In other words, practically every one of the twenty-one consonant letters of our alphabet quite regularly represents a single consonant phoneme. Only *C, G*, and *S* have any considerable amount of use representing a second phoneme, and thus overlap the regular use of another consonant letter. *C* regularly represents the same phoneme as *K* and *Q* do; but sometimes represents /s/, thus overlapping the regular use of the letter *S*. *G* regularly represents /g/ but sometimes represents /ǰ/ thus overlapping the regular use of the letter *J*. *S* regularly represents /s/, but sometimes represents /z/, thus overlapping the regular use of the letter *Z*.

In addition to the single consonant letters there are combinations of two letters each which regularly represent other consonant phonemes than the ones listed above.

CH regularly represents /č/ as in *chest, rich, church, bachelor*, but often with *T* as in *hatch, stretch*.

SH regularly represents /š/ as in *sharp, bush*.

DG regularly represents /ǰ/ as a medial or final consonant, as in *judge, edge*.

NG regularly represents /ŋ/, which occurs only as a medial or final consonant, as in *sing, singer* /sɪŋər/, *wringer* /rɪŋər/, but also *finger* /fɪŋgər/ and *longer* /lɔŋgər/; *ginger* /ǰɪnǰər/.

TH regularly represents both /θ/ and /ð/, as in *thin* and *then, moth,* and *mother, cloth* and *clothe.*

Again as we make rather general statements about English spelling, we must stress the difference between the needs of the *reader* and those of the *writer.* The reader starts from the sequences of letters as they are given to him in the materials he wants to read. He must recognize these sequences of letters as representing certain contrastive sequences of phonemes which identify for him certain word-patterns of the language. For the reader the recognition responses to the consonant letters present very little difficulty, for of these consonant letters almost every one regularly represents one phoneme only. A few represent two but the spelling-patterns in which these few appear mark the distinctive situation for each.

For the writer, however, to learn to supply for each particular word he wants to use, the special sequence of letters by which it is identified, whether it is a regular pattern or one that is quite unusual, is a very different and a much more complex problem. We are here concerned only with the limited special needs of the reader.

For the reader, then, the chief problems in learning the major spelling-problems concern the vowels rather than the consonants. On the whole the consonant letters offer a fairly regular one-for-one correspondence with the consonant phonemes. There are, in the analysis for English used here, twenty-four consonant phonemes. The English alphabet has twenty-one consonant letters. Two of the consonant letters, *X* and *Q,* duplicate the uses of other letters, leaving but nineteen useful consonant letters. In addition to these nineteen consonant letters there are four combinations of two letters each that represent consonant phonemes: *TH* /θ, ð/, *SH* /š/, *CH* /č/, *NG* /ŋ/. These consonant letters and consonant letter combinations constitute the frames of the spelling-patterns in which to use the *five vowel letters to represent* the *eleven vowel phonemes* of English. The major spelling-patterns consist of consonant frames which contain one or more of the five vowel letters. The consonant letters of the frames have a rather simple and regular correspondence with consonant phonemes, and the vowel letters within these frames occur in special arrangements that identify them as representing one of the eleven vowel phonemes or three phonemic dipthongs.

(3) The major sets of spelling-patterns which constitute the substantive body of material to which beginning readers must develop high speed recognition responses, are best organized for the necessary practices in accord with *the contrastive letter sequences that identify each of the various kinds of vowel phonemes.*[4] This principle refers to the ordering or the progression established for the basic material to be embedded in the exercises, not to the content meanings that should occupy the conscious attention of the pupils. In other words the exercises, the practices for the pupil, should center his attention upon making firm connections between the individual sequences of specific letters he has already learned to "see," and *words* from his own vocabulary that he has learned to understand when talking. *His success in each step of making such a connection* will build up the interest of the pupil at this stage. Seeking an extraneous interest in a story as a story, during the earliest steps of the transfer stage is more likely to hinder than to help the efforts put forth by the pupil himself. The cumulative satisfaction of accomplishment in each "word" and combination of "words" that is recognized as written will create a powerful incentive that needs only to be fed by a series of materials so well chosen and organized in simple contrastive sequences that each small new step takes up and uses all the recognition connections that have been made, and never causes any confusion or frustration. It is in *this selection and ordering of the material to be put into these exercises, not only for the first steps but for the complete processes of the entire "transfer stage"* that modern linguistic knowledge can make one of its chief contributions to the teaching of reading. The confusions and frustrations arising out of a struggle with reading materials deficient in kind and in sequence *throughout the transfer stage* furnish one of the causes of the situations that make remedial reading necessary.

(4) In developing the understanding of the connections between "words" as represented by spelling-patterns and "words" as spoken in live utterances, it misleads the pupil and sets up habits that may cause confusion later to seek constantly to match each of the individual letters with which a word is spelled with the particular sounds that make up its pronunciation. The assumption that learning to read is learning to match words, as written,

letter by letter, with words, as pronounced, sound by sound, constitutes the basic difficulty with *phonics* as a method of teaching reading. It is perfectly true that in a variety of spelling-patterns one can match the individual letters with the separate "sounds" of the word. The word *m a n* furnishes an example, with its three letters and three "sounds" [m] [æ] [n]. And the same would be true to a large extent of the words included in the first set of spelling-patterns described in Chapter Six. And with the words of this great spelling-pattern a "phonics" approach has proved helpful. As a matter of fact the persistence of the methods of "phonics" in spite of the many articles of condemnation furnishes some evidence that these phonic methods have a certain validity.

This "phonics" approach, however, and the assumption upon which it rests does not lay the basis for the kind of responses to spelling-patterns that can be used for all the materials. In spite of the widespread familiarity with the "phonics" way of approaching reading and its continuous use we must cast it out here for a more thoroughly successful way.

Because most of the thinking about connecting the sound-patterns of words with the spelling-patterns has been channeled through the phonics way, it has become difficult to set forth another approach to building responses to the connection between spellings and sounds in such a way that the full significance of the difference may be fully realized. Teaching the "sounds the letters make" in the familiar way seems the simpler way. And the objector could point to the discussion earlier in this chapter, in which I pointed out that nearly all the consonant letters represent quite regularly a single consonant phoneme.

Instead of the approach through trying to match individual letters and separate sound units, we must develop the automatic habits of responding to the contrastive features *of spelling-patterns as identifying the word-patterns* they represent. For example, even in the three letter word used above, *man,* it is not the single letter *A* that indicates the vowel sound [æ]. It is the spelling-pattern *m a n* in contrast with the spelling-pattern *m a n e* or that of *m e a n* that signals the different vowel phonemes that make these three different words. Each of these three is one of the major regular spelling-patterns of English. These three words have the same number of phonemes in each—/mæn/ /men/ /min/. The reader must learn through great practice to respond automatically to the contrastive features that separate these three patterns each of which contains a large number of words.

MAN	MANE	MEAN
DAN	DANE	DEAN
BAN	BANE	BEAN
HAT	HATE	HEAT
FAT	FATE	FEAT
MAT	MATE	MEAT

Perhaps at this point those familiar with some of the common methods of teaching reading would insist that this approach through the spelling-patterns as a whole, rather than through individual isolated letters, is really an example of the much debated "word-method." And, in a way, they would be correct. The spelling-pattern approach, learning to respond to the contrastive features that separate and identify whole word-patterns is indeed a "word-method." The essential difference between this spelling-pattern approach and the usual "word-method" lies in the kind of identifying characteristics used to recognize the words. The systematic materials used here to build up the habits of automatic recognition responses to the contrasts of the major spelling-patterns leave no uncertainty in the identifying characteristics that mark off one written word from another. These are the identifying characteristics of the language itself as incorporated in the patterns of our alphabetic spelling.

The spelling-pattern approach here employed does develop the connections between alphabetic signs of reading and the sound-patterns of talk. This spelling-pattern approach also does treat the "words" as wholes. The significant identifying criteria used in the spelling-pattern approach differ greatly from those used by any common "phonics" method or by any common "word" method.

(5) In order to make the path of the beginning reader through the transfer stage as smooth and as free as possible from unnecessary difficulties, the actual substantive material for the

practice activities must be subjected to rigid criteria of selection and programmed into a progression of small, coherent steps through the major spelling-patterns.

For selection of the substantive material:

(a) The words used, that is, the sound-patterns of the words themselves and the particular meanings selected, must include only those within the *actual linguistic experience* of the pupil. The beginning reading stage must use only the language material already in the full control of the pupil; it is not the time to strive to increase the range of that control.

(b) The grammatical signals must also include only those within the pupil's linguistic experience. By the age of four or five, however, most native speakers of English will have full control of practically all the basic grammatical signals of their language. The grammatical limitations of the materials for English pupils of that age need be very few. As fast as the control of spelling-patterns makes adequate vocabulary available the full range of the pupil's stock of grammatical signals should be employed.

(c) Not all the words familiar to the pupil in the transfer stage of reading can be used for the materials of practice. It is essential *throughout this stage* that the words selected for the practice materials be only those for which the *spelling-patterns fit those that have been introduced and practiced or those that are being introduced.*

(d) The progression of the materials must be so programmed that each new item of whatever length is tied by a simple contrast to an item formerly practiced. The simple contrasts used should always be of items within a whole pattern, never of items less than a word. The basic principle of the learning and the teaching should always be contrast within a frame. For all the work with spelling-patterns we assume that the alphabet has been *learned* so well that the recognition-responses have become rapid and correct.

The following list of material will furnish an example of such a progression for beginning. The "items" for contrast are indicated by a dash between them and are included within double slashes. Items that make a structure are also included within double slashes.

//AT—CAT//   //CAT—RAT//
//A CAT—A RAT//   //AT—CAT—RAT—PAT//
//PAT A CAT//   //PAT A RAT//

//RAT—PAT—FAT//
//A FAT CAT//   //A FAT RAT//
//PAT A FAT CAT//   //PAT A FAT RAT//

//PAT—RAT—BAT//   //A RAT—A BAT//
//PAT A RAT//—//BAT A RAT//
//PAT A FAT CAT//—//BAT A FAT RAT//

//FAT—HAT//   //RAT—BAT—HAT—PAT//
//A BAT—A HAT—A RAT—A CAT//
//AT BAT//   //A CAT AT BAT//

//BAT—BATS//   //PAT—PATS//   //CAT—CATS//
//RAT—RATS//   //HAT—HATS//
//A CAT BATS AT A RAT//
//CATS BAT AT RATS//

(e) It is perhaps unnecessary to point out that the materials just given constitute a bare list of words and structures put into a teachable sequence of contrasts and structures. The actual specific procedures for handling such materials in order to build up recognition responses to the spelling-patterns as representing the spoken words they already know, and to the contrastive items and sequences of items within pairs of word-patterns that separate and identify each of the word-patterns, are the function of teachers guides to accompany a specific set of basic readers. Here we would suggest only a very few matters for the beginning that have some general import.[5]

At the beginning and for considerable time thereafter the teacher pronounces *in normal talking fashion* each new word and each pair of contrastive words as it is introduced and makes sure that the pupil, from that pronunciation, identifies the words as ones he knows.

Only complete words are pronounced. The pronunciation for the "word" is thus attached to the total spelling-pattern that represents that word. The spelling-pattern *cat* represents the word

/kæt/ as pronounced. Sounds are not given to the separate letters of a spelling-pattern. The understanding of the difference that any particular letter makes in the spelling-pattern is built up out of the experience of pronouncing a variety of word pairs with minimum differences in their *spelling-patterns.*

CAT—AT
CAT—RAT
CAT—PAT

We avoid completely such a question as "What does the letter *C* say?"

For the spelling sequences that represent words the pupils will develop recognition responses connecting the consonant letters with individual phonemes, but with these phonemes as phonetically realized in their various positions. But for the vowel letters, the pupils should develop responses connecting the whole distinctive spelling-pattern with one of the eleven vowel phonemes as phonetically realized in its particular position, rather than connect single vowel letters with single vowel phonemes.

The handling of even these beginning materials need not be mechanical, but it must be systematic, leading by the easiest sets of contrasts through all the major spelling-patterns and some of the minor patterns. Even from the beginning there must be complete meaning responses, including the spontaneous social-cultural responses of realizing the near absurdity or humor of a situation with "a cat at bat."

THE STAGE OF "PRODUCTIVE" READING

The preceding discussion has centered attention upon the first stage in learning to read—called here the "transfer" stage. During this period the child learns to change from auditory signs for his language signals, which he has already learned, to a set of visual signs for the same language signals. His task is to learn to *read* the visual signs, not to *write* them. In other words his task is limited to the so-called receptive side of language in its communicative function. He must develop recognition responses (high-speed recognition responses to read efficiently) to the bundles of graphic shapes that now represent the language signals formerly represented for him only by bundles of vocal noises. This first stage of learning to read, the transfer stage, is complete when within his narrow linguistic experience the child can respond rapidly and accurately to the visual patterns, the spelling-patterns, that represent the language signals of this limited linguistic experience, as fully as he does to the auditory patterns they replace.

The next, the second stage, covers the period during which the reader's responses to the visual patterns, the bundles of graphic shapes, become habits so automatic that the significant identifying features of the graphic shapes themselves sink below the threshold of conscious attention. He seems to respond to the meanings that are signalled without the use of the signals themselves. Finally, the *cumulative comprehension* of the meanings becomes so complete that as reader he can as he goes along supply those portions of the language signals which the bundles of spelling-patterns alone do not represent.

That the recognition responses of reading, which at first demand conscious attention to the significant details of identification, as they become habits, should require less and less conscious direction to such details is nothing unusual. This process seems to coincide with the normal progress of learning. In a number of the discussions of the teaching of reading, however, the habits of the successful adult reader are sometimes taken as the model upon which to build the practices of the beginner. It seems to be argued that, if the successful adult reader does not in his maturity use the details of the spelling, then these details are unnecessary. The beginning reader, therefore, it is further argued, could probably speed up his reading and achieve more efficiency if he learned from the very beginning to ignore such details. Certainly the habits and the achievement of the most successful readers should be thoroughly examined. But, to be of value in determining the methods for beginners, all the background of the methods and the amount of the practice, through which the superior reader's present standard of achievement was attained, must certainly be taken into account. All the experience lying back of the conclusions presented in this book seems to justify the assertion that only a tremendous amount of practice on reading materials that have been adequately programmed and streamlined to lead the developing reader by small steps through all the important sets of spelling-patterns will lead to the high-speed recognition responses of efficient reading.

The materials must also make provision for making conscious to the developing reader the range of language signals that at the present time our system of graphic devices does not represent, or represents very inadequately. Contrary to ordinary belief our writing represents *less* of the language signals than does speech. In writing this book, on page after page I have sought vainly for satisfactory devices to make the reader aware of the kind and amount of stress he needs to give to particular words in special sentences or to particular sentences in special paragraphs or to whole paragraphs. I have used italics as I did for *less* in the second sentence preceding this one, and at times asked for boldface type. But these crude devices can show nothing of the range of degrees of emphasis speech is capable of. Time after time, sentences, strategic for my meaning, sentences upon which I have labored in order to make them unmistakably clear, have been completely misunderstood because the reader evidently read them with a distribution of intonation and stress entirely different from that which I was "hearing" as I wrote.

These features of intonation and stress which attach to every utterance are, for the most part, unconsciously used by most of us. Actors only usually have given them considerable attention. Only comparatively recently have linguists made progress in describing the significant structural contrasts of the intonation of American English.[6] But although we now know more concerning *the kinds of meaning that the patterns of our intonation and stress add* to the basic linguistic meanings that correlate with the word patterns and grammatical structures, we have not yet developed a complete and flexible set of graphic devices to signal many of these additional meanings to the reader.

And yet if the reader is to learn to read well, that is, if the graphic devices are to function as fully for him as reader as all the sound-patterns of speech do for him as hearer, there must be some way by which he can learn to supply with some degree of fullness and accuracy the meanings contributed to speech by the patterns of intonation and stress. As a matter of fact, all of us who read with some maturity and the few who read with extraordinary insight and understanding, do, as they read, carry along and build up such a cumulative comprehension of so much of the total meanings of a discourse that their automatic recognition-responses *fill in the appropriate intonation and stress patterns.* The evidence for this supplying of the appropriate intonation and stress patterns shows itself in the fact that these good readers read orally "with expression." Reading "with expression" seems to be nothing other than this supplying of the signals that lie in the appropriate intonation and stress patterns for word groups marked by pitch pauses.

For many years, teachers of reading and reading specialists have discussed the relative merits of programs that stress primarily silent reading and those that devote large portions of time to oral reading. Most of the "research" upon this problem has given no consideration whatever to the significance of the linguistic facts noted here. The case for a very considerable amount of *properly directed and properly used oral reading from the very beginning* throughout the transfer stage and through this second stage of development rests primarily on the need to develop, along with the automatic responses to the bundles of contrastive graphic shapes that actually are present in the writing, the ability to supply or produce the appropriate, or at least an appropriate, set of intonation and stress patterns that *fit* and display evidence of a total cumulative understanding.

Teachers should never allow to pass any oral reading of any sentence that does not display in the features of pitch sequence and stress an understanding or some understanding of the total meaning. The very least that teachers should accept at the beginning, is the "saying" of a sentence, after it has been "mechanically read," as the child would "talk" it to a companion. Later, intonation patterns can be marked on material that is to be read aloud. Children can very soon quite consciously judge the significance or the fitness of an intonation sequence, for they are *not,* at the age of five or six, learning to *use* intonation sequences. They have already learned to produce them in their speech and have learned to respond to them as they have learned to understand speech directed to them. Now, in their learning to read, they are simply becoming conscious of their existence as they are brought to realize that "reading" must substitute for the "understanding of talk."

More and more as the pupil's power of reading develops and he grows in reading consecutive discourse with its sequence signals, he will learn that intonation and stress patterns have their special significance, not for an individual isolated sentence but for the meanings that grow out of the cumulative contribution of whole series of sentences. He will learn, for example, that he cannot mark the isolated sentence considered alone, with the proper intonation-stress pattern, but that most of these particular signal patterns demand that each utterance be grasped in relation to the sequence of utterances in which it occurs.

In other words, the second stage of the development of reading ability is complete not only when the responses to the spelling-patterns have become so automatic that the contrastive features of these bundles of the graphic shapes themselves sink below the threshold of attention leaving only consciousness of the body of meaning as it develops, but especially when the cumulative understanding of this body of meaning enables the reader to supply, to produce for materials read "at sight," those portions of the language signals, the appropriate patterns of intonation and stress that are not represented or only partially represented in the graphic materials given for the eye. We have, therefore, called this stage of reading development the "productive" stage. The case for oral reading today rests primarily on the need to develop "productive" reading.

THE STAGE OF "VIVID IMAGINATIVE REALIZATION"

The third, the last stage in developing the ability to read, begins when the reading process has become so automatic for the reader that he uses reading equally with or even more fully than the live language of speech in acquiring and assimilating new experience. Reading at this level stimulates a vivid imaginative realization of vicarious experience. Reading responses of this kind fulfill the "literary" purpose. The discussion for this section will therefore deal briefly with the reading of literature as somewhat distinct from what is commonly regarded as utilitarian reading.

Earlier in this book we referred to language as the storehouse of all the knowledge and understanding that the experience of *man* has accumulated. With the invention of writing the capacity of that storehouse became greatly extended, and the ability to read the only key to that tremendous addition to the accumulation of human knowledge and understanding. Of these accumulated materials, accessible only to those who can read with considerable freedom, we must distinguish two major types: first, the great collection of information, the knowledge of how to do things and the knowledge of the physical properties of all that has been explored, all that we call science; and, second, the great body of "literature."

These two bodies of material differ rather fundamentally in their dealing with human experience. For the purposes of science, attention centers upon the common features of differing experience—the features that can form the bases of generalizations and such predictions as will increase man's practical control of his environment. For the purposes of literature, these common features of differing experience become insignificant in the effort to grasp the unique features of individual experience and communicate the experience itself. As DeWitt H. Parker puts it, "History may tell us what men did, but only the poet or other artist can make us relive the values of their experience."

The literary purpose is, I believe, the use of language to communicate *not* facts and information but vivid imaginative realizations of actions, of emotions, of values. The literary artist carries a capacity for vivid impressions into every part of man's experience, and then we share the sensitiveness of his keener insight through his power to communicate vivid realizations of his experience.

. . . each one of us has within him capacities of action and emotion and thought unrealized—the actual self is only one of many that might have been—hundreds of possible lives slumber in our souls. And no matter which of these lives we have chosen for our own, or have been forced upon us by our fate, we always retain a secret longing for all the others that have gone unfulfilled, and an understanding born of longing. Some of these we imagine distinctly—those that we consciously rejected or that a turn of chance might have made ours; but most of them we ourselves have not the power even to dream. Yet those too beckon us from behind, and the artist provides us with their dream. Through art we secure an imaginative realization of interests and latent tendencies to act and think and feel which, because they are contradictory among themselves or at variance with the conditions of our existence, cannot find free play within our experience.[7]

The ability to read "literature," that is, the ability to build up from the written materials of the literary artist a complete vivid imaginative realization, must be learned. Little has been done in the way of describing the details of the paths through which to reach this goal.

The goal has been discussed frequently—at times from the point of view of the philosophy of art, aesthetics, as in the quotation from DeWitt H. Parker above; at times from the point of view of the literary critic, as in the chapters "The Nature of Literature" and "The Function of Literature" by René Welleck and Austin Warren;[8] and at times from the point of view of the producers of literature as it is set forth in the statements they have made concerning their own work. John Masefield's *Dauber* furnishes an example.

> That that was what his work meant; it would be
> A training in new vision—a revealing
> Of passionate men in battle with the sea,
> High on an unseen stage, shaking and reeling;
> And men through him would understand their feeling,
> Their might, their misery, their tragic power,
> And all by suffering pain a little hour;
>
> High on the yard with them, feeling their pain,
> Battling with them; and it had not been done.
> He was a door to new worlds in the brain,
> A window opening letting in the sun,
> A voice saying, 'Thus is bread fetched and ports won,
> And life lived out at sea when men exist
> Solely by man's strong brain and sturdy wrist.'
>
> So he decided, as he cleaned his brasses, . . .
> To share man's tragic toil and paint it true.[9]

H. G. Wells makes his case for the novel in the following.

You see now the scope of the claim I am making for the novel: it is to be the social mediator, the vehicle of understanding, the instrument of self-examination, the parade of morals and the exchange of manners, the factory of customs and ideas, the criticism of laws and institutions and of social dogmas and ideas. It is to be the home confessional, the initiator of knowledge, the seed of fruitful self-questioning. Let me be very clear here. I do not mean for a moment that the novelist is going to set up as a teacher, as a sort of priest with a pen who will make men and women believe and do this and that. The novel is not a new sort of pulpit; humanity is passing out of the phase when men sit under preachers and dogmatic influences. But the novelist is going to present conduct, devise beautiful conduct, discuss conduct, analyze conduct, suggest conduct, illuminate it through and through. . . .

We are going to write, subject only to our own limitations, about the whole of human life. We are going to deal with political questions and religious questions and social questions. We cannot present people unless we have this free hand, this unrestricted field. . . .

We are going to write about it all . . . until a thousand pretenses and ten thousand impostures shrivel in the cold clear air of our elucidations. We are going to write of wasted opportunities and latent beauties, until a thousand new ways of living open to men and women.[10]

Many believe that the linguist, especially the modern linguist, would exclude all the essential literary qualities from his consideration.

All devices for securing emphasis or explicitness can be classed under stylistics: metaphors, which permeate all languages, even of the most primitive type; all rhetorical figures; syntactical patterns. Nearly every linguistic utterance can be studied from the point of view of its expressive value. It seems impossible to ignore this problem as the "behavioristic" school of linguistics in America very consciously does.[11]

As a matter of fact, however, the linguist's proper field of study consists of the whole of language. Whitney expressed this view in 1867.

Every fact of every language, in the view of the linguistic student, calls for his investigation, since only in the light of all can any be completely understood. To assemble, arrange, and explain the whole body of linguistic phenomena, so as thoroughly to comprehend them, in each separate part and under all aspects, is his endeavor.[12]

And others have not only shown a general interest but have tried to find scientifically acceptable approaches to the study of the "expressive values" of language. The fact that at present "the study of meanings is the least satisfactory of the areas of linguistic study" means simply that competent linguists have been busy elsewhere in the feeling that a variety of other studies must first lay the foundation.[13]

The practical question can be stated simply. In the effort to develop the ability to respond to literary materials with a complete and vivid imaginative realization can the linguistic knowledge that we have furnish any help? More specifically we might attempt to answer questions such as the following.

(a) Modern linguistics has developed an increasingly vigorous and exact way of talking about both the form and the content of language. Can this way of talking—this method of linguistic statement—help in the meeting of minds, in understanding, that should come from the discussion of, or the "teaching" of literature?

(b) Can the methods, principles, assumptions of modern linguistics be extended and developed in any way and applied to a literary work (a poem, for example) so as to stimulate new responses to it as an artistic product?

Basically, of course, literature uses the language of the community. The linguistic meanings of the written materials will thus be the "same" for the linguistic community and must be reckoned with. At times, however, certain social-cultural meanings will constitute the chief communication of a literary piece. These may be quite apart from or even oppose the linguistic meanings of the language signals. Special symbolism, private or traditional, known only to a limited group may be attached to particular utterances. Here, however, we shall not attempt to deal with any of the broader and less linguistic features of literary materials. We can make only a very few observations concerning some of the formal matters of poetry, to illustrate several linguistic features of which the "literary code" makes significant use.

(1) In the English language itself, with its utterances of sequences of sounds in a time dimension, there are no *lines*. Graphic signs to represent the language, using direction in space to represent the time dimension, can, of course, continue spirally around a column without any "line end" until the final word of a text. Or they can move without "line end," as the news bulletins have on the *Times* building in New York. Most written texts appear in "lines," however, because of the physical limitations of the materials on which the writing appears. The length of these lines is arbitrarily determined by the width of the page or the number of "columns" on a page. Printers have usually "justified" the "lines" of their pages—by adjusting the width of "spaces"

they have made all the "lines" on a page the same length. The lines of typewritten pages have not usually been so "justified." In other words, these "lines" of written, or printed, or typed material have been wholly arbitrary in length within the practical needs of efficient reading. For most people a line 80 millimeters (3.2 inches) long can, with a small amount of tolerance, be most easily read. A line shorter by 12 millimeters reduces the speed by 4 percent, and a line longer by 35 millimeters reduces the speed by 7 percent. A line arbitrarily shortened at the beginning (by indentation) has been used in modern times to signal the grouping of "sentences" into a "paragraph." But on the whole the "lines" in ordinary prose have had no signalling significance.

In the literary code of poetry, however, the "line" is used structurally to achieve a number of artistic effects. To *read* poetry one must learn to respond automatically to the signals of these structural uses of the lines. Some examples follow.

(a) In general the "rhythm" of the poetic expression is a function of the line. Languages differ greatly in respect to their rhythm. English seems to be a "stress" timed rhythm rather than a syllable timed rhythm. In English poetry, therefore, the "lines" are not only indicated graphically; they are usually marked by a particular number of "stressed" syllables in patterns of stressed and unstressed syllables. In English, the length or duration of the vowels seems to be tied to the "stress." Syllables given special prominence by "stress" or "intonation" are usually lengthened; they are shortened and "crushed" when several syllables occur between "stresses." Vowel length in English is thus not phonemic as it was in Greek and Latin. English, therefore, cannot duplicate the quantitative patterns of verse characteristic of the literary "code" of Greek or Latin. Nor can it easily imitate poetry in which the number of the syllables marks the "line."

(b) Lines in English poetry may also be marked by rhymes. Linguistically, rhymes consist essentially of minimum or near-minimum contrasting word pairs similar to those used above in Chapter Three. For rhymes, however, two or more words must have the same vowel in the last prominent syllable, and the same sound features following that vowel; the sound features preceding the vowel must be different: /stɛdɪ/ *steady*, /rɛdɪ/ *ready*; /ɔn kɔl/ *on call;* /ɪn fɔl/ *in fall;* /ɪnstɪtut/ *institute*, /rɛzəlut/ *resolute*.

Such minimum pairs do occur in the language as it is used in everyday communication. But their occurrence there is unpredictable and seldom noticed. In the literary code this feature of the language is greatly heightened and used for various kinds of "pointing" that have an artistic significance.

The "code" of literature is limited to the linguistic material that the language possesses. Modern English can use rhymes effectively because of the rather large number of significant contrastive vowel qualities. In languages with small numbers of such vowel contrasts, rhyme has not developed as a literary device. The literary "code" of English includes rhyme as a significant pointing signal: an arbitrarily increased frequency of contrastive word pairs in parallel positions—word pairs that have the same vowel phoneme in a prominent syllable, with similar phonemes following and contrasting phonemes preceding.

(2) The discussion above (Chapter Three) concerning the signals of the meanings carried by the lexical items made a special point of the fact that in learning his language the child builds up not only an understanding of the various bundles of experience connected with a lexical form, he learns also the items of the lexical sets that serve to identify each particular meaning of a word with multiple meanings. In other words, he learns the usual or regular distribution of the lexical forms—the regular co-occurrence of other linguistic items of the lexical sets. In using our native language, we seldom realize the particular items that on each occasion signal for us the precise meaning out of the many a lexical item could have. The literary "code" takes advantage of this sensitiveness to the regular or usual distribution of vocabulary items to achieve effective expression of meaningful connections of the social experience not usually brought together. Metaphor is thus characteristic of the language of poetry. The cue to metaphor is the unusual distribution of a lexical item. It brings together in effective minimum statement two different but joinable distributions.

Part of the many signals of the meanings that literary art communicates with particular force consists of special uses of linguistic material for effects that fulfill the literary purpose. The ability to respond to the artistic materials of literature, like other abilities, must be won by effort. It does not come freely. Part of the task must be learning the special code of poetry. That code for English has not as yet been fully described in such linguistic terms as to make possible the laying out of a program of specific teaching.

Learning to read has no end. We believe we now know better than formerly where to begin and how. We believe that we must give thorough and systematic practice not only through the transfer stage but through the building up of a superior ability to read productively. Nor must we stop before we go as far as possible in teaching our students to *really read* literature.

Notes

CHAPTER ONE

1. Unfortunately a comprehensive history of the teaching of reading has never been achieved. We have only fragments and these are sometimes misleading. Among the more complete historical treatments are the following:

(a) *The Historical Development of School Readers and Methods in Teaching Reading* by Rudolph R. Reeder. A doctoral dissertation (93 pages) completed in the Faculty of Philosophy of Columbia University, New York, in 1900.

(b) *A History of the Teaching of Beginning Reading* by Harold B. Lamport. An unpublished doctoral dissertation (516 manuscript pages) completed in the Department of Education at the University of Chicago in August 1935. (Pages 487–516 give a chronological summary.)

(c) *A Historical Analysis of American Reading Instruction* by Nila Banton Smith. A book of 287 pages published by Silver Burdett and Company, Morristown, N. J., 1934.

(d) *The Improvement of Reading in Elementary Schools* by Emmett Albert Betts. A brief survey of the shifting centers of attention in the study of reading problems during the first half of the twentieth century—an article published by the American Council on Education, in Supplement Number 17, of *The Educational Record*, 1948.

(e) *The Teaching of Reading and Writing.* An International Survey by William S. Gray. A book of 286 pages, published by UNESCO, Paris, 1956.

Some of the more useful bibliographical aids for those interested in the tremendous number of professional publications concerning the problems of teaching reading during the last sixty years are the following.

(a) William S. Gray's *Summary of Investigations Relating to Reading* began with a monograph of that name published in 1925 by the University of Chicago Press. This monograph summarized 435 studies—14 from 1885 to 1900; 30 from 1901 to 1910; but 391 from 1911 to 1925. The first number of the yearly publication of the "Summary of Investigations Relating to Reading" appeared in the Elementary School Journal (February and March) in 1927. In 1933 the "Summary" was transferred to the *Journal of Educational Research* and has been an annual feature of that journal to the present time. Helen M. Robinson was finally responsible for the "Summary" as it appeared in February 1961; and Theodore L. Harris for that which appeared in February 1962. Altogether these summaries, justifiably called the "Gray Summaries," contain descriptive statements concerning 4158 studies. Beginning in 1963 these annual *Summaries* are to appear in *The Reading Teacher* published by the International Reading Association. See the "Summary of Investigations" for July 1, 1961 to June 30, 1962, by Helen M. Robinson, in Vol. 16, No. 4 (January 1963), 285–322. 180 items.

(b) More highly selected and more fully analyzed are the materials contained in the four volumes of *Research in Reading* compiled by Arthur E. Traxler, with the assistance of the Educational Records Bureau Staff, and published by the Educational Records Bureau, New York, N.Y., in 1941, 1946, 1955, 1960. These four volumes covering the "Reading Research" from 1930 to the end of 1957 deal with 2343 items.

(c) Much wider in range and less selective in character is *An Index To Professional Literature on Reading and Related Topics* (to January 1, 1943) by Emmett A. Betts and Thelma M. Betts, published by the American Book Company in 1945. The Betts and Betts *Index* not only lists with satisfactorily complete bibliographical information more than 8200 items, it also very helpfully groups these articles (by index number) under some 168 different topics (with many cross-references).

(d) *The National Society for the Study of Education* has devoted a number of its *Yearbooks* to the "Teaching of Reading." The yearbooks, especially the later ones, do attempt to summarize and draw conclusions from the published studies of reading problems, but on the whole they have addressed themselves to the practical problems of the teachers and have sought to prepare recommendations especially on the "debatable issues." Each of the committees responsible for the preparation of these several yearbooks has represented the outstanding "reading experts" of the time the yearbook was prepared and published.

(1) *Report of the National Committee on Reading, Twenty-Fourth Yearbook*, Part I, Public School Publishing Company, Bloomington, Illinois, 1925.

(2) *The Teaching of Reading: A Second Report, Thirty-Sixth Yearbook*, Part I, Public School Publishing Company, Bloomington, Illinois, 1937.

(3) *Reading in the High School and College, Forty-Seventh Yearbook*, The University of Chicago Press, Part II, 1948.

(4) *Reading in the Elementary School, Forty-Eighth Yearbook*, Part II, The University of Chicago Press, 1949.

(5) *Adult Reading, Fifty-fifth Yearbook*, Part II, The University of Chicago Press, 1956.

(e) Other organizations of school personnel have issued special cooperative yearbooks on the problems of teaching reading. The Department of Elementary School Principals (National Education Association) has, for example, published two yearbooks on reading, one in 1938 and the other in 1955.

(1) *Reading for Today's Children, Thirty-fourth Yearbook*, published as Volume XXXV, No. 1 of the Bulletin of the Department of Elementary School Principals, 1955.

(f) For useful surveys and bibliographies of the studies and professional materials dealing with particular kinds of reading problems there are publications like the following.

(1) *The Psychology of Teaching Reading*, by Irving H. Anderson and Walter F. Dearborn, 1952, New York, The Ronald Press Company. A book of 382 pages, with a bibliography list of 386 selected items.

(2) *Bibliography of Vocabulary Studies* (Revised Edition 1957) by Edgar Dale and Donald Reichert. Bureau of Educational Research, The Ohio State University, Columbus, Ohio.

(3) *Readiness for Reading and Related Language Arts*, A Digest of Current Research, Prepared by a Committee of the National Conference on Research in English, Nila Banton Smith, Chairman. Issued by the National Council of Teachers of English, 1950.

2. W. S. Gray, "Reading," in Walter Scott Monroe, ed., *Encyclopedia of Educational Research*, New York, The Macmillan Company, 1950, p. 966.

3. Arthur E. Traxler, Agatha Townsend, and Staff, *Eight More Years of Research in Reading*, New York, Educational Records Bureau, 1955, pp. 5, 6, 4.

4. C. Winfield Scott, "A 'Forest' View of Present Research in Reading," *Educational and Psychological Measurement*, XIV:1 (Spring 1954), 208–214.

5. Nila B. Smith, Professor of Education and Director, The Reading Institute, New York University, at the Public Relations Seminar sponsored by the National School Public Relations Association (a department of the National Educational Association), Lake Forest, Ill., July 14, 1955, *Why Do the Schools Teach Reading as They Do?*, pp. 2, 4, 5, 7, 8, 15. See also "Some Answers to Criticisms of American Reading Instruction" by Nila Banton Smith in *The Reading Teacher* 16 (December 1962), pp. 146–150.

6. Lyman Cobb, *Juvenile Reader No. 1, containing Interesting, Moral, and Instructive Reading Lessons composed of easy words of One and Two Syllables. Designed for the Use of Small Children in Families and Schools*, Ithaca, N. Y., 1831.

7. *The Works of Benjamin Franklin*, ed. by Jared Sparks, Philadelphia, Childs and Peterson, 1840, VII, 2.

8. John Hart, *The Opening of the Unreasonable Writing of Our English Toung*, 1551. There is now an excellent edition of *John Hart's Works* with biographical and bibliographical introductions by Bror Danielsson, Stockholm, Almquist and Wiksell, 1955.

9. John Hart, *A Methode or comfortable beginning for all vnlearned, whereby they may bee taught to read English, in a very short time, with pleasure*, London, 1570, fol. IVa.

10. He illustrates the absurdity of requiring the pupil to pronounce the names of the letters of a word as a preliminary to reading it by using the combination *t h r*. Pronouncing the names of these letters in order would produce *te-ache-er*, which should according to "right reason" represent the word *teacher* (*ibid.*, fol. IXa).

11. He says:

> It is a sophisticall maner of teaching when the letters apart must be named in one sort, and being put together, in another, it is a maner of Metamorphosis, or work of Circes, so to transforme them from their natures and offices. Wherefore (though nowe in the latter dayes, being better late than neuer) here followeth a certain rule with demonstrations, so as the first breath or sound or both togither, of the name of the thing figured [presented in pictures] vnder eche letter, is the breath or sounde, or both togither of the letter aboue it, with examples thereafter in diuers wordes. Which euery one that is able to read, may at first sight understand, and so be able to teach it to others.
>
> The ease wherof is such, that so soone as one is able to name the .xxv. letters perfitly and readily, whersoeuer they present themselues to his eye, so soone shall he be able to reade. Which may be

in so short a time, or shorter, than he shall be able to learne to know .xxv. diuers men, women, and children (though he neuer saw them before) and to name them readily and perfitly wheresoeuer he might méete them [*ibid.,* fol. IVb].

12. Charls Butler, *The English Grammar,* Oxford, Wm. Turner, 1633–1634.

13. See the list in C. C. Fries, "The Rules of the Common School Grammars," *Publications of the Modern Language Association,* XLII (1927), 223–224.

14. Hart, *A Methode* . . . , fol. IIb.

15. Samuel Putnam, *The Analytical Reader,* Portland, Me., William Hyde, Publisher, 1836, Preface, p. 3.

16. William H. McGuffey, *The Eclectic Third Reader,* improved ed. of 1838, Cincinnati, Truman & Smith, 1838, p. 8.

17. *The Common School Journal,* IV (1842), 20.

18. George L. Farnham, M.A., Superintendent of Schools, Council Bluffs, Iowa, late Superintendent of Schools at Binghamton and Syracuse, N.Y., *The Sentence Method of Teaching Reading, Writing and Spelling, A Manual for Teachers,* Syracuse, N.Y., C. W. Bardeen, Publisher, 1881, pp. 13–14.

19. E. H. Butler, *The First Reader,* Philadelphia, Sherman & Co., 1883, p. 5.

20. *The Common School Journal,* IV (1842), 27, 29.

21. *Ibid.,* pp. 90–96.

22. "I could not have made him remember them by making this analysis the first time he saw them for in my former groping after a true method, I have often tried this" (*ibid.,* p. 96).

23. J. Russell Webb, *Normal Series of School Readers,* New York, 1850.

24. *Webb's Normal Reader, No. 1. A New Method of Teaching Children to Read,* New York, 1856, Preface, p. v.

25. *Ibid.,* "Directions for Teaching," p. vii.

26. *Ibid.,* "Directions for Teaching," p. viii.

27. *Ibid.,* pp. 37–39.

28. *Ibid.,* p. 51.

29. E. H. Butler, *op. cit.,* p. 5.

30. *Ibid.,* p. 4.

31. See advertisement for the *Eclectic Series* on the back cover of *The Eclectic Third Reader* of the edition of 1838, printed in Cincinnati in 1839.

32. *McGuffey's First Eclectic Reader,* rev. ed., Cincinnati, Van Antwerp, Bragg & Co., 1879, pp. iii–iv.

33. *Ibid.,* p. ii.

34. *The Eclectic Third Reader* (improved edition, 1838), p. 8.

35. Farnham, *The Sentence Method of Teaching Reading, Writing and Spelling, A Manual for Teachers* (1881).

36. *Ibid.,* Preface, pp. iii–v, xii.

37. Farnham, *The Sentence Method,* pp. 13–19, 20–24.

38. *Ibid.,* pp. 28, 34, 35, 36.

39. *Ibid.,* pp. 57–58, 63.

40. In the 1881 edition (p. 61) the word *reproductive* appears here, but it has been corrected to *reproduction* in the 1895 edition.

41. Farnham, *op. cit.,* pp. 60–62, 55.

42. *Feeds* in the 1895 edition; an error, *feels,* in the 1881 edition.

43. Farnham, *op. cit.,* p. 66.

44. For a somewhat different point of view regarding the studies of reading problems from 1910 to 1960 see the article by Nila Banton Smith, "What Have We Accomplished in Reading?—A Review of the Past Fifty Years," in *Elementary English,* XXXVIII (March 1961), 141–150.

45. Émile Javal, *"Essai sur la physiologie de la lecture,"* in *Annales d'oculistique,* LXXXII (1879), 242–253.

46. For a survey of these materials, see Edmund B. Huey, *The Psychology and Pedagogy of Reading,* New York, The Macmillan Company, 1908, pp. 15–184; Irving H. Anderson and Walter F. Dearborn, *The Psychology of Teaching Reading,* New York, The Ronald Press Company, 1952, pp. 101–137; and William S. Gray, *The Teaching of Reading and Writing: An International Survey,* Monographs on Fundamental Education X, Paris, UNESCO, 1956, pp. 43–60.

47. For an extensive bibliography covering the work done in the various aspects of the study of eye movements see the 608 titles given by Earl A. Taylor as an appendix to his book *Eyes, Visual Anomalies, and the Fundamental Reading Skill,* New York, Reading and Study Skills Center, 1959. The author of this book indicated that the program described here has been in operation for eighteen years.

Another book dealing with the problems of severe reading disability is Donald E. P. Smith and Patricia M. Carrigan, *The Nature of Reading Disability,* New York, Harcourt, Brace & World, Inc., 1959.

48. See the brief summaries of the research studies on "Eye-movements and Reading Ability" in Traxler's four volumes (New York, Educational Records Bureau): Arthur E. Traxler, *Ten Years of Research in Reading* (*1930–1940*), 1941, pp. 31–33; Arthur E. Traxler and Agatha Townsend, *Another Five Years of Research in Reading* (*1940–1945*), 1946, pp. 45–48; Arthur E. Traxler and Agatha Townsend, *Eight More Years of Research in Reading* (*1945–1953*), 1955, pp. 56–58; and Arthur E. Traxler and Ann Jungeblut, *Research in Reading During Another Four Years* (*1953–1957*), 1960, pp. 48–51.

49. William C. Morse, "A Comparison of the Eye-Movements of Average Fifth- and Seventh-Grade Pupils Reading Materials of Corresponding Difficulty," in *Studies in the Psychology of Reading,* Ann Arbor, University of Michigan Monographs in Education, Number 4 (April 1951), p. 64.

50. Traxler, Townsend, *Eight More Years of Research in Reading,* p. 6.

51. But see Traxler in *Eight More Years of Research in Reading,* p. 5: "The findings in studies of reading speed and comprehension confirm earlier

findings in that fast and slow readers appear to comprehend reading material about equally well. There is a small amount of evidence that fast reading is of advantage in the comprehension of pupils with high intelligence but is not advantageous for pupils of average and low mental ability."

52. The discussion here has been limited to the teaching of reading in English. The members of the Summer Institute of Linguistics have constructed primers and taught reading for some 150 different languages. These linguists have reported on their work and discussed their problems. See Sarah Gudschinsky, *Handbook of Literacy*, first published in 1953 (an extensive revision of materials originally prepared in 1951, and again revised in 1957). See also her *Recent Trends in Primer Construction*, 1959. There was also the little booklet by Henry Lee Smith, Jr., *Linguistic Science and the Teaching of English* (Cambridge, Harvard University Press, 1956, 61 pages), which touched the problem of reading.

53. Published in the *Elementary English Review*, XIX (1942), 125–130, 183–186.

CHAPTER TWO

1. One author writes:

> The great cry is for improved communication, and yet under the pretext of being free and easy and above quibbling, those who do the most talking and writing indulge themselves in the very obscurities and ambiguities that cause the outcry. They are abetted, moreover, by another offspring of the scientific spirit, the professional student of language. In his modern embodiment the linguist takes the view that whatever occurs in anybody's speech is a fact of language and must not be tampered with, but only caught in flight and pinned on a card. This is "scientific detachment," and it has gone so far that under its influence in many schools all the categories of grammar, syntax, and rhetoric have been discarded. The modern way to learn English or a foreign language is to absorb a phrase-by-phrase enumeration of all that might conceivably be said in ordinary talk—a directory instead of a grammar. . . . The linguists themselves pay lip service to "effective" speech, approving the end while forbidding discrimination among the means.

Jacques Barzun, "English as She's Not Taught," *The Atlantic Monthly*, December 1953, p. 25.

> Frivolously, the would-be scientists argued the other way, saying that democracy and their science alike called for a policy of "Hands Off." As scientists they maintained that the speech of any group is good speech for that group; as democrats and progressives they maintained that the child should not be made to feel inferior (or superior) by changing his speech. "There can . . . never be in grammar an error that is both very bad and very

common." Thus spoke Charles Carpenter Fries, the theorist who engineered the demise of grammar in the American schools. Yet this doctrine and his crusade were not, as he thought, objective and detached in the spirit of science. Rather, philanthropy and egalitarianism inspired him. To teach one kind of usage, pronunciation, and grammar seemed to him tantamount to reintroducing social distinctions of the most artificial kind. Wanting the opposite gave him his first principle: Accept what comes and in time we shall have a classless speech corresponding to the usage of the most numerous.

Jacques Barzun, *House of Intellect,* New York, Harper & Row, Publishers. 1959, p. 241.

In the two quotations above Jacques Barzun (Professor of History in Columbia University and Dean of the Faculties and Provost) is wrong, in respect to the facts, in practically every statement he makes concerning "the linguist," and the single section of direct quotation he makes from me is not only taken out of context, but out of a context that develops a point of view just the opposite of the point of view he attributes to me.

The sentence Barzun quotes comes from my *Teaching of the English Language* (New York, Thomas Nelson & Sons, 1927). In the brief summary of the immediately preceding chapter, an historical survey of "The Rules of Grammar as the Measure of Language Errors," I had used as examples "It is me" and "It is you," pointing out that historically *me* and *you* were both dative-accusative forms, that the dative-accusative form *you* had displaced the earlier nominative form *ye* in "It is you" and is now completely accepted "solely because we use it in that situation," and that "obviously the rule that 'The verb *to be* takes the same case after it as is used before it' is not the final measure to be applied in this case, but must yield, as rules have always done, to the drift and development of the language." The sentence Barzun quotes comes in the very first paragraph of the next chapter in which as a means of connection with the earlier discussion I used "It is you." I wrote as follows:

> Where that usage is practically unanimous, as it is in respect to "It is you," there is no possible appeal despite any rules that may come into conflict with it. In such cases, if the rule of grammar does not harmonize with the general usage of the language it has no validity. Rules or laws of grammar are like laws of botany, or physics, or biology; they are general statements attempting to describe the ways in which language operates to express ideas, and valid only in so far as they are accurate generalizations. But the facts of usage are in all cases fundamental. If these facts are not in harmony with the rules or generalizations we have had in our grammars hitherto, then these rules must be restated and expanded to include all the facts. There can thus never be in grammar an error that is both very bad and very common. The more common it is, the nearer it comes to being the best of grammar.

But difficulties do not arise in cases where the usage is fairly unanimous. "It is you" is not a problem; but with the pronoun of the first person there is a problem because some people insist upon using "It is I," and others "It is me." The trouble arises where usage is thus divided, in those cases in which adult English-speaking people differ in their practice. Here, obviously, the appeal to usage is futile because it is the very fact of the division of usage which creates the difficulty. . . . It is probably much more sound to decide that the spontaneous usage of that large group who are carrying on the affairs of English-speaking people is the usage to be observed and to set the standard. Certainly this would seem sound as far as the teaching of the schools is concerned if we agree that education must bear directly upon and prepare for life. When, then, this usage is practically unanimous in respect to any form or construction that form or construction is correct and acceptable English grammar. When this usage differs in respect to any form or construction we must set up some other principle of decision. To do that is the purpose of the rest of this chapter. . . .

To avoid possible misunderstanding let me call attention to the fact that we are not here discussing the artistic use of language nor are we attempting to define any ideal of the highest reaches of our language in beauty and effectiveness. We are here trying to outline some practical standards of *acceptable* English. The artistic point of view will be discussed in Chapter V and the significance of differing speech habits in the various groups will be dealt with in Chapter VI.

Mr. Barzun could not possibly have read the book from which he quotes, especially Chapter V, which deals with "The Scientific and Artistic Points of View in Language" (showing that they are complementary and not conflicting), and Chapter VI, which deals with the problems of the teachers in developing in their pupils "the language habits of those we have called the socially acceptable group" (p. 137). Nor could he have looked at the first chapter of my *American English Grammar* (1940), entitled "The Social Significance of Differences in Language Practice and the Obligation of the Schools," and Chapter XI, "Some Inferences from This Study for a Workable Program in English Language for the Schools." In fact the subtitle of the book itself should provide an obvious clue for one who has any interest in discovering what I really believe concerning usage. The whole title is the following: *American English Grammar: The Grammatical Structure of Present-Day English with Especial Reference to Social Differences or Class Dialects.*

Nor could anyone attribute to me the views given in the Barzun quotations if he had looked at the introduction to my *Structure of English* (New York, Harcourt, Brace & World, Inc., 1952, pp. 3–7). The following quotation again contradicts several of Barzun's assertions.

A linguist records and studies all the actual forms and uses of the language that occur, but that recording and that study, of Vulgar English as well as Standard English, *should certainly not be taken as evidence that he therefore recommends or believes that the forms of Vulgar English can or should be substituted for the forms of Standard English.* If he is a good linguist he is very careful to note the precise areas of use in which the language forms are recorded, and he understands the problems of trying to learn to substitute the forms of one "dialect" for another. He understands, perhaps more completely than others, the nature of the task that the schools have undertaken when they assume the burden of teaching every child to use Standard English and, accordingly, he sometimes urges the limitation of that teaching to the actual forms of Standard English, as a scientific description reveals them, and the abandoning of attempts to teach forms that do not occur in the actual speech of native speakers of Standard English, forms that have become shibboleths of the classroom.

For the principles of a "linguistic" approach to the teaching of a language see my book *Teaching and Learning English as a Foreign Language* (Ann Arbor, Mich., University of Michigan Press, 1945).

Every one of these four books was published and had very wide circulation before 1953. Historically, for the influences that contributed to what Mr. Barzun calls "the demise of grammar in the American schools," I believe that Mr. Barzun must look at some of the publications giving the results of studies using educational tests and measurements, as, for example, Franklin S. Hoyt in *Teachers College Record*, VII (1906), 467–500, and some of those listed in R. L. Lyman's *Summary of Investigations Relating to Grammar, Language, and Composition*, Chicago, University of Chicago Press, 1929.

2. *Undersögelse om det gamle Nordiske eller Islandske Sprogs Oprindeke.*

3. For the details to demonstrate these two features in the beginnings of the "modern scientific study of language" see Chapter VII of Holger Pedersen, *Linguistic Science in the Nineteenth Century: Methods and Results,* Copenhagen, University of Copenhagen, 1924, trans. by John Webster Spargo, Cambridge, Mass., Harvard University Press, 1931.

4. *The Report of the Smithsonian Institution for 1863,* Washington, D.C., 1864, pp. 95–118. In England, Friedrich Max Müller delivered his "Lectures on the Science of Language" at the Royal Institution of Great Britain in 1863. His book was published in the United States in 1864.

5. William Dwight Whitney, *Language and the Study of Language: Twelve Lectures on the Principles of Linguistic Science,* New York, Charles Scribner and Co., 1867, Preface, pp. vii–viii.

6. William Dwight Whitney, *The Life and Growth of Language: An Outline of Linguistic Science,* 1875, p. 5.

7. *Ibid.,* pp. 315–316.

8. See the great mass of evidence concerning the history of one important aspect of this authoritarian approach, summarized by Andrew D. White, the first President and Professor of History of Cornell University, in *A History of the Warfare of Science with Theology,* 1895, Vol. II, Chapter XVII, 168–208, "From Babel to Comparative Philology."

9. B. Delbrück, *Introduction to the Study of Language,* trans. by E. Channing, Jena, 1880, p. 33.

10. Pedersen, *op. cit.,* p. 231.

11. Whitney, *Language and the Study of Language,* p. 5.

12. *Ibid.,* p. 6.

13. Whitney, *The Life and Growth of Language,* pp. 33–34.

14. *Ibid.,* pp. 177–178.

15. *Oxford English Dictionary,* 1888, Preface, Vol. I, v, vi.

16. See the booklet by Richard Chenevix Trench, Dean of Winchester, entitled *On Some Deficiencies In Our English Dictionaries, Being the Substance of Two Papers Read Before the Philological Society,* Nov. 5 and Nov. 19, 1857, London, John W. Parker and Son, 1857. These two papers shed considerable light upon the thinking that led the Philological Society soon after (Jan. 1858) to undertake the collection that finally made the *Oxford English Dictionary* possible.

17. See Harold B. Allen, *Samuel Johnson and the Authoritarian Principle in Linguistic Criticism,* University of Michigan doctoral dissertation, No. 1662, 1940.

18. Verner's paper was entitled *Eine Ausnahme der ersten Lautverschiebung,* referred to in English as "An Exception to the First Consonant Shift" or "Verner's Law."

19. Pedersen, *op. cit.,* p. 282.

20. *Ibid.,* p. 292, Note 1.

21. That is, spelled with *s,* but, in sound, phonetically adjusted to the character of the sound immediately preceding. After voiced sounds it is the sound [z], after voiceless sounds it is the sound [s], after the sounds [s], [z], [š], [č], [ǰ], it is a separate syllable, [ɪz], or [əz].

22. Edward Sapir, "The Status of Linguistics as a Science," *Language,* V (1929), 207, 208. Reprinted by permission. See also note by Leonard Bloomfield, attached to his article "On the Sound-System of Central Algonquian" in *Language,* I (1925), 130.

> I hope, also, to help dispose of the notion that the usual processes of linguistic change are suspended on the American continent (Meillet and Cohen, *Les langues du monde,* Paris, 1924, 9). If there exists anywhere a language in which these processes do not occur (sound-change independent of meaning, analogic change, etc.) then they will not explain the history of Indo-European or of

any other language. A principle such as the regularity of phonetic change is not of the specific tradition handed on to each new speaker of a given language, but it is either a universal trait of human speech or nothing at all, an error.

23. Whitney, *Language and the Study of Language,* p. 6.

24. See "Bibliography of Linguistic Geography," in Hans Kurath *et al., Handbook of the Linguistic Geography of New England,* Providence, R.I., Brown University, 1939, 55–61.

25. For a critical analysis of phonetic theory from the middle of the nineteenth century to 1940, see Kenneth L. Pike, *Phonetics,* Part I, Ann Arbor, Mich., University of Michigan Press, 1943, pp. 1–79. For a new constructive system of phonetic analysis, see Part II, pp. 83–156.

26. Edward Sapir, *Language,* New York, Harcourt, Brace and Co., 1921, Chapter III, "The Sounds of Language."

26a. G. B. Shaw, *Pygmalion.* Reprinted by permission of the Public Trustee and The Society of Authors.

27. See Chapter Five for a statement of some of the difficulties that arise out of interchanging the words *phonetics* and *phonics* in discussions concerning the teaching of reading. In that section I bring together and try to clarify the distinctions among the four terms *phonics, phonetics, phonemics,* and *alphabet.*

28. See the scholarly edition of *John Hart's Works* by Bror Danielsson, Stockholm, Almquist and Wiksell, 1955, pp. 117–118.

29. For further discussion of the principles and use of phonetic alphabets see the following: Charles C. Fries and Agnes C. Fries, *Foundations for English Teaching,* Tokyo, Kenkyusha Ltd., 1961, pp. 347–373 (distributed in the United States by Wahr's University Bookstore, Ann Arbor, Mich.); Leonard Bloomfield, *Language,* New York, Holt, Rinehart and Winston, Inc., 1933, pp. 86–89; Hans Kurath *et al.,* "The Phonetic Alphabet and Other Symbols Used on the Maps," Chapter IV, pp. 122–146, in *Handbook of the Linguistic Geography of New England,* Brown University, Providence, Rhode Island, 1939; Robert W. Albright, *The International Phonetic Alphabet: Its Background and Development,* Part III of Vol. 24 (1958) Number 1 of *International Journal of American Linguistics,* Indiana University Research Center.

30. See page 47 for three of the basic features of the nature of language achieved by 1875.

31. During the last ten or twelve years there has been a growing awareness of the differences between American and European linguists. Differences are to be expected and should cause no concern unless they make impossible or difficult a mutual understanding of the scientific contributions produced by either group. Europeans have had difficulty in thoroughly grasping the significance of American studies, and Americans have not given enough patient effort to understanding the European work. (See Einar Haugen, "Directions in Modern Linguistics," *Language,* XXVII [1951], 211–222.)

Achieving such mutual understanding is part of the function of the International Congress of Linguists. The volume on *Trends in American and European Linguistics,* published for the 1962 meetings of the ninth International Congress, is one step toward this goal.

32. For a list of the American Indian languages in North America and the language families to which they belong see Memoir 9 of the *International Journal of American Linguistics,* entitled *Indian Tribes of North America,* by Harold E. Driver, *et al.,* Bloomington, Ind., Indiana University Publications, 1953, 30 pages and a detailed map. Most of those who have contributed to the development of structural linguistics (through "descriptive" linguistics) in America have been either linguistic anthropologists, like Edward Sapir, Charles Hockett, Carl Voegelin, and Harry Hoijer or linguists who have spent considerable time working with Indian languages, like Leonard Bloomfield, Zellig Harris, and Kenneth Pike.

33. Leonard Bloomfield, review of Ferdinand de Saussure's *Cours de linguistique générale,* 2nd ed., 1922, in *Modern Language Journal,* VIII (1924), 318, 319.

34. Leonard Bloomfield, review of Edward Sapir's *Language,* in *The Classical Weekly,* XV (1922), 142.

35. There is still some confusion in the use of this term. There are those who regard the developments since 1925 as constituting "descriptive linguistics" in contrast with the work of the preceding hundred years which was primarily devoted to "historical linguistics." It is true that the new approach of the last thirty-five years arose in connection with the descriptive analysis of living languages—chiefly the many diverse languages of the American Indians. The term "structural linguistics" came later in an effort to name more precisely the organizing principle of the "descriptive" methods of the new approach. Some still use as interchangeable equivalents the two names "descriptive linguistics" and "structural linguistics." Many, however, have come to believe that the principles of our new "structuralism" apply to the complete range of linguistic data and they are restudying historical linguistic data in terms of the principles and techniques that arose in the new "descriptive" analyses. Moreover, older scholars have insisted that the data upon which to construct language "history" must be soundly "descriptive." In order to avoid confusion, it seems best to follow the more recent practice of using the phrase "structural linguistics" to cover the principles and methods of "structural analysis" whether applied to working with a living informant or working with ancient texts. It is the work with these techniques and methods which has unexpectedly given us a new view and understanding of the nature and functioning of human language. This "structural linguistics" then, applies to both the "descriptive linguistics" of living languages and also the "historical linguistics" of older linguistic forms. The basic difference between the two will be the nature of the evidence and the goal to be achieved. The "structuralism" of the Cercle linguistique de Prague and that of the Cercle linguistique de Copenhagen, differs in a variety of respects from that developed in the United States.

36. Sapir, *Language*, p. 57.

37. Edward Sapir, "Sound Patterns in Language," *Language*, I (1925), 42, 43, 50.

38. *Language*, II (1926), 153–164.

39. *Modern Philology*, XXV (1927), 211–230.

40. Bernard Bloch, "Leonard Bloomfield," *Language*, XXV (1949), 92.

41. Leonard Bloomfield, *Introduction to the Study of Language*, New York: Holt, Rinehart and Winston, Inc., 1914, Preface.

42. See C. C. Fries, "The Bloomfield 'School,'" in *Trends in European and American Linguistics*, Utrecht, The Netherlands; Antwerp, Belgium, Spectrum Publishers, 1961, pp. 196–224; "Meaning and Linguistic Analysis," *Language*, XXX (1954), 57–68; *The Structure of English*, 1957.

43. Sapir, *Language*, p. 234.

44. The purpose of this chapter, which seeks to give only a summary sketch of certain significant achievements of linguistic science during the last 140 years, makes it advisable to exclude extended discussion of the signals which constitute a language code. These matters will be dealt with later in the chapters specifically devoted to analyzing the reading process in the light of the linguistic knowledge of today. See especially Chapter 3, "Language Meanings and Language Signals," and Chapter 4, "The Nature of the Reading Process."

45. The representations in phonemic notation /tɪn/, /kæn/, /nat/, /nak/, identify the sequences of "sounds" (sound contrasts) which constitute the word-patterns; the ordinary letters *tin, can, knot, knock,* represent the spelling-patterns.

46. Richard Grant White, *Words and Their Uses, Past and Present*, New York, Sheldon and Company, 1872 (entered according to Act of Congress, in the year 1870, by Richard Grant White) pp. 297–298.

47. William S. Gray, *The Teaching of Reading and Writing*, Monographs on Fundamental Education X, Paris, UNESCO, 1956, p. 68.

48. A linguistic community is any group of speakers that make the "same" responses to the same set of linguistic stimuli.

49. See the increasing number of studies that seek to restudy and reinterpret historical linguistic data in terms of a "structural" approach, for example, Henry Hoenigswald, *Language Change and Linguistic Reconstruction*, Chicago, University of Chicago Press, 1960. See also other titles listed by Kenneth L. Pike and Eunice V. Pike in *Live Issues in Descriptive Linguistics*, 2nd ed., Santa Ana, Cal., Summer Institute of Linguistics, 1960, VI, 33–34.

50. Sapir, "The Status of Linguistics as a Science," p. 209. See also Harry Hoijer, "Cultural Implications of Some Navaho Linguistic Categories," *Language*, XXVII (1951), 111–120; Harry Hoijer, ed., *Language in Culture: Conference on the Interrelations of Language and Other Aspects of Culture*, Chicago, University of Chicago Press, 1954; John B. Carroll, ed., *Language Thought and Reality, Selected Writings of Benjamin Lee Whorf*, Cambridge, Mass., Massachusetts Institute of Technology, 1956; Robert

Lado, *Linguistics Across Cultures,* Ann Arbor, Mich., University of Michigan Press, 1957. For earlier statements see the following:

The style in which we shall do our thinking, the framework of our reasonings, the matters of our subjective apprehension, the distinctions and relations to which we shall direct our chief attention, are thus determined in the main for us, not by us. In learning to speak with those about us, we learn also to think with them: their traditional habits of mind become ours. In this guidance there is therefore something of constraint, although we are little apt to realize it. Study of a foreign language brings it in some measure to our sense. He who begins to learn a tongue not his own is at first hardly aware of any incommensurability between its signs for ideas and those to which he has been accustomed. But the more intimately he comes to know it, and the more natural and familiar its use becomes to him, so much the more clearly does he see that the dress it puts upon his thoughts modifies their aspect, the more impossible does it grow to him to translate its phrases with satisfactory accuracy into his native speech. The individual is thus unable to enter into a community of language-users without some abridgment of his personal freedom—even though the penalty be wholly insignificant as compared with the accruing benefit. Thus, too, each generation feels always the leading hand, not only of the generation that immediately instructed it, but of all who have gone before, and taken a part in moulding the common speech; and, not least, of those distant ages, whose action determined the grand structural features of each tongue now spoken. Every race is, indeed, as a whole, the artificer of its own speech, and herein is manifested the sum and general effect of its capacities in this special direction of action; but many a one has felt through all the later periods of its history the constraining and laming force of a language unhappily developed in its first stages of formation; which it might have made better, had the work been to do over again, but which now weighs upon its powers with all the forces of disabling inbred habit. Both the intellectual and the historical career of a race is thus in no small degree affected by its speech.

Whitney, *Language and the Study of Language,* pp. 445–446.

The chief intellectual classifications that constitute the working capital of thought have been built up for us by our mother tongue. Our very lack of explicit consciousness in using language that we are employing the intellectual systematizations of the race shows how thoroughly accustomed we have become to its logical distinctions and groupings.

John Dewey, *How We Think,* Boston, D. C. Heath and Co., 1910, p. 175.
51. Sapir, *Language,* p. 8.

52. Whitney, *The Life and Growth of Language*.

53. Fries, *The Teaching of the English Language*.

54. *Ibid.*, p. 44.

55. C. C. Fries, *The Structure of English*, New York, Harcourt, Brace & World, 1952.

56. C. C. Fries, *English Word Lists*, Washington, D.C., American Council on Education, 1940.

57. Kenneth L. Pike, *Pronunciation* (Vol. I of the three volumes of *An Intensive Course in English for Latin-American Students*), Ann Arbor, Mich., English Language Institute of the University of Michigan, 1942, pp. 25–97.

58. C. C. Fries, *The Teaching and Learning of English as a Foreign Language*, Ann Arbor, Mich., University of Michigan Press, 1945.

59. A recent article in *Language Learning*, X (1960), 67–88, Mary Jane Norris, "A List of Descriptions of Present-Day Languages," shows something of the extent of the activity in this type of exploration, and furnishes a helpful list of some of the descriptive analyses useful for further work.

60. Charles C. Fries and Agnes C. Fries, *Foundations for English Teaching*, published for the English Language Exploratory Committee, by Kenkyusha Ltd., Tokyo, 1961. (Distributed in the United States by Wahr's University Book Store, Ann Arbor, Michigan, and by the National Council of Teachers of English.)

61. In *Trends in European and American Linguistics, 1930–1960,* edited on the Occasion of the Ninth International Congress of Linguists, Utrecht, The Netherlands, Spectrum Publishers, 1961.

62. Kenneth L. Pike, *Language in Relation to a Unified Theory of the Structure of Human Behavior,* Glendale, Calif., Summer Institute of Linguistics, Part I, 1954; Part II, 1955; Part III, 1960.

63. Kenneth L. Pike, Presidential address for the Linguistic Society of America, December 28, 1961, published in *Language* XXXVIII (1962).

64. Kenneth L. Pike, "Language as Particle, Wave, and Field," *The Texas Quarterly,* II (1960) 37–54.

65. Bloomfield, *Language,* Chapter 28, "Applications and Outlook," pp. 496–509.

66. Sol Saporta, ed., *Psycholinguistics: A Book of Readings,* New York, Holt, Rinehart and Winston, Inc., 1961, Preface, p. v.

67. John W. Gardner, Foreword, in Charles E. Osgood and Thomas A. Sebeok, eds., *Psycholinguistics: A Survey of Theory and Research Problems,* Publications in Anthropology and Linguistics, Memoir 10, Bloomington, Ind., Indiana University, 1954.

68. See Note 66, above.

69. The memorandum written by Warren Weaver has been reprinted in William N. Locke and A. Donald Booth, eds., *Machine Translation of Languages,* Cambridge, Mass., The Technological Press of the Massachusetts Institute of Technology, 1955, pp. 15–23.

70. See the reports by Paul L. Garvin and Erwin Reifler in *Proceedings of the Eighth International Congress of Linguists,* Oslo, Oslo University Press, 1958, pp. 502–539.

71. *Ibid.,* pp. 503, 505–506.

72. For the many publications on various aspects of the research dealing with the linguistic problems involved, see E. Delavenay and K. Delavenay, *Bibliography of Mechanical Translation* (1959), International Study Group on Mechanical Translation, Paris, UNESCO.

73. Warren Plath, "Mathematical Linguistics," in *Trends in European and American Linguistics, 1930–1960,* pp. 21–57. See also Yuen Ren Chao, "Models in Linguistics and Models in General," in *Logic, Methodology and Philosophy of Science: Proceedings of the 1960 International Congress,* ed. by E. Nagel, P. Suppes, and A. Tarski, Stanford, Calif., Stanford University Press, 1962.

74. Zellig S. Harris, "Discourse Analysis," *Language,* XXVIII (1952), 1–30, and "Discourse Analysis: A Sample Text," *Language,* XXVIII (1952), 474–498.

Other approaches to the problems of dealing with portions of discourse larger than single "sentences" have been shown by Kenneth L. Pike. (See *Language in Relation to a Unified Theory of the Structure of Human Behavior,* Part I, 5, 63, "On Linguistic Units Larger than Sentences.") See also Fries, Chapter XI, " 'Sequence' Sentences and 'Included' Sentences," and Chapter VIII, Section III, pp. 164–172, in *The Structure of English, op. cit.*

75. Harris, "Discourse Analysis," p. 19.

76. *Ibid.*

77. *Ibid.*

78. Zellig S. Harris, "Co-occurrence and Transformation in Linguistic Structure," *Language,* XXXIII (1957), 335. See also his later publication *Strings and Transformations in Language Description,* Papers on Formal Linguistics, Number 1, Philadelphia, The University of Pennsylvania, Department of Linguistics, 1961.

79. Harris, "Co-occurrence and Transformation in Linguistic Structure," pp. 338–399.

80. Harris, *Strings and Transformations in Language Description,* p. 10.

81. Henry Hiż, "Congrammaticality, Batteries of Transformations and Grammatical Categories," in *Proceedings of the Symposia in Applied Mathematics,* Providence, American Mathematical Society, 1960, XII, 1, 13.

82. Noam Chomsky, *Syntactic Structures,* The Hague, The Netherlands, Mouton and Co., 1957, p. 13.

83. Noam Chomsky, "Some Methodological Remarks on Generative Grammar," *Word,* XVII (August 1961), 221–223. For a list of materials of transformation and generative grammar, see Noam Chomsky "On the Notion 'Rule of Grammar,' " in *Structure of Language and Its Mathematical Aspects,* Vol. XII of *Proceedings of the Symposia in Applied Mathematics,* Providence, R.I., American Mathematical Society, 1961, p. 16, n. 14.

CHAPTER THREE

1. See selected quotations given in Chapter One, under the heading "Meaning."

2. Donald D. Durrell, "Development of Comprehension and Interpretation," Chapter IX in *Reading in the Elementary School,* Part II of *The Forty-eighth Yearbook of the National Society for the Study of Education,* Chicago, University of Chicago Press, 1949, p. 199.

3. Arthur I. Gates, "The Nature of the Reading Process," in "Reading in the Elementary School," Part II of *ibid.,* p. 3.

4. C. K. Ogden and I. A. Richards, *The Meaning of Meaning,* first edition 1923, second impression of tenth edition 1952.

5. Leo Abraham, "What Is the Theory of Meaning About?", *The Monist,* XLVI (1936), 228–256.

6. W. B. Pillsbury, "Meaning and Image," *Psychological Review,* 1908, p. 156.

7. C. W. Morris, *Signs, Language and Behavior,* Englewood Cliffs, N.J., Prentice-Hall, Inc., 1946, p. 19.

8. J. R. Firth, "General Linguistics and Descriptive Grammar," in *Transactions of the Philological Society* (1950), London, 1951, p. 82.

9. John B. Carroll, *A Survey of Linguistics and Related Disciplines,* Cambridge, Mass., Harvard University Press, 1950, p. 15.

10. Leonard Bloomfield, *Language,* New York, Holt, Rinehart and Winston, Inc., 1933, pp. 139–140.

11. Bernard Bloch, "A Set of Postulates for Phonemic Analysis," *Language,* XXIV (1948), 5–6, note 8.

12. Leonard Bloomfield, *Linguistic Aspects of Science,* Chicago, University of Chicago Press, 1944, p. 13.

13. Leonard Bloomfield, "Language or Ideas," *Language,* XII (1936), 92, note 6. Bloomfield followed A. P. Weiss in objecting to the term *behaviorism* and believed that the word *physicalism* indicated much better the essential quality of the kind of descriptive statements he sought.

14. Bloomfield, *Language,* p. 27.

15. Leonard Bloomfield, "Linguistics as a Science," *Studies in Philology,* XXVII (1930), 555.

16. The use of this diagram and the fact that the words *stimulus* and *response* occur in the explanation of the illustration must not be taken as evidence of any general underlying psychological theory.

17. Here we shall refer to the older American Morse code as simply the Morse code, and the present international telegraph code as the international code.

18. For the particular purpose here it seems unnecessary to complicate the picture and spoil the usefulness of the illustration by commenting on the fact that, of course, our telegraphic codes depend upon language and essentially upon the writing system of a language. They are codes of codes

several times removed. More than that, simply from the point of view of code features, a language is a much more complicated structure.

19. See also Chapter Two, the section entitled "Structural Units and Word Patterns."

20. See also Chapter Two, the section entitled "Structural Units and Grammar," and C. C. Fries, *The Structure of English,* New York, Harcourt, Brace & World, Inc., 1952.

21. In discussing the problems of the "parts of speech"—the major form-classes of a language like English—it is necessary to make a distinction between

(a) the procedures and the criteria which the analyst uses to determine what the "parts of speech" (the functioning form-classes) of a particular language are, and,

(b) the "markers" or the signals by means of which the users (speakers and hearers) of that language identify these various "parts of speech" as the functioning units in the patterns that signal grammatical meanings.

As for (a), the linguistic analyst must discover for each separate language how many and what particular parts of speech (word-classes that are functioning units in the contrastive patterns of grammatical signals) must be identified. The structural system of each language will demand its own special kind and number of "parts of speech" (if any) and the precise procedures for determining and identifying the kind and the number will vary in their usefulness from language to language. In my *Structure of English* (1952), Chapter V attempted to give something of the procedure I used for this purpose as I approached a body of fifty hours of mechanically recorded conversation in English. Chapter V does *not* present the "markers" by which the users of the language (the speakers and the hearers) identify these form-classes as functioning units of grammatical patterns. The significant "markers" for English form-classes (see (b), following) are presented in Chapter VIII of *Structure of English.*

As for (b), the markers of the "parts of speech," there seem to be no common features that will be applicable to all languages. Lexical meaning has not provided (in English, for example) any really useful criteria for the speaker-hearer to use in identifying these contrastive units of the patterns that signal the structures to which grammatical meanings are attached. The meaning of *thing* does not attach to a bare vocabulary entry in a dictionary. The shape *stone* takes on a "thing-word" or "action-word" meaning only as certain markers such as "a stone" or "two stones" or an "action-word" meaning as in "to stone a . . ." or "he stoned a . . ." identify a particular form-class for it, and then the shape *stone* takes on the form-class meaning.

The meaning of "thing" or "action" cannot be the basis of identifying the words as belonging to certain form-classes, for these meanings attach to the words only after the markers have identified the words as belonging to the form-class.

22. See Fries, *The Structure of English*, Chapter VIII, "Structural Patterns of Sentences"; Chapter IX, " 'Subjects' and 'Objects' "; Chapter X, " 'Modifiers' "; and Chapter XII, "Immediate Constituents."

23. The conventional view that a "rising intonation" at the ends of questions signals the distinction between questions and statements, seems untenable in the light of the facts brought out in recent studies of intonation (see Kenneth L. Pike, *The Intonation of American English*, Ann Arbor, Mich., University of Michigan Press, 1945, and C. C. Fries, *On the Intonation of "Yes-No" Questions in English*, London: Longmans Green, in press). The facts seem to support the conclusion that in English there is no *question intonation pattern*, as such. When one brings together a large number of instances of all types of questions the proportion of falling intonation patterns they will bear is overwhelming. Of course, when one compares the intonation patterns of all yes-no questions with the intonation patterns of all other types of questions, he will find that, even with the ratio of three to two in favor of falling intonation patterns for yes-no questions, which the evidence supports, there will be a higher proportion of rising intonation patterns on yes-no questions than on other question types. But there seem to be no intonation sequences on questions as a whole that are not also found on other types of utterances, and no intonation sequences on other types of utterances that are not found on questions.

24. In America, the ground-breaking study by Kenneth L. Pike (1941–1942) was the first to approach the problems of English intonation in terms of the assumptions and principles of the "structural linguistics" especially stimulated by Edward Sapir and Leonard Bloomfield. The results of this study were published in a book entitled *Pronunciation* which he contributed as Volume I of the three-volume *Intensive Course in English*, copyrighted in June 1942, by the English Language Institute of the University of Michigan. In this book of 1942 (pages 26 to 97), Pike summarized his significant conclusions. These results were incorporated in the revised *Intensive Course* published in 1943, and then expanded and published in the spring of 1945 in his book entitled *The Intonation of American English*. A few of the especially significant conclusions set forth in the book of 1942 are given below, briefly and with oversimplification.

(1) The absolute pitch of a syllable (the number of vibrations per second) as such, is not significant. The relative pitch of one syllable to another is all important.

(2) English has four significant contrastive levels:
    (1) extra-high (two steps above the usual voice level)
    (2) high (one step above the usual voice level)
    (3) mid (the usual level of the speaker's voice)
    (4) low (one step below the usual voice level)
    "It makes no difference how far apart 1 and 4 may be; English intonation will come out quite satisfactorily if 2 and 3

are spaced between. Personal habits and differences, and various styles of speaking partially determine the particular set
of intervals in use at a particular time" (p. 33).

(3) The significant intonation patterns, in general, cover phrases,
that is, groups of syllables or words, rather than single syllables
(p. 32).

(4) Primary intonation patterns occur at the ends of utterances. A
pattern begins at the "peg," the place of the "intonation turn," and
extends to the end of the phrase (p. 35).

(5) The syllables immediately following the "peg" form the "post-
peg" section of the intonation pattern. The semantic feature is
expressed only as a result of the total peg–post-peg effect. It demands the complete peg–post-peg intonation phrase (p. 35).

(6) "Pre-peg" variations of pitch are not structurally significant for
the primary contours.

(7) The marking of the significant intonation patterns can thus be
schematic and relative rather than an attempt to represent the
precise tones of each of the syllables. For the primary contours
or intonation patterns, the notation can, therefore, be limited to
the following:

(a) the direction of the tone immediately following the beginning
of the "peg" or intonation "turn,"

(b) the tone level reached by this change,

(c) the direction of the final change from this tone level, and

(d) the tone level reached by the final movement of tone.

(8) Such a schematic representation can ignore the variations of tone
in the material preceding the peg syllable and identify only the
distinctive features of the intonation pattern, as listed in the preceding paragraph (no. 7). The following are examples, marked
with the notation developed in 1943 for the intonation material
of the *Intensive Course*

	Pattern
He went to the office	3–2–4
What did you tell him	3–2–4
When will he come	3–2–4
Do you know him	3–2–1
Is he a young man	3–2–4
You have no books	3–2

25. The term "social-cultural" meaning is by no means a completely
satisfactory name for the rather wide range of meanings to be included
here. As a matter of fact, all the meanings attaching to any of the features
of language—the "words," the grammatical structures, the intonation sequences—can truly be said to arise out of and depend upon the social-

cultural situations in which the particular language materials are used. Here, however, I seek to designate in some way the many kinds of meanings that attach to the utterances as unique wholes rather than to any or all of their replaceable parts. Instead of trying to define "social-cultural" meaning by further general statements, I shall depend upon the instances to which the label is here attached, to build up an understanding of the varieties of meaning I would include under this semi-technical use of the term.

CHAPTER FOUR

1. William S. Gray, "How Well Do Adults Read?", in *Adult Reading, Part II of The Fifty-fifth Yearbook of the National Society for the Study of Education,* Chicago, University of Chicago Press, 1956, p. 38. See Table 2 on p. 37, quoted by Gray from Ambrose Caliver, *Literacy Education: National Statistics and Other Related Data,* United States Office of Education Circular No. 376, Washington, D.C., Government Printing Office, 1953.

2. Part I of *The Twenty-fourth Yearbook of the National Society for the Study of Education,* Bloomington, Ill., Public School Publishing Company, 1925 (especially Chapter II).

3. *The Teaching of Reading: A Second Report,* Part I of *The Thirty-sixth Yearbook of the National Society for the Study of Education,* Bloomington, Ill., Public School Publishing Company, 1937 (especially Chapter II). Quotations following are from pp. 25–28.

4. William S. Gray, "Reading and Factors Influencing Reading Efficiency," Chapter II in *Reading in General Education,* Washington, D.C., American Council on Education, 1940, p. 50.

5. William S. Gray, Chapter III in *Reading in the High School and College,* Part II of *The Forty-seventh Yearbook of the National Society for the Study of Education,* Chicago, University of Chicago Press, 1948, pp. 27–45.

6. Gray, "How Well Do Adults Read?", pp. 33–34. See also William S. Gray, *The Teaching of Reading and Writing, an International Survey,* Monographs in Fundamental Education X, Paris, UNESCO, 1956, Chapter III, especially pp. 59, 60.

7. Ruth Strang, "The Nature of Reading," in Ruth Strang, Constance M. McCullough, and Arthur E. Traxler, eds., *Problems in the Improvement of Reading,* 2nd ed., New York, McGraw-Hill Book Company, Inc., 1955, p. 62.

8. Arthur I. Gates, "The Nature of the Reading Process," in *Reading in the Elementary School,* Part II of *The Forty-eighth Yearbook of the National Society for the Study of Education,* Chicago, University of Chicago Press, 1949, pp. 3, 4.

9. The view expressed here is in opposition to that expressed by Rudolf Flesch in *Why Johnny Can't Read, and What You Can Do About It,* New York, Harper & Row, Publishers, 1955, p. 23:

Many years ago, when I was about fifteen, I took a semester's course in Czech; I have since forgotten everything about the language itself, but I still remember how the letters are pronounced, plus the simple rule that all words have the accent on the first syllable. Armed with this knowledge, I once surprised a native of Prague by reading aloud from a Czech newspaper. "Oh, you know Czech?" he asked. "No, I don't understand a word of it," I answered. "I can only read it."

10. Because of the fact that in 1929 only about fifteen percent of the Turkish population could read and write, this change in the writing system to represent their language did not constitute so great a revolution as it would in countries with much higher proportions of literacy.

11. Dr. Henry Bradley, the senior editor of the *Oxford English Dictionary* from 1915 until his death in 1923, learned to read at the age of four, without any instruction, but simply by watching his father as he read the Bible aloud at family prayers. In the reading his father moved his finger along the lines of print. But Henry sat around the corner from his father at the table and thus learned to read with the book held upside down. Later he learned to read print that was right side up. But all his life he read with complete ease and efficiency books which he held upside down. His daughters also read in similar fashion with equal ease.

12. John Hart, *A Methode or comfortable beginning for all vnlearned, whereby they may bee taught to read English, in a very short time, with pleasure,* London, Henrie Denham, 1570, Preface, fol. IVa.

13. Irving H. Anderson and Walter F. Dearborn, *The Psychology of Teaching Reading,* New York, The Ronald Press Company, 1952, p. 204. Copyright 1952 The Ronald Press Company.

14. The simplification here is somewhat like that of the newer international telegraphic code with only two basic contrastive elements, in contrast with the older American Morse code with four. See Chapter Three, section on "Language Signals."

15. *Report of the President of Columbia University for the Year Ending June 30, 1943,* 44th Series, Number 3, New York, December 2, 1943. See also Fries, *The Structure of English,* Chapter II, pp. 9–28, for a discussion of "What Is a Sentence?"

16. See, however, the discussion of "lines" in Chapter Seven.

CHAPTER FIVE

1. Leonard Bloomfield, "Linguistics and Reading," *The Elementary English Review,* XIX (April 1942), 125–130, and XIX (May 1942), 183–186. See also Bloomfield's *Language,* New York, Holt, Rinehart and Winston, Inc., 1933, pp. 500–503, and Chapter 17, "Written Records."

2. From *Why Johnny Can't Read* by Rudolf Flesch, pp. 9–10. Copyright © 1955 by Harper & Row, Publishers, Incorporated. Reprinted by permission of the publishers.

3. Flesch, *Why Johnny Can't Read,* pp. 120–122.

4. Bloomfield, "Linguistics and Reading," p. 129. Reprinted with the permission of the National Council of Teachers of English.

5. Flesch, *op. cit.,* pp. 100, 108.

6. Irving H. Anderson and Walter F. Dearborn, *The Psychology of Teaching Reading,* New York, The Ronald Press Company, 1952, pp. 210–211. Copyright 1952 The Ronald Press Company.

7. Paul Witty, "Phonics Study and Word Analysis—I," *Elementary English,* XXX (May 1953), 296–305, and "Phonics Study and Word Analysis—II," *Elementary English,* XXX (October 1953), 375–383.

8. See the reports of the *International Congresses of Phonetic Sciences* held in Amsterdam, The Netherlands, in 1932; in London, England, in 1935; in Ghent, Belgium, in 1938; in Helsinki, Finland, September 4–9, 1961. See also Kenneth L. Pike, *Phonetics,* Ann Arbor, Mich., University of Michigan Press, 1943; R. M. S. Heffner, *General Phonetics,* Madison, Wis., University of Wisconsin Press, 1949; Daniel Jones, *An Outline of English Phonetics,* 8th ed., Cambridge, England, W. Heffer and Sons, Ltd., 1957; Martin Joos, *Acoustic Phonetics,* Language Monograph No. 23, Linguistic Society of America, 1948; and Eli Fischer-Jorgensen, "What Can the New Techniques of Acoustic Phonetics Contribute to Linguistics?", in *Proceedings of the Eighth International Congress of Linguists,* Oslo, Oslo University Press, 1958, pp. 433–438.

9. Irving H. Anderson, "The Psychology of Learning to Read," *School of Education Bulletin* (University of Michigan), XIX (December 1947), 36.

10. Anderson and Dearborn, *op. cit.,* p. 209.

11. E. W. Dolch, "Phonics in the First Grade," *Elementary English,* XXXII (December 1955), 515.

12. E. W. Dolch, "Am I Teaching Phonics Right?" in *Elementary English,* XXXIV (April 1957), 228.

13. Witty, "Phonics Study and Word Analysis—II," p. 374. The last sentence of this group is quoted by Witty from A. I. Gates, *The Improvement of Reading,* New York, The Macmillan Company, 1947.

14. William S. Gray, *The Teaching of Reading and Writing,* Monographs on Fundamental Education X, Paris, UNESCO, 1956, p. 79.

15. H. E. Waits, *Course in Phonics,* Milwaukee, The Bruce Publishing Company, 1925, pp. 2, 57–58, 60. For the stress on "ear training" see also Donald D. Durrell and Helen A. Murphy, "The Auditory Discrimination Factor in Reading Readiness and Reading Disability," *Education,* LXXIII (1953), 556, 560:

> The child who learns to read easily is one who notices the separate sounds in spoken words. . . .
> The ability is not assured by a high mental age or by elaborate exercises in "phonics" which consist in giving sounds of letters and blends. An excellent illustration of this point was a ten-year-old with an I.Q. of 166, a mental age of 17, and enviable clarity

and fluency of speech, but with a reading vocabulary of sixty words. This boy had been in school five years and could give the sounds of letters and blends with high facility. He did not have the slightest notion, however, of the first letter in the spoken words *magic, machine,* and *motion.* After the words had been repeated, he said hesitantly, "Is it T?" After lessons in ear training, he caught the idea and its importance. His report is revealing. "I knew there was some trick to it. The words have sounds in them and you just match the sound with the way the word looks. I suppose that's why they taught me phonics all these years." It is pleasing to report that this exceptional boy made eight years' progress in reading in the following three months.

Of course, ability to identify sounds in spoken words is not the sole requisite for learning to read. Other abilities are required, such as visual discrimination of word elements, ability to sustain attention in beginning reading, relating words to meanings, etc., but the skill in which the child is usually most deficient is in noticing the separate sounds in spoken words.

16. Arthur I. Gates and David H. Russell, "Workbooks, Vocabulary Control, Phonics, and Other Factors in Beginning Reading," in C. W. Hunnicutt and William J. Iverson eds., *Research in The Three R's,* New York, Harper & Row, Publishers, 1958, pp. 88–89.

17. Lucille D. Schoolfield and Josephine B. Timberlake, *Sounds the Letters Make,* Boston, Little, Brown & Company, Inc., 1940, pp. 2, 4, 27, 36. Copyright 1940, by Lucille D. Schoolfield and Josephine B. Timberlake.

18. Romalda Bishop Spalding, with Walter T. Spalding, *The Writing Road to Reading,* New York, Whiteside, Inc., and William Morrow & Company, Inc., 1957, p. 27.

19. Mabel Aspden, "Phonetics Related to Listening and Reading Skills," *The Reading Teacher,* XIV (November 1960), 112. The word *phonetics* appears throughout this article; the practices are those of *phonics.*

20. Gertrude Hildreth, "Some Misconceptions Concerning Phonics," *Elementary English,* XXXVI (January 1957), 26, 27.

21. Known especially for his *On Early English Pronunciation,* published by the Early English Text Society, Extra Series, 2, 7, 14, 23, 56.

22. "Report on Phonetics," *The Massachusetts Teacher,* VI (1853), 25–28. See also "The Phonetic Method with Pronouncing Orthography in It's Relations to Other Methods," *The Addresses and Journal of Proceedings of the National Educational Association,* 1873, pp. 207–219.

23. George Farnham in the Preface to his book, *The Sentence Method of Teaching Reading, Writing and Spelling, a Manual for Teachers,* Syracuse, N.Y., C. W. Bardeen, Publisher, 1881, writes the following:

In 1858, the phonetic system was introduced into the schools of Syracuse, New York, and for a time it was thought that the true method of teaching children to read had been discovered. After a trial of five years, however, it was seen that while pupils learned to read by this method in much less time than usual, and attained a high state of excellence in articulation, their reading was nearly as mechanical as before, and few of them became good spellers. The two systems of analysis, phonic and graphic, had so little in common that permanent confusion was produced in the mind.

He probably means the "phonetic method" as described here, in spite of the word *phonic* in the same paragraph. The contrast of *phonic* with *graphic* as two systems of analysis would seem to support that view.

24. In *A Methode or comfortable beginning* . . . , fols. Ib–IIb, Hart writes concerning his alphabet as follows:

> Then followeth the newe maner of teaching, whereby who so can read English onely, may alone learne the order folowing, and so bee able to teach the same to others that knowe no letter, to reade thereafter in a very short time. . . .
> . . . méete for any man that would write the Welsh. As by the way of pastime, I haue done from a Welshmans mouth, though I vnderstood no worde thereof, and did reade it againe to him, and diuers others of that language, so as one amongst them (which knew me not) sayde vnto the rest in Welsh, that I coulde speake Welsh so well as he. But the rest knowing the contrary, laughing tolde me what he sayde, whom I forthwith certified, that I did it, by an order and certaine knowledge what I did write, and not by any acquaintance with the tongue. The like haue I done to the Irishe, and may as easily doe of the Barbarian, or Russian speaches, or any other so straunge as they, hearing them distinctly spoken. And though I vse not their letters or maner of writing, I would well hope so to write, as at any time thereafter séeing it, I should be able to reade and pronounce it againe, euen as he that I heard it of, spake it vnto me. And I haue of late experimented and prooued the certaintie and profite, in the ease and readinesse of the sayde newe maner of teaching, to the comfort of diuers which are extant and liuing, to certifie such as maye doubt thereof: and so the same is most profitable for such as can not read, and are otherwise out of al hope euer to be able to attain to read.

25. The following is from *The Works of Benjamin Franklin*, ed. by John Bigelow, 1904, II, 30–41.

Diir Madam :—ḥi abdſiekſiyn.iu meek to rektifyiiŋ aur alfabet, "ḥat it uil bi atended uiḥ inkanviniensiz and difikyltiz," iz e natural uyn ; far it aluaz akyrz huen eni reſarmeſiyn is propozed ; hueḥyr in rilidſiyn,

gyvernment, laz, and iven daun az lo az rods and huil
karidfiiz.   Ꭷi tru kuestfiyn Ꭷen, is nat hueꭷyr Ꭷaer
uil bi no difikyltiz ar inkanviniensiz, byt hueꭷyr Ꭷi
difikyltiz mê nat bi syrmaunted; and hueꭷyr Ꭷi kan-
viniensiz uil nat, an Ꭷi huol, bi grêtyr Ꭷan Ꭷi inkanviniensiz.   In Ꭷis kes, Ꭷi difikyltiz er onli in Ꭷi biginiŋ
av Ꭷi praktis; huen Ꭷê er uŋns ovyrkym, Ꭷi advan-
tedfiez er lastiŋ.—To yiꭷyr iu ar mi, hu spel uel in
Ꭷi prezent mod, yi imadfiin Ꭷi difikylti av tfiendfiiŋ
Ꭷat mod far Ꭷi nu, iz nat so grêt, byt Ꭷat ui myit
pyrfektli git ovyr it in a uiik's ryitiŋ.—Az to Ꭷoz hu
du nat spel uel, if Ꭷi tu difikyltiz er kympêrd, viz.,
Ꭷat av titfiiŋ Ꭷem tru speliŋ in Ꭷi prezent mod, and
Ꭷat av titfiiŋ Ꭷem Ꭷi nu alfabet and Ꭷi nu speliŋ
akardiŋ to it, yi am kanfident Ꭷat Ꭷi latyr uuld bi
byi far Ꭷi liist.   Ꭷê natyrali fal into Ꭷi nu meꭷyd
alrehdi, az mytfi az Ꭷi imperfekfiyn av Ꭷêr alfabet
uil admit av; Ꭷêr prezent bad speliŋ iz onli bad,
bikaz kantreri to Ꭷi prezent bad ruls; yndyr Ꭷi nu
ruls it uuld bi gud.—Ꭷi difikylti av lyrniŋ to spel uel
in Ꭷi old uê iz so grêt, Ꭷat fiu atên it; ꭷauzands
and ꭷauzands ryitiŋ an to old edfi, uiꭷaut ever biiŋ
ebil to akuyir it.   'T iz, bisyidz, e difikylti kantinuali
inkriisiŋ, az Ꭷi saund graduali veriz mor and mor
fram Ꭷi speliŋ; and to farenyrs¹ it mêks Ꭷi lyrniŋ
to pronauns aur laŋuedfi, az riten in aur buks, almost
impasibil.

Nau az to "Ꭷi inkanviniensiz" iu menfiyn.—Ꭷi
fyrst iz, Ꭷat "aal aur etimalodfiiz uuld bi last, kan-
sikuentli ui kuld nat asyrteen Ꭷi miiniŋ av meni
uyrds."—Etimalodfiiz er at prezent veri ynsyrteen;
byt sytfi az Ꭷê er, Ꭷi old buks uuld stil prizyrv Ꭷem,
and etimalodfiists uuld fyind Ꭷem.   Uyrds in Ꭷi
kors av tyim, tfiendfi Ꭷer miiniŋs, az uel az Ꭷer speliŋ

*and pronynsiefiyn; and ui du nat luk to etimalodfii
far 'her prezent miiniŋs. If yi fiuld kal e man e neev
and e vilen, hi uuld hardli bi satisfyid uih myi teliŋ
him, 'hat uyn av 'hi uyrds oridfiinali signifyid onli e
lad ar syrvant; and 'hi yhyr, an yndyr plauman, ar
'hi inhabitant av e viledfi. It iz fram prezent iusedfi
onli, 'hi miiniŋ av uyrds iz to bi dityrmined.*

*Iur sekynd inkanviniens iz, 'hat "'hi distinkfiyn
bituiin uyrds av difyrent miiniŋ and similar saund
uuld bi distrayid."—'hat distinkfiyn iz alreadi distrayid in pronaunsiŋ 'hem; and ui rilyi an 'hi sens
alon av 'hi sentens to asyrteen, huitfi av 'hi several
uyrds, similar in saund, ui intend. If 'his iz syfifient
in 'hi rapidtti av diskors, it uil bi mutfi mor so in
riten sentenses, huitfi mê bi red lezfiurli, and atended
to mor partikularli in kes av difikylti, 'han ui kan
atend to e pafit sentens, huyil e spikyr iz hyryiiŋ ys
alaŋ uih nu uyns.*

*Iur hyrd inkanviniens iz, 'hat "aal 'hi buks alredi
riten uuld bi iusles."—'his inkanviniens uuld onli kym
an graduali, in e kors av edfies. Iu and yi, and yhyr
nau liviŋ ridyrs, uuld hardli farget 'hi ius av 'hem.
Piipil uuld loŋ lyrn to riid 'hi old ryitiŋ, 'ho 'hê praktist
'hi nu.—And 'hi inkanviniens iz nat greter 'han huat
hes aktuali hapend in e similar kes, in Iteli. Farmerli
its inhabitants aal spok and rot Latin; az 'hi laŋuedfi
tfiendfid, 'hi speliŋ falo'd it. It iz tru 'hat, at prezent,
e miir ynlern'd Italien kanat riid 'hi Latin buks; 'ho
'hê er stil red and yndyrstud byi meni. Byt, if 'hi speliŋ had nevyr bin tfiendfied, hi uuld nau hev faund it
mytfi mor difikylt to riid and ryit hiz on laŋuadfi;
far riten uyrds uuld heve had no rilêfiyn to saunds,
'hê uuld onli hev stud far 'hiŋs; so 'hat if hi uuld
ekspres in ryitiŋ 'hi yidia hi hez huen hi saunds 'hi*

uyrd Vescovo, *hi myst iuz ħi letterz* Episcopus.—*In ħart, huatever ħi difikyltiz and inkanviniensiz nau er, ħê uil bi mor iizili syrmaunted nau, ħan hiraftyr; and sym tyim ar yħyr, it myst bi dyn; ar aur ryitiŋ uil bikym ħi sêm uiħ ħi Tħyiniiz,¹ az to ħi difikylti av lyrniŋ and iuzing it. And it uuld alredi hev bin sytfi, if ui had kantinud ħi Saksyn speliŋ and ryitiŋ, iuzed byi our forfaħers.*

yi am, myi diir frind, iurs afekfiynetli,

B. FRANKLIN.

Lyndyn,
Kreven-striit, Sept. 28, 1768.

26. See Chapter Two, the section "Phonetics" and the section "Structural Units and Word Patterns."

27. A. Sterl Artley, "Controversial Issues Relating to Word Perception," *The Reading Teacher,* VIII (April 1955), 198.

28. Evelyn Wenzel, "Common Sense in Spelling Instruction," *Elementary English,* XXV (1948), 517.

29. Julie Hay and Charles E. Wingo, *Teacher's Manual for Reading with Phonics,* Philadelphia, J. B. Lippincott Company, 1948, pp. 10–11.

30. F. H. Vizetelly, *A Desk-Book of 25,000 Words Frequently Mispronounced.*

31. J. W. Barlow, *Basic Spanish,* New York, Appleton-Century-Crofts, 1940, pp. 1, 2. For an opposite point of view using a phonetic approach to the actual pronunciation without regard for the spelling, see Henry Sweet, *A Primer of Spoken English,* 4th ed., Oxford, Clarendon Press, 1906 (1st ed. 1890).

32. Dolch, "Phonics in the First Grade," p. 515.

33. See the descriptive analysis of the "production mechanisms" and the "controlling mechanisms" in K. L. Pike's *Phonetics,* pp. 83–156.

34. See "The Phonetic Alphabet and Other Symbols Used on the Maps," in Hans Kurath *et al., Handbook of the Linguistic Geography of New England,* Providence, R.I., Brown University, 1939, Chapter IV, pp. 122–146.

35. See the discussion "Structural Units of Word Patterns" in Chapter Two.

36. See the following publications and the bibliographies they contain: Marcel Cohen, *La grande invention de l'écriture et son évolution,* Texte, Plances, Documentation et Index. Paris, Imprimerie nationale, Librairie C. Klincksieck, 1958; I. J. Gelb, *A Study of Writing: The Foundation of Grammatology,* Chicago, University of Chicago Press, 1952; C. F. Voegelin and

F. M. Voegelin, "Typological Classification of Systems with Included, Excluded, and Self-Sufficient Alphabets," *Anthropological Linguistics,* III (January 1961), 55–96; David Diringer, *The Alphabet: A Key to the History of Mankind,* New York, Philosophical Library, Inc., 1948; John Chadwick, *The Decipherment of Linear B,* New York, Random House, Inc., With Postscript 1959 (first printing Cambridge, England, Cambridge University Press, 1958); Samuel Noah Kramer, *History Begins at Sumer,* New York, Doubleday & Company, Inc., 1959 (first printing, Indian Hills, Colo., The Falcon's Wing Press, 1956); J. Berry, "The Making of Alphabets," in *Proceedings of the Eighth International Congress of Linguists,* pp. 752–770; Holger Pedersen, "Inscriptions and Archeological Discoveries, the Study of the History of Writing," *Linguistic Science in the Nineteenth Century,* Copenhagen, University of Copenhagen, 1924, trans. by John Webster Spargo, Cambridge, Mass., Harvard University Press, 1931; Leonard Bloomfield, "Written Records," *Language,* pp. 281–296.

37. Dr. Samuel Noah Kramer (Clark Research Professor of Assyriology at the University of Pennsylvania and Curator of the tablet collections at the University Museum there), *History Begins at Sumer.* Reprinted by permission of The Falcon's Wing Press. The following statements are especially significant.

> One remarkable fact is that only a century ago nothing was known even of the existence of these Sumerians in ancient days. The archeologists and scholars, who, some hundred years ago, began excavating in that part of the Middle East known as Mesopotamia were looking not for Sumerians but for Assyrians and Babylonians. On these peoples and their civilizations they had considerable information from Greek and Hebrew sources, but of Sumer and the Sumerians they had no inkling. There was no recognizable trace either of the land or of its people in the entire literature available to the modern scholar. The very name Sumer had been erased from the mind and memory of man for more than two thousand years.
>
> Yet today the Sumerians are one of the best-known peoples of the ancient Near East. We know what they looked like from their own statues and steles scattered throughout several of the more important museums in this country and abroad. Here, too, will be found an excellent representative cross section of their material culture—the columns and bricks with which they built their temples and palaces, their tools and weapons, pots and vases, harps and lyres, jewels and ornaments. Moreover, Sumerian clay tablets by the tens of thousands (literally), inscribed with their business, legal, and administrative documents, crowd the collections of these same museums, giving us much information about the social structure and administrative organization of the ancient Sumerians. Indeed—and this is where archeology, because of its

mute and static character, is usually least productive—we can even penetrate to a certain extent into their hearts and souls. We actually have a large number of Sumerian clay documents on which are inscribed the literary creations revealing Sumerian religion, ethics, and philosophy. And all this because the Sumerians were one of the very few peoples who not only probably invented a system of writing, but also developed it into a vital and effective instrument of communication.

It was probably toward the end of the *fourth* millennium B.C., about five thousand years ago, that the Sumerians, as a result of their economic and administrative needs, came upon the idea of writing on clay. Their first attempts were crude and pictographic; they could be used only for the simplest administrative notations. But in the centuries that followed, the Sumerian scribes and teachers gradually so modified and molded their system of writing that it completely lost its pictographic character and became a highly conventionalized and purely phonetic system of writing. In the second half of the third millennium B.C., the Sumerian writing technique had become sufficiently plastic and flexible to express without difficulty the most complicated historical and literary compositions.

38. See Chadwick, *op. cit.*, p. 67 (the following quotation is from an address by Ventris in June 1952):

> During the last few weeks, I have come to the conclusion that the Knossos and Pylos tablets must, after all, be written in Greek— a difficult and archaic Greek, seeing that it is 500 years older than Homer and written in a rather abbreviated form, but Greek nevertheless.

The following quotation, on p. 86, is from Professor Sittig, who earlier had advanced a different line of decipherment:

> "I repeat: your demonstrations are cryptographically the most interesting I have yet heard of, and are really fascinating. If you are right, the methods of the archaeology, ethnology, history, and philology of the last fifty years are reduced *ad absurdum*." And a week later: "I am extremely grateful to you for your most interesting news of the new inscription, which removes all doubt and completely verifies your assumption."

And on p. 133:

> It [the decipherment of Linear B] has pushed back some seven centuries the date of the earliest Greek inscriptions, and thus extended our knowledge of the Greek language, which now has a continuous recorded history totalling thirty-three centuries, a record rivalled only by Chinese.

The significance for the Greek language of this accomplishment would be comparable to the discovery of a text in "English" of a period about 700 years before our only text of Beowulf, dated about A.D. 1000.

39. Gelb, *op. cit.,* p. v.

40. There has been considerable confusion concerning graphic units of this kind. The older practice of calling such units *ideograms* and the writing that uses them *ideographic* ("idea"-writing) has been misleading. As Bloomfield states it, "The important thing about writing is precisely this, that the characters represent not features of the practical world ('ideas'), but features of the writers' language; a better name accordingly would be *word-writing* or *logographic-writing*" (*Language,* p. 285).

41. *Antiquity,* XXVII (1953), 202.

42. Gelb, *op. cit.,* pp. 164, 115.

43. These syllables make the following words:

> Oh Abie see de two bees
> Hell, them ain't no bees
> Oh yes they are, one is

An example of the same type of syllabary use of letters of the French alphabet is the following (Cohen, *op. cit.,* p. 367):

l n n é	o p y	l i a é t	l v	l i a
Hélène est née	au pays grec,	elle y a été	élevée,	elle y a

m é	l i a	v q	l i é	d c d	a g	é k c
aimé,	elle y a	vécu,	elle y est	décédée,	agée	et cassée.

44. Voegelin and Voegelin, *op. cit.,* p. 89. This typological classification of alphabetic systems, although technical, repays patient study.

CHAPTER SIX

1. See Kenneth L. Pike, *Phonetics,* Ann Arbor, Mich., University of Michigan Press, 1943, 3rd printing 1947, pp. 149–156, for a brief statement of the many items to be considered in a systematic description of any sound. See also the following excerpt from Leonard Bloomfield, *Language,* New York, Holt, Rinehart and Winston, Inc., 1933, pp. 84–85:

> Some persons have an aptitude for hearing and reproducing foreign speech-sounds; we say that such persons are good imitators or have a "good ear." Most other people, if they hear enough of a foreign language, or if they are carefully instructed, will in time learn to understand and make themselves understood. Practical phoneticians sometimes acquire great virtuosity in discriminating and reproducing all manner of strange sounds. In this, to be sure, there lies some danger for linguistic work. Having learned to discriminate many kinds of sounds, the phonetician may turn to some language. new or familiar, and insist upon recording all the

distinctions he has learned to discriminate, even when in this language they are non-distinctive and have no bearing whatever. Thus, having learned, say in the study of Chinese, to hear the difference between an aspirated *p, t, k* (as we usually have it in words like *spin, stick, skin*), the phonetician may clutter up his record of English by marking the aspiration wherever he hears it, while in reality its presence or absence has nothing to do with the meaning of what is said. The chief objection to this procedure is its inconsistency. The phonetician's equipment is personal and accidental; he hears those acoustic features which are discriminated in the languages he has observed. Even his most "exact" record is bound to ignore innumerable non-distinctive features of sound; the ones that appear in it are selected by accidental and personal factors. There is no objection to a linguist's describing all the acoustic features that he can hear, provided he does not confuse these with the phonemic features. He should remember that his hearing of non-distinctive features depends upon the accident of his personal equipment, and that his most elaborate account cannot remotely approach the value of a mechanical record.

Only two kinds of linguistic records are scientifically relevant. One is a mechanical record of the gross acoustic features, such as is produced in the phonetics laboratory. The other is a record in terms of phonemes, ignoring all features that are not distinctive in the language. Until our knowledge of acoustics has progressed far beyond its present state, only the latter kind of record can be used for any study that takes into consideration the meaning of what is spoken.

2. See the following quotations for a discussion of the problem concerning West Semitic syllabaries.

Perhaps the single most important revolutionary concept in this book is Gelb's assignment of the West Semitic systems to the syllabic stage. Others have preceded Gelb in alluding to the syllabic character of the West Semitic systems; Gelb names F. Praetorius, S. Yeivin, E. Schwyzer, A. Poebel, and H. Pedersen, with E. H. Sturtevant and Bloomfield to be included also. But it is to Gelb alone that we now owe the full proof of the syllabic character of West Semitic writing. Very briefly his argument may be summed up as follows. (1) Since the alphabet as such was developed by the Greeks out of material borrowed from West Semitic sources, what existed prior to this alphabetic invention must have been a stage of writing other than alphabetic. (2) The syllabic character of the West Semitic systems is to be understood as the type where each symbol stands for a consonant plus any vowel or zero. The proof for the inherent vowel within each West Semitic sign is to be found in the systems of vocalic indication developed in later times, when a distinct symbol was invented to indicate the absence of vowel: if the basic sign had been merely consonantal, no such separate sign would have been needed. . . . This thesis, the high point of Gelb's volume, illustrates the value of the structural approach in the study of writing.

Herbert H. Paper, review of I. J. Gelb's *The Study of Writing,* in *Lingua,* IV (April 1954), pp. 91–92.

The Phoenician inscriptions are written in the so-called Phoenician alphabet to which perhaps all other alphabets are in one way or another related. The script is simple and linear, written from right to left. It contains twenty-two letters, all representing consonants (a peculiarity which requires definite explanation), and each letter has an acrophonic name, that is, a name which begins with the sound of that letter. . . .

There existed, then, at this early date an alphabet constructed on the acrophonic principle, by which every letter has the value of the initial sound of its name. The source of this alphabet is not far to seek. In Egypt, and as far as is known there only, alphabetic signs were in use at that time. They had risen naturally in the development of Egyptian writing. Because of the Hamito-Semitic character of Egyptian, in which roots are composed of consonants only, a word with a set consonantal root would have a number of different vocalizations in its various grammatical forms. The Egyptian signs which represented the whole root group ("the root idea") had therefore the phonetic value of the root consonants only. There thus existed a large number of signs that made up Egyptian writing; the vowels were not indicated. To words with roots of only one consonant there naturally corresponded signs with the value of that one consonant alone. While these signs were in effect alphabetic (uni-consonantal) letters, they formed merely a fraction of the total number of hieroglyphic signs, uni-consonantal, bi-consonantal and tri-consonantal, and were not felt to differ from the others. No separate lists of such "alphabetic" signs appeared. In some cases there existed more than one sign with the same phonetic value; each could then be used for that sound, although the complicated conventions of Egyptian writing would usually prefer one as against the other. . . .

The mechanical application of this acrophonic method resulted in a true phonetic alphabet, for in applying it a sign was set for every sound with which any word began, that is, for every initial phoneme, or significant speech-sound, in the language. It may be assumed that in the development of such an acrophonic alphabet every linguistically distinct sound which could occur initially would sooner or later come to be represented. This is of practical importance, for the alphabet can thus be used as a test of the phonemic equipment of the language in which it was constructed, which is not the case in other languages in which the alphabet was borrowed from outside.

But this very method is also the source of the chief peculiarity of the alphabet, its much-debated lack of any indication for the vowels. In Semitic all words could originally begin only with a consonant. Following the acrophonic method one could never come upon a vowel, for no word began with one. The lack of vowel indication in the Semitic alphabet is thus a direct and mechanical corollary of the method by means of which the alphabet was constructed.

Finally, it is the same acrophonic principle which explains the appearance of vowels when the Greek borrowing of the Phoenician alphabet gave vocalic value to the Phoenician laryngal signs. This change is not to be understood as an intentional dropping of the laryngals "because the Greeks had no use for them," but rather as a purely mechanical development. From the fact that the Greeks took over, together with the letters, also their names, it follows that the Greek borrowing consisted not so much of a set of signs with their phonetic values, as of a set of signs with their acrophonic names.

Zellig Harris. *A Grammar of the Phoenician Language,* Series 8, New Haven, American Oriental Society, 1936, pp. 11, 13, 15. Reprinted by permission of the American Oriental Society.

3. There is not yet available a complete satisfactory history of English in terms of the developments within the English sound system. Useful materials are listed in the bibliographies for the various periods of English given in A. G. Kennedy's *Bibliography of Writings on the English Language from the Beginning of Printing to the End of 1922,* Cambridge, Mass., Harvard University Press, and New Haven, Conn., Yale University Press, 1927, pp. 2,072–2,354, 3,580–3,691, 4,945–5,082, 7,796–8,016, 8,094–8,262, 12,202–12,316. See also the *Linguistic Bibliographies,* published by the Permanent International Committee of Linguists, Utrecht, Spectrum Publishers (14 volumes to 1960).

The brief sketch of "Modern English Spelling" in W. W. Skeat, *Principles of English Etymology,* First Series, *The Native Element,* 2nd ed., Oxford, Clarendon Press, 1892, pp. 294–333, although old, is still useful. For the "borrowed" words in English, see Skeat's *Principles of English Etymology,* Second Series, *The Foreign Element,* Oxford, Clarendon Press, 1891, pp. 37–43, 129–136, 355–371, and various other sections.

For Middle English, see Hans Kurath, ed., *Middle English Dictionary,* Ann Arbor, Mich., University of Michigan Press, 1954, I, 4–10.

See also H. C. Wyld, *A Short History of English,* 3rd ed., New York: E. P. Dutton, 1927, pp. 94–221; H. C. Wyld, *History of Modern Colloquial English,* New York, E. P. Dutton and Co., 1920, pp. 62–313; and W. A. Craigie, *English Spelling, Its Rules and Reasons,* New York, F. S. Crofts and Co., 1927.

4. For more information concerning the Greek alphabet in its various forms, see David Deringer, *The Alphabet,* New York, Philosophical Library, 1948, pp. 449–506.

5. "Old English" as used in this book means English from the earliest records to 1050; "Middle English," from 1050 to the beginning of printing, 1475; "Early Modern English," 1475 to 1700.

6. A clear statement of the important details of this phonemic and orthographic situation is given by Hans Kurath in the introductory section, "Plans and Methods," in *op. cit.,* I, 6:

> The phonemically long stops and sonorants, which in late OE were confined to the position between a short stressed vowel and a following unstressed vowel, as in *sittan, sunna,* survived as separate phonemes until c1400 in the dialects that retained short *i* and *u* in the open syllable, e.g. inf. *sitten:* ppl. *biten; sonne* sun; *sone* son. Long consonants lost their phonemic status (though retaining phonetic length) in the dialects that lengthened OE *i* and *u* along with *e, a* and *o* in the open syllable (by 1200), so that thereafter in such dissyllabics every long vowel was followed by a phonetically short consonant, every short vowel by a phonetically long consonant. This stage had been attained in Orm's dialect before his time and permitted him to use double consonants as an orthographic device for indicating short vowels. This usage was current from Norfolk northward and was not unknown in London by Chaucer's time.
>
> The history of the ME fricatives is much more complicated. OE had (1) a set of *short* fricatives, *f, þ, s, h,* which were voiceless except between voiced sounds, as in *næfre* never, *baþian* bathe, *wīse* manner; and it had (2) a set of *long* voiceless fricatives occurring in later OE only medially between voiced sounds, as in *offrian* offer, *moþþe* moth, *missan* miss, *hlihhan, hlæhhan* laugh. The phonetic difference between short and long medial fricatives, as in *næfre: offrian; baþian: moþþe; wīse: missan,* was thus very marked in OE, since in this position the short consonants were voiced and the long ones voiceless.

7. See B. J. Wallace, *A Quantitative Analysis of Consonant Clusters in Present-Day English,* University of Michigan dissertation, 1950; C. C. Fries, *Teaching and Learning English as a Foreign Language,* Ann Arbor, University of Michigan Press, 1945, pp. 16–20.

8. P. Luckombe, *The History and Art of Printing,* 1771, p. 441.

9. See Chapter Two, "Structural Units and Word Patterns," and Chapter Three, "Language Signals."

10. For the purpose here, it seemed unnecessary to call attention to the fact that the phonemic symbols are not the phonemes themselves but another way of graphic representation.

11. See Chapter Four, "The Nature of the Reading Process."

12. A set of such texts with the materials for the first stage of reading instruction will be issued shortly after the publishing of this book.

13. A detailed description of spelling-patterns for the writer rather than for the reader has been excluded from this book and will be treated elsewhere.

14. Most of the spellings that do not fit any of the spelling-patterns given here, or any combination of these patterns, are remnants of some of the older patterns (*know, gnaw, Thomas*). Some of these older spelling-patterns have been pointed out earlier in this chapter. They constitute a special learning problem, to be discussed in the next chapter.

15. The particular "irregularities" of *mutt* with the double *t* here, and *putt* in contrast with *put*, will be commented on below.

16. It should be understood that the lists given here are not exhaustive. The aim has been not completeness but rather sufficient examples to give some understanding of the range and huge number of items the patterns of this basic set contain.

17. In this series and for some other word-patterns beginning with /n/ an old spelling-pattern still persists: *knack, knock, knuck(le)*. *For the reader*, this spelling-pattern presents no real problems. He learns to ignore the letter *k* whenever these spellings occur. *For the writer*, however, there is the problem of learning each particular item that must begin with this letter *k*.

18. Words like *boss, hoss, loss, floss, gloss, moss, cross, dross, toss*, may not, in any particular dialect area, have the vowel phoneme that rimes with that of the words *hot, dot, rock, doll*. If so, they should be treated as a separate spelling-pattern. In similar fashion, the words *roll, toll, poll* (as in *poll-tax*), *scroll, droll, troll, stroll*, should not be included in the set of patterns listed in (1) g. Neither should *bull, full* nor *pull* be included here.

19. The spelling-pattern of "double" *l* after the vowel letter *a* as in *all, ball, call*, does not completely fit the large set of patterns brought together under (1). The *a* in this particular pattern represents the phoneme /ɔ/, not the phoneme /æ/. It is regular in itself, however, and fits into the contrasts of (2).

20. Once such a live spelling pattern as *gale, hale, pale* is established it is often extended without limit to spellings of words for which there is no one particular contrastive word actually in use, as *yale, kale, vale*. Nor is it to be assumed that the particular spellings brought into contrast here are necessarily historically related.

21. There are a few words that have a similar *ea* spelling-pattern for the phoneme /ɛ/. This is one of the minor sets that will be commented on later. bread—breed; stead—steed; head—heed; dead—deed; sweat—sweet.

Some other similar *ea* spelling patterns for /ɛ/ without the contrasting words with /i/ are: dread, tread, spread, threat, breath.

22. There are, however, more words of this kind that fit the more regular spelling pattern contrasts illustrated in (2):

bar—bar e	mar—mar e	scar—scar e
car—car e	par—par e	spar—spar e
far—far e	tar—tar e	star—star e

23. Some of these minor patterns need special attention, as, for example, the following:

rod—rood	rot—root	shot—shoot	prof.—proof
cot—coot	hot—hoot	tot—toot	

There have been some changes of sound in the words that have this *oo* spelling that appear in dialect differences for such words as *root, roof, hoof; foot, good, hood, stood, wood;* and the further changes in *blood* and *flood.*

24. *A New English Dictionary on Historical Principles* (1888), I, xxiv (later named the *Oxford English Dictionary*).

CHAPTER SEVEN

1. See Romalda Bishop Spalding with Walter T. Spalding, *The Writing Road to Reading,* New York, Whiteside, Inc., and William Morrow & Company, Inc., 1957, pp. 8, 27:

> The core of the method is a technique by which the child learns how to write down the sounds used in spoken English as they are combined into words. Thus, conversely he can pronounce any printed word. Meaning is thoroughly taught hand-in-hand with the writing and by using new words in original sentences. It begins with correct pronunciation of words and the writing of their component sound in accordance with the rules of English spelling. By this means the saying, writing, reading and meaning of words are well learned and understood. After this initial grounding, a child in his reading recognizes words at a glance—very soon without any resort to their phonetic composition. For reading there is no resort to pictures or any other aids except the use of phonics. After a new word has been read aloud its meaning is discussed and pictures are used if they can help explain the meaning. . . .
>
> This method differs basically from other phonic methods in that it does not start with reading, which is, in phonics, the translating of printed letters or words into the sounds of spoken words. Instead it first teaches the child the *writing* of the sounds by using the letters which say the sounds. This direct approach from the *sounds* of the words the child knows and uses in speaking into the *written characters* which represent the sounds is a direct, simple, logical explanation to him of the whole writing and reading process. As soon as he can write a word he can usually read it, often at a glance wherever he sees it. In fact, reading as such need not be taught to many children, but training in the blending of the sounds

in a syllable is needed for some. When a child has once mastered the phonic tools, he is able to decipher and pronounce and understand any printed words which come within his speaking vocabulary.

2. The present English names for the letters of our alphabet are not as hopelessly illogical as writers from Hart in the sixteenth century to the reading specialists of today have claimed. Most of the names have as a basis the acrophonic principle, that is, that each letter has a name which begins with the sound of that letter.

For English, the one syllable names /bi/ for *B*, /di/ for *D*, /pi/ for *P*, /ti/ for *T*, /vi/ for *V*, /zi/ for *Z* are strictly acrophonic. The names /si/ for *C*, and /ǰi/ for *G* are also acrophonic, but only for special sounds for *C* and *G*. The names /ǰe/ for *J*, and /ke/ for *K*, although they use a different vowel from that used by the eight preceding letters, are still acrophonic. The names for the following consonants begin with a vowel rather than with the sound of the consonant: /ɛf/ for *F*, /ɛl/ for *L*, /ɛm/ for *M*, /ɛn/ for *N*, /ɛs/ for *S*, /ɛks/ for *X* (a consonant cluster), and /ar/ (with a different vowel in accord with an Early Modern English development) for *R*. The names /e/ for *A*, /i/ for *E*, /o/ for *O* represent the sounds for the so-called "long" English vowels, *after the Early Modern English vowel shift*, as do also the diphthongs /ai/ for *I* and /yu/ for *U*. The names /eč/ for *H*, /dǝbǝlyu/ for *W*, and /waɪ/ for *Y* are not based on the acrophonic principle.

3. Dr. Henry Bradley was the second editor-in-chief of the Oxford English Dictionary, following Sir James Murray and succeeded by Sir William Craigie, who brought the work of this great dictionary to completion in 1928. See Chapter Four, Note 11.

4. See the description of major spelling-patterns in Chapter Six, the section entitled "Present Patterns of English Spelling."

5. Such a series of beginning texts has been developed in accord with these principles and should appear soon after the publication of this book.

6. See Kenneth L. Pike, *Intonation of American English,* University of Michigan Press, 1945. See also Pike's earlier statement in the volume entitled *Pronunciation* of the three volume series, *Intensive Course in English for Latin American Students,* English Language Institute, (1942) Vol. I, 64.

7. DeWitt H. Parker, *The Principles of Aesthetics,* New York (1920) 41. See also C. C. Fries *et al.,* the chapters "Objectives," "Principles of Teaching," "Organization of a Course" in *The Teaching of Literature,* New York, Silver Burdett and Company, 1926.

8. René Welleck and Austin Warren, *Theory of Literature,* New York, Harcourt, Brace & World, Inc., 1949.

9. John Masefield, *Dauber,* London, William Heinemann, Ltd., 1913, V, 18, 19, 20.

10. H. G. Wells, "The Contemporary Novel" in *Atlantic Monthly,* 109 (1912) 6, 10, 11.

11. René Welleck and Austin Warren, *Theory of Literature, op. cit.,* p. 181. See, however, C. C. Fries, "The Bloomfield School" in *Trends in European and American Linguistics,* 1962, edited for the Ninth International Congress of Linguists, Spectrum Publishers, Utrecht, The Netherlands, Antwerp, Belgium.

12. William Dwight Whitney, *Language and the Study of Language, Twelve Lectures on the Principles of Linguistic Science,* New York, 1867, p. 6.

13. See for example the studies by Roman Jakobson, being published by Mouton and Co., N.V., Publishers, The Hague. See also those listed in Kenneth L. Pike and Eunice V. Pike, *Live Issues in Descriptive Linguistics,* Santa Ana, Cal., Summer Institute of Linguistics, 1960, under the heading "The Relation of Linguistics to the Analysis of Literature."

INDEX OF NAMES

SUBJECT INDEX

DATE DUE

JUN 1 3 1984			